# Supervision in Coaching

Supervision, ethics and continuous professional development

Edited by
Jonathan Passmore

ASSOCIATION
forCOACHING

KoganPage

LONDON   PHILADELPHIA   NEW DELHI

*This book is dedicated to Florence*

First published in Great Britain and the United States in 2011 by Kogan Page Limited

| | | |
|---|---|---|
| 120 Pentonville Road | 1518 Walnut Street, Suite 1100 | 4737/23 Ansari Road |
| London N1 9JN | Philadelphia PA 19102 | Daryaganj |
| United Kingdom | USA | New Delhi 110002 |
| www.koganpage.com | | India |

© Association for Coaching, 2011

ISBN      978 0 7494 5533 0
E-ISBN   978 0 7494 6297 0

Association for Coaching – formed in the United Kingdom in 2002, the Association for Coaching is a non-profit and independent professional body whose aim is to promote best practice and to raise awareness and standards of coaching while providing value-added benefits to its members – whether they are professional coaches or organizations involved in coaching.
www.associationforcoaching.com 'promoting excellence & ethics in coaching'

**British Library Cataloguing-in-Publication Data**

A CIP record for this book is available from the British Library.

**Library of Congress Cataloging-in-Publication Data**

Supervision in coaching : supervision, ethics and continuous professional development / Association for Coaching, Jonathan Passmore.
     p. cm.
  ISBN 978-0-7494-5533-0 – ISBN 978-0-7494-6297-0  1. Employees–Coaching of.  I. Passmore, Jonathan. II. Association for Coaching.
  HF5549.5.C53S87 2011
  658.3'124–dc22

                                                                 2011001106

Typeset by Saxon Graphics Ltd, Derby
Printed and bound in India by Replika Press Pvt Ltd

# CONTENTS

**PART 4** Personal reflection 263

# FOREWORD

Coaching has undoubtedly come of age, with this next period of growth moving it from being a young, emergent profession, to one that establishes itself on a global scale.

What I believe makes this fruitful, growing field so appealing, is the ongoing development we personally gain from our clients; for as we know, being a coach allows us the opportunity to develop a greater level of learning and understanding about ourselves along the way.

In other words, the person we started off as, when our coaching journey began, may look different to the person we are today – we grow! This is not too dissimilar to the aims, or journey, that we take our clients on. There is both a *give* and a *get* from the experience.

One of the disciplines or mechanisms for a coach to draw out these deeper levels of learning and to develop further as a professional is through reflective practice and coach supervision, so richly illustrated here in this book, from a number of thought leaders in this space.

Additionally, as we continue to define, shape and raise the standards of coaching on a wider scale – now becoming more readily available as research and contributions are being shared amongst the various coaching bodies, academic/training institutions, and practitioners alike – we are getting a much *clearer* picture of what makes up good coaching practice.

This healthy 'push' coming from groups of professionals within the industry seeking to raise their game, promote excellence, and make coaching sustainable, is also being complemented by a 'pull' from buyers of coaching within organizations looking for greater measures of performance, consistency, and value, as they roll-out coaching programmes on a global scale.

It is also pleasing to see an increasing amount of coaches participating in different forms of supervision, now essential to many accreditation schemes. They are starting to recognize first-hand the benefits they are gaining in their practices, as well as their effectiveness as a coach.

Therefore, if we accept that coaching is a *learning journey* for all participants, and that part of our responsibility as coaches is to ensure the highest levels of success for our clients – as well as our own sense of fulfilment and wellbeing – then this is where coach supervision plays a part.

Furthermore, as the demand and appetite for coaching ripples throughout businesses, societies, and people's personal lives, there is both a moral and ethical obligation that we have as a collective group of professionals to ensure we are doing all we *can to be our best, do the right thing*, and to *protect* those that we serve.

On this basis *Supervision in Coaching* is certainly worth a read, as it addresses some of the key needs and issues our profession now faces. The intent, like our previous books in the series, is to embrace the different approaches used within this important area so readers can see the different perspectives, and choose what is most suitable for their practices.

I would also like to personally thank Kogan Page and Jonathan Passmore, the editor of all the Association for Coaching (AC) books to date, who once again masterfully compiled and edited this valuable piece of work, to support coaches, and the profession, as we continue on our learning journey into the next global era.

*Katherine Tulpa, CEO & Founding Chair, Association for Coaching*

# NOTES ON THE CONTRIBUTORS

## Editor

**Dr Jonathan Passmore**  Jonathan is one of the UK's leading coaches. He is a chartered occupational psychologist, an accredited AC coach, a coaching supervisor and fellow of the CIPD. He has wide business consulting experience having worked for PricewaterhouseCoopers, IBM Business Consulting and OPM, and as a chief executive and company chairman in the sports and leisure sector. He is based at the School of Psychology, University of East London and is director for the coaching and coaching psychology programmes. He is the author of 13 books including titles on the psychology of social networking, *The Facebook Manager* and on organizational change, *Appreciative Inquiry for Organizational Change*. He is also the editor of four previous books in this series: *Excellence in Coaching, Psychometrics in Coaching, Diversity in Coaching* and *Leadership Coaching*. He can be contacted at: **jonathancpassmore@yahoo.co.uk**.

## Contributors

**Julie Allan**  Julie is a chartered and registered psychologist who works with people in organizational contexts to promote successful transition and change. An accredited coach, coaching psychologist and supervisor, she serves as Ethics and Social Policy Liaison Officer for the British Psychological Society's Special Group in Coaching Psychology and is a member of the BPS Ethics Committee. Her practitioner research is the development of corporate wisdom. She can be contacted at: **www.irvingallan.com**.

**Diane Brennan**  Diane is an executive coach working with individuals and teams in healthcare, engineering, science and technology. She served as the 2008 ICF Global President. Diane holds a Master's in Business Administration, the ICF Master Certified Coach Credential and distinction of Fellow in the American College of Medical Practice Executives. She is co-editor and contributing author of *The Handbook of Knowledge Based Coaching*. Diane can be reached at: **diane@coachdiane.com**.

**Dr Max Blumberg**  Max is a Chartered Psychologist and Research Fellow at Goldsmiths, University of London where he investigates the impact of applying academic research methodologies in organizational contexts. He is particularly interested in assessing the effectiveness of coaching interventions on business performance. Max can be contacted at: **max@maxb.com**.

**Dr Francine Campone**  Francine provides executive and personal coaching and is engaged in coaching-related research. She is the Director of the Evidence-Based Coaching Program at Fielding Graduate University and a founding faculty member in the graduate coaching certification program at the University of Texas at Dallas. Francine presently serves as vice-chair of the ICF Research Committee. Francine can be contacted at: **francine@reinventinglife.net**.

**Roy Childs**  Roy is Managing Director of Team Focus and a Chartered Psychologist. He works as a coach, facilitator and trainer and his main focus is building sustainable relationships that enhance wellbeing and performance. His reputation of challenging orthodox thinking has been applied to developing an innovative range of psychometric instruments (the Profiling for Success range). His publications include *The Psychometric Minefield; So You Want to be an ENFJ; Emotional Intelligence and Leadership* and *Coaching using FIRO Element B*. He is contactable at: **teamfocus@teamfocus.co.uk**.

**Barbara Christian**  Barbara is an executive coach and talent management consultant at Mercer. Before joining Mercer, Barbara worked with Robert J Lee, the director of iCoachNewYork. Barbara's experience includes positions in financial services in the United States, and with an HR and Talent consultancy in Austria focusing on teamwork, communications, negotiations, marketing and business development. Barbara can be contacted at: **coach4action@gmail.com**.

**Sue Congram**  Sue Congram is a Chartered Psychologist specializing in organizational work. She teaches, coaches and supervises consultants, coaches, managers, directors and students, individually and in groups. Sue is currently researching leadership from a field theory perspective for a PhD at Cardiff University. She has published and co-authored a range of books. Sue's website is: **www.suecongram.co.uk**.

**Anne Davidson** Anne is a coach and consultant specializing in leadership development and organizational and community change projects. She works internationally with executives, management groups, work teams and boards. Anne is an Associate with Roger Schwarz & Associates, co-author of two books on coaching and facilitation, and a certified somatic coach. Anne can be contacted at: **anne@schwarzassociates.com**.

**Marion Gillie** Marion Gillie is a coach, consultant and supervisor and a Chartered Occupational and Counselling Psychologist with Master's degrees in Organizational Psychology and Gestalt Psychotherapy. She is Programme Director of the Diploma in Advanced Executive Coaching and the Master Practitioner Programme at the AoEC, a coach supervisor for Oxford Brookes University Business School and is a faculty member of the Gestalt International Study Center, Cape Cod, Massachusetts. Marion can be contacted at: **Marion.Gillie@thegilliepartnership.co.uk**.

**David Hain** David Hain is a director of Transformation Partners (Wales) Ltd. David has been a business executive coach for over 20 years and specializes in helping leaders to make sense of the complex environment that surrounds them for themselves and their team, particularly in collaborative situations. David can be reached at: **david@transformationpartners.co.uk**.

**Philippa Hain** Philippa is a Chartered Occupational Psychologist and director of Transformation Partners (Wales) Ltd where she leads the coaching team. Philippa specializes in the coaching and development of individuals, teams and businesses and has been coaching clients for nearly 20 years. She is also a council member of the Society of Coaching Psychology and sits on the committee of the Society's Special Group in Coaching Psychology managing their events. Philippa can be reached at: **philippa@transformationpartners.co.uk**.

**Professor Peter Hawkins** Peter Hawkins is chairman of Bath Consultancy Group and Emeritus Professor of Leadership at Henley Business School. Peter is President of the Association of Professional Executive Coaching and Supervision (APECS) and leads the international modular training programme in the Supervision of Coaches, Mentors and Consultants through Bath Consultancy Group. He is the author and co-author of several books including *Supervision in the Helping Professions, Coaching* and *Mentoring; Organizational Consultancy: Supervision and development* and *Leadership Team Coaching*. He can be contacted at: **peter.hawkins@bathconsultancygroup.com**.

**Professor David Lane**   David is Director of the Professional Development Foundation and Research Director of the International Centre for the Study of Coaching at Middlesex University. He was Chair of the British Psychological Society Register of Psychologists Specialising in Psychotherapy and Convened the Psychotherapy Group of the European Federation of Psychologists Associations. He was a founder member of the steering group for the Global Convention on Coaching. His contributions to psychology led to the senior award of the BPS for Outstanding Scientific Contribution to Counselling Psychology and in 2010 for Distinguished Contribution to Professional Psychology. David can be contacted at: **davidlane@pdf.net**.

**Robert J Lee**   Bob Lee is an executive coach in New York City. He is Managing Director of iCoachNewYork, which provides coach training programs and supervision. Previously he was president of the Center for Creative Leadership, and founder and president of Lee Hecht Harrison. He co-authored *Discovering the Leader in You* and *Executive Coaching: A Guide for the HR professional*. Bob can be contacted at: **bob@bobleecoach.com**.

**Angy Man**   Angy has worked with senior executives in the business arena for 23 years. Her experience includes work with clients in the UK and Europe, ranging from major banks through international car manufacturers, pharmaceuticals, insurance, healthcare and the media. Through her work, she has established coaching as a fundamental skill that underpins personal effective performance management, implementation of strategy, functional team work and best management practices. She works both as a coach and a coach supervisor and has a Master's degree in psychodynamic counselling.

**Gladeana McMahon**   Gladeana is considered one of the leading personal development and transformational coaches in the UK. She holds the position of Fellow and Chair, Association for Coaching UK. She is accredited as a coach, therapist and supervisor and is one of the UK founders of Cognitive Behavioural Coaching. She is currently

Director of Professional Coaching Standards for Cedar Talent Management and Director of Gladeana McMahon Associates.

**Dr Lisa Matthewman**   Lisa is a Chartered Occupational Psychologist and an Associate Fellow of the British Psychological Society. She is a Member of the Division of Occupational Psychology within the British Psychological Society. Lisa is Past Chair of the Division of Occupational Psychology Training Committee and is a member of the Special Group in Coaching Psychology. She is also a founding council member of the Society for Coaching Psychology and is an Accredited Member. Lisa is a Principal Lecturer in Occupational and Organizational Psychology at the Westminster Business School. Lisa can be contacted at: **L.J.Matthewman@westminster.ac.uk**.

**Lance Mortimer**   Lance is a director and co-founder of a Mind to Perform Ltd (**www.amtp.co.uk**), a business and sport psychology coaching and consultancy firm that works with organizations, athletes and individuals to coach them to realize their true potential. Combining over 25 years' experience of working in finance and telecoms with large companies such as Barclays Bank, ABB and Cadbury, Lance has a BSc in Psychology from the University of Greenwich and an MSc in Occupational and Organizational Psychology from the University of East London (UEL). He can be contacted at: **lance.mortimer@sky.com**.

**Dr Barbara Moyes**   Barbara is a coach, learning and development consultant and researcher. A former therapeutic supervisor, she has supervised internal coaches across government. Previously the head of people and leadership development in two central government departments, she is currently a Senior Visiting Fellow at Cass Business School and an associate with the National School of Government. She holds a Master's degree in coaching with distinction and has published from her research and practice.

**Elaine Patterson**   Elaine is a national and international executive coach, coach trainer, and coach supervisor with over 20 years' practical leadership experience. She is an accredited EMCC Master Practitioner Coach Mentor with an Advanced Certificate in Coaching and Mentoring from The OCM and a Diploma in Coaching Supervision from the Coaching Supervision Academy.

**Kevin M Rogers** Kevin M Rogers LLB, LLM is a Senior Lecturer in Law, University of Hertfordshire, School of Law and a member of the Law Society's Technology and Law Reference Group. He is a consultant for various law firms on data protection issues and speaks widely on these and related areas. He can be contacted at: **K.Rogers@herts.ac.uk.**

**Dale Schwarz** Dale is a personal and business coach, workshop leader, Registered Art Therapist and Licensed Mental Health Counselor. She is co-author of *Facilitative Coaching: A toolkit for expanding your repertoire* and *Achieving Lasting Results,* co-founding director of the Center for Creative Consciousness and an associate at Roger Schwarz & Associates. Dale can be contacted at: **dale@tocreate.org.**

**Michelle Tenzyk** Michelle is the owner of East Tenth Group, Inc, an HR consultancy and executive coaching practice based in New York City. Michelle also held the position of Chief HR and Marketing Officer at Healthcare Consulting Group. Michelle was an executive team member of Trip Network, which currently operates as part of Orbitz Worldwide. Michelle can be contacted at: **michelle@ easttenthgroup.com.**

**Bob Thomson** Bob is a Learning and Development Adviser at the University of Warwick, where he acts as coach, supervisor, facilitator and mediator. He leads the University's Certificate and Diploma in Coaching. He describes his primarily non-directive approach in his book, *Don't Just Do Something, Sit There,* and on his website **www.bobthomsoncoaching.com.**

**Claire Townsend** Claire Townsend is a business psychologist, coach and learning and development specialist who has worked with managers and leaders throughout the UK and Europe. She uses her business background to work with her clients to develop pragmatic, solution-focused outcomes. She holds a Master's Degree in Occupational Psychology and a degree in Psychology. Claire can be contacted at: **claire@impact.uk.net.**

**David Willcock** David combines over 25 years' experience of developing people in organizations with specialist skills in supporting personal and organization change. His work involves leadership, management and team development to support change and the development of caring and high performing organization cultures. He works both under his own company name of Liberating Potential and as an associate of Team Focus Ltd. He has considerable experience of developing leaders and their teams through coaching, facilitation and consultancy work in the UK and abroad. David is a fellow of the CIPD and an AC accredited coach.

**Declan Woods**   Declan is an executive coach, business psychologist and leadership developer and Director of Penna plc's Board and Executive Coaching practice. He coaches highly talented leaders across the private and public sectors. Declan holds qualifications in business (Executive MBA, Warwick) and Psychology (MEd, Cambridge University) and is an accredited coach with Ashridge and the Association for Coaching (AC). He has designed and taught Master's level qualifications in coaching and designed the AC's individual coach accreditation scheme up to Master Coach level, all of which involve coaches reflecting upon their practice.

**Martin Woods**   Martin has worked in organization and people development for the last 20 years. In corporate life he has been responsible for leadership, management and organization development in the UK and abroad. As an independent consultant his work has been centred on the development of the business through people using organization development as a prime focus. He works as an associate of Team Focus and focuses on one-to-one coaching and team development. Martin is an accredited coach and a qualified counsellor.

# PART 1
# Approaches to supervision

# Supervision and continuous professional development in coaching

**JONATHAN PASSMORE**

## Introduction

Continuous professional development is becoming an essential part of practice for professionals. While coaching has yet to fully emerge as a profession, its progress over the past decade suggests that coaching has many of the features of a profession on a par with counselling. However, before becoming a profession a number of challenges need to be overcome.

The first of these challenges is the need for a distinct and unique body of knowledge. We can track the linage of coaching back to the 1930s (see for example Bigelow, 1938; Gorby, 1937). In the early period of coaching's history, before 1990, research was sporadic (see, for example, Grant *et al*, 2010). From 1995 coaching practitioners and researchers have been working hard to build a research base. In the early period, 1995–2001, this focused on case studies, stories and descriptions of what coaches found worked for them (Kampa-Kokesch and Anderson, 2001). More recently we have seen a growth in quantitative studies and the use of more formalized qualitative research methods. We have also seen a development in research methods with papers using recognized methods such as Grounded Theory and Interpretative Phenomenological

Analysis (IPA) and well described method statements, which are characteristics of a developing research maturity (Passmore and Fillery-Travis, 2011).

A second challenge is the development of recognized and formalized training. The status of a profession is often measured by the level of training demanded. High status professions often require practitioners-in-training to study for five to seven years and through this process to obtain postgraduate qualifications. Examples include doctors and accountants, where entry is through rigorous university and professional examination. In contrast healthcare workers and accounts clerks may require more limited training, which is in turn reflected in the status and financial rewards they obtain.

A third challenge is an agreed code of conduct, such as an ethical code. Such codes set out publicly the standards required of members of the profession. These codes set expectations for the public and also offer members of the public protection through a formal complaints mechanism. Such complaints mechanisms can ultimately lead to members of the profession being barred from practice.

A fourth challenge is a perception among members that they belong to a single group with a shared definition of their practice. A dentist knows, as does the public, what his or her role is and what the limits of practice are. This is not to say there are not grey areas or boundaries, but dentists have an identity that binds them together.

A fifth challenge is the role of continuous professional development (CPD). In short this involves undertaking ongoing development after completion of the formal training. CPD has become accepted in coaching as an important aspect for coaching practitioners. There has been a growth in coaching supervision, coach training and publications. This book focuses on the emerging area of coaching CPD, with a specific focus on supervision as an approach that has become widely accepted as a useful model for coaching practitioners for reviewing and enhancing their practice.

This chapter will reviews the sections of the book and offer a short insight into the developing nature of coaching CPD and supervision.

## Supervision in coaching

The first section of the book focuses on alternative models for supervision practice – little has been written on this topic to date. One exception is Peter Hawkins' (2007) 'Seven-eyed model', which is summarized in

*Excellence in Coaching.* The majority of models including Hawkins' are drawn from social work, nursing or counselling practice. While there are clear parallels with these professions, there are also important differences which should be reflected by coaching developing models of practice to suit the demands of coaching.

The chapters in this section offer varying perspectives on supervision approaches, from a reflective practitioner model through action learning to more traditional psychological approaches used in coaching such as Gestalt and humanistic. We hope to stimulate debate through the inclusion of chapters on the imagined field and the role of presence in supervision which are relatively new to many in coaching.

As an emerging profession coaching needs to develop its own body of knowledge suited to the unique demands and clients in the field. Such knowledge can of course be inspired by and grounded in other domains of practice, but for coaching to describe itself as a profession this knowledge must be distinct. A failure to create unique knowledge and models will lead to coaching being considered a sub-set of counselling or mentoring.

As yet we do not have universally agreed models of practice. Even the relevance of supervision has been in question. Given the diverse nature of coaching, diversity in continuous professional development can be considered to be a strength. Such diversity recognizes that coaching works in many different spheres, from individuals at work to those outside, from personal coaching for health and education and for one-to-one and for groups.

# Coaching ethics and the law

In this section we have three chapters that focus on the development of ethical standards and the law. In the first of these, Claire Townsend reviews the development of ethical codes of practice in coaching. The development of these codes is a relatively new phenomenon. Most of the coaching professional bodies' codes only date back to around the millennium and some are newer than this. Further, given the unregulated nature of coaching, few of the codes have been tested through public complaints and the need to remove members. The chapter compares and contrasts the codes adopted by the main coaching professional bodies to guide coaches in understanding the subtle but important differences that regulate their practice.

In the second chapter we present a model for ethical decision making. Given the complex, changing and contradictory nature of codes of ethical practice, plus the variable level of awareness among coaching practitioners of the contents of such codes, we have tried to develop a model to frame ethical decision making. The ACTION model, like GROW, aims to be easily remembered and is grounded in research with coaching practitioners. In this way coaching is gradually building its own unique field of knowledge.

The third chapter focuses on the legal issues which can impact on coaches, from data protection to confidentiality. These are rarely discussed in the literature but are a foundation of ethical practice, as coaches need to ensure they comply with the legal requirements of the government or the State in which they operate as a minimum requirement.

Taken together the three chapters aim to offer an overview of the issues facing coaches and a structure for continuous professional development.

# Continuous professional development

In the third section we draw on the thinking of two groups of writers, one from the UK, the other from the United States on their ideas about continuous professional development. In the first chapter David Hain and his colleagues argue the case for CPD's role in coaching. They note that while CPD is sometimes regarded as an additional pressure in a time-constrained world, it has a vital role to play in helping coaches keep up to date. We share these views.

Continuous professional development is a vital part of coaching and a critical aspect if coaching is to establish itself as a separate profession. Some might hold the view that it is a foregone conclusion that coaching will become a profession. In my view the jury is still out. Coaches and coaching bodies, such as the Association for Coaching and the International Coaching Federation, have some choices to make. One route leads to a continuation of growth and aspects of professionalization, but not professional status. A second route leads to coaching becoming a recognized and respected profession.

In the 1950s academics in the United States debated the role of management and its growing professionalization. Over the past 60 years management has become acknowledged as an important skill for people leading other people. Management has developed a body of unique knowledge, training courses exist at postgraduate level such as the MBAs, but it has failed to become a profession. We might consider why this is the case.

One reason why management has failed to establish itself as a distinctive profession is that management is diverse. The term can be applied in many situations from the person managing an assistant to the role of the chief executive of Microsoft. Both may be managers but their roles are different. Management lacks a single bond that ties together these diverse groups.

A second hurdle that 'management' has not overcome is an agreement on training to enter the profession. In accounting or medicine, an agreed qualification offers entry to the profession. Without the qualification and registration, a recognized title cannot be used. Such titles often come about because of trade bodies arguing the case to protect a title that is subsequently protected by law.

A third challenge that has blocked the development of management towards professional status is the lack of a body to represent its interests with a single voice. While diversity can be a positive step, for example accounting has a number of different bodies, it can lead to infighting and introspection as members look to differentiate themselves from one another, as opposed to seeking uniting common themes in their practices and definitions.

Coaching suffers from similar challenges. So far efforts to bring together and gain agreement between professional bodies have failed. Even in relatively small and more regulated states such as Norway the experiences of collaboration have proved negative (Svaleng and Grant, 2010). The relatively large number of professional bodies can be seen as a weakness if the aim is to establish a single profession, particularly if members of those bodies see themselves as unique or different from members of other bodies.

Furthermore, coaching has yet to fully resolve issues of training and access to the profession. Almost all of the professional bodies have established accreditation arrangements. These largely remain practitioner focused, reflecting the dominance of practitioners and independent coaches on professional committees within coaching. To make further progress coaching needs to increase the level of qualifications it is seeking from undergraduate to postgraduate and move from practice-based qualifications, such as hours of practice, to ones based on knowledge and skills. One challenge to this argument is that coaching is practice and not a theory-based 'profession'. However, while surgeons certainly need to undertake training on how to perform a task, the profession also demands they have a solid body of knowledge about the human body and use evidence to guide their practice, which is shared with each other first through formal training and later through journals, videos and books.

In the last chapter in this section, David Lane and Max Bloomberg review the nature of coaching research: methods and approaches. In their chapter the two writers note the value of coaching research and highlight the particular role played by practitioner-based research. In this way research becomes liberated from the academic, and can be embraced by all. In a domain such as coaching, practitioners need to move from pure practice to reflective practitioners, skilled and able to share their growing knowledge and experiences with others, in the same way that academics need to remain grounded in practice; continuing to undertake coaching and client work, as a way of remaining connected to the essence of coaching.

So where does this leave coaching in its aspirations towards professional status? It leaves it with a significant amount of work to do, some difficult challenges to overcome, but with a growing base of practitioners with the energy and desire for learning and development.

# Personal reflection

The fourth section of the book offers a series of chapters to aid continuous professional development through personal reflection. In the first chapter Declan Woods reviews the role that reflective logs and diaries for learning can play in CPD. I have previously argued that for some, supervision is a useful and essential process as they gain value from openly discussing with others their work. However, for others, reflective logs can play a useful role, either alongside supervision or, for some coaches, in place of supervision. The log offers a formal time and space to reflect on what has happened, to check information and form a view about future action.

In the next chapter Peter Hawkins discusses how coaches can enhance their own ethical maturity. Hawkins notes that coaches' frame of reference both enables and limits their ability to develop those they coach. To become more effective, coaches need to develop themselves, as well as to develop their coaching practice. This means coaches need to work simultaneously on three aspects of their personal development:

their relational engagement capacity, their ethical capacity and their cognitive capacity to embrace and work with complexity.

The final chapter of the book offers a series of case studies. Case studies can offer highly useful material for both classroom-based discussions and personal reflection. They are widely used in counselling and in education. Rather than gather together a host of these drawing solely from my own experience, we have asked different writers and practitioners from the UK, United States and Europe to share a case study and comment on the case.

# Conclusions

The nature of coaching practice is changing. Coaches need mechanisms to keep up and to continually reflect and update their knowledge and skills. This book offers a review of the diverse ways coaches are achieving this goal.

Alongside this, coaching is moving forward with the aspirations of becoming a profession. This chapter raises a number of the challenges that stand in its way and how such challenges have foiled others who came before.

## *References*

Bigelow, B (1938) Building an effective training program for field salesmen, *Personnel*, 14, 142–50

Gorby, C B (1937) Everyone gets a share of the profits, *Factory Management & Maintenance*, 95, 82–3

Grant, A M, Passmore, J, Cavanagh, M and Parker, H (2010) The state of play in coaching, *International Review of Industrial & Organizational Psychology*, 25, 125–68

Hawkins, P (2007) Coaching supervision, in (ed) J Passmore, *Excellence in Coaching*, Kogan Page, London

Kampa-Kokesch, S and Anderson, M Z (2001) Executive coaching: a comprehensive review of the literature, *Consulting Psychology Journal: Practice and Research*, 53 (4), 205–28

Passmore, J and Fillery-Travis, A (2011) A critical review of executive coaching research: a decade of progress and what's to come, *Coaching: An International Journal of Theory, Practice & Research*

Svaleng, I and Grant, A (2010) Lessons from Norwegian coaching industry's attempt to develop a joint coaching standards: an ACCESS pathway to a mature coaching industry, *The Coaching Psychology*, 6 (1), 4–13

# The reflective coaching practitioner model

## FRANCINE CAMPONE

## Introduction

**R**eflective practitioners intentionally draw upon their experiences in practice to refine and extend their knowledge and skills. The development of reflective practice has long been integral to the preparation of professionals in several fields that share with coaching a reliance on a combination of practice skills and theoretical foundations combined with some degree of artistry. This chapter explores the core principles of reflective practice and suggests a model relevant to the ongoing development of coaching practitioners.

The learning potential of reflective practice is especially salient for coaches, practitioners in a relatively new field with a nascent body of theoretical literature. Reflective practice invites the coaching practitioner to regard coaching engagements as opportunities for the development of judgement artistry. Such judgement artistry may be defined as 'the capacity to make highly skilled micro-, macro- and metajudgements that are optimal for the circumstances of the client and the context' (Paterson *et al*, 2006).

The reflective practitioner (Schön, 1983) engages in a conversation with a situation for purposes of contextualizing the technical expertise applied in practice. Since Schön's original formulation the model has been adapted, researched and revised for use in the preparation of professionals in many fields, including education, psychotherapy, nursing and social work. This chapter offers a model of reflective practice that comprises an iterative cycle of action and underlying cognitive and emotional processes which frame the coach's work in a context consistent with Schön's original theory. The three-step model presented here begins with the coach documenting experiences that serve as learning opportunities and applying a systematic strategy for meaning-making. In the second step of the process the practitioner engages more deeply with the experiences applying principles of reflective and critical judgement to surface underlying mental models and reframe and revise beliefs assumptions, expectations and decision protocols. The third step invites practitioners to formulate coaching processes and strategies that incorporate the newly acquired insights and knowledge. The chapter sets out both theories and practices for each step of the model and concludes with a sample of a reflective practice journal.

# Origins of the reflective practitioner

Reflective practice is a structured, intentional process of examining one's own experience in order to gain insight. The model of reflective practice offers a means for professionals to surface the often tacit knowledge and mental models that guide their choices in professional practice. This section offers an overview of Schön's (1983) model as well as exploring parallels between the current status of coaching and the status of related fields in the early 1980s.

As Schön (1983) observed at the time of his writing, the fields of psychology, engineering and education appeared to be experiencing a rift between the hard knowledge of science and scholarship and the soft knowledge of artistry within those disciplines. Concomitantly, there was need for understanding how technical knowledge (whether theory or structured strategy) translates into effective personal action. At that time, teachers, social workers, industrial managers and others were engaged in reconciling sometimes competing commitments of professional depth, technical skills and client wellbeing with the demand for rapid and significant return on investment. One result was a diversity of opinions in the field about best methods and measures of professional practice. This is analogous to the circumstances which executive coaches find in reconciling the sometimes competing needs of individual and organizational clients, limits on service and delivery access, externally determined methods of intervention and the expectations of measurable outcomes.

As an additional challenge, coaches who are unaware of their own underlying coaching ideologies and theoretical assumptions may find the unarticulated mindset takes a toll on their practice. A continual focus on improvement, for example, may lead to client exhaustion. Without a clear understanding of the subtle forms and degree of the coach's influence, the power dynamics of the relationship may be hidden (Askeland, 2009). Other potential risks exist as well, including possible conflicts between individual and organizational perspectives and the ability to help clients manage complexity. Consequently, coaching practitioners are confronted with sometimes competing expectations and role definitions. Additionally, each unique client and coaching engagement requires the coach to have a set of implicit or explicit protocols for formulating well grounded decisions about the most appropriate processes and tools to use.

A further parallel can be found in considering that the reflective practitioner model was developed at a time when professions of counselling, education and public administration were confronting a crisis of confidence in professional knowledge. This crisis was catalyzed by visible failures of professional action in several public arenas. Evidence of crisis included calls for external regulation. At present, the various schools of thought among coaching, continued debate about coaching/therapy boundaries, and periodic initiatives towards the regulation of coaches and coaching (see, for example, Svaleng and Grant, 2010) suggest the potential for a similar crisis of confidence in the coaching field. While coaching is not recognized as a profession, nonetheless efforts on the part of various organizations – including the International Coach Federation, the European Mentoring and Coaching Council and the Association of Coaching – suggest a positive approach to ensuring professional knowledge of coaches is sufficient to meet the expectations these associations are helping to create.

Given the complexity of coaching contexts, an executive coach cannot rely on a single learnt system of coaching techniques or follow a one-size-fits-all protocol. Rather, it is incumbent on coaches to engage in active consideration of knowledge in their field of practice and to continually evolve the artistry that is a synthesis of science and skill. This reflective coach practitioner model is proposed as an epistemology of professional practice: ie as a way to make explicit what is known and unknown in a given situation to determine the most appropriate course of action.

# The case for reflective practice in coaching

Coaching is an interactive, context-dependent process for helping people develop themselves and meet their goals. The challenges confronting coaches in real-world practice rarely conform to the well-formed problem and solution patterns learnt in their training. To engage in this practice, coaches rely on their coach training as well as practices, theories and models learnt in prior professional fields and practices (Liljenstrand and Nebeker, 2008). This is not without its drawbacks as coaching seeks to achieve status as a unique professional practice. The traditional view of a professional is someone who possesses some expertise in techniques, eg in coaching as distinguished from consulting, therapy and training 'The professionals claim to extraordinary knowledge is rooted in techniques and theories derived from scientific research undertaken for the most part in institutions of higher learning.' (Schön, 1983). The reliance on technique is especially true of coaching, as evidenced by an emphasis on skills-based standards compared rather than theory and knowledge-based standards in coach training and assessment. Education in and reliance upon theories derived from scientific research are evident in coaching, which has a very slim body of empirical research to which theory-oriented practitioners can refer and lacks an agreed body of theoretical knowledge. As an epistemology of practice, an intentional practice of considered reflection serves as a means for an individual practitioner to identify and make responsive and appropriate changes to habitual practice derived from over-learning or repetitive experience with a narrow set of techniques; applications of received models and theories.

Reflective practice is useful not only in terms of correcting habitual coaching behaviours but as a support for the cognitive development of the coach. Basseches (1984) suggests that reflective practice is essential to self-management by developing a concept of self as competent and capable of self-invention and strengthening the ability to reconcile different perspectives to create a balanced and functioning system of problem-solving.

The field of coaching offers practitioners many opportunities to engage in formal professional development. However, the practice of coaching itself offers coaches an opportunity for meaningful self-development and potentially transformative learning. Two characteristics make this possible. First, the nature of coaching work is consistent with work conditions identified by Basseches (1984) as work contexts that support critical reflection; for example, workers whose tasks involve:

1 adapting services and processes to new circumstances (eg contracts and contexts, client characteristics);

2 improving relationships between interdependent systems;

3 coordinating activities of workers within organizations.

In addition, the coaching relationship is a personal one and often significant, a condition that Brookfield (1987) proposes offers an ideal opportunity for 'significant personal learning'. Specifically, personal relationships are those that are 'self-consciously perceived as profoundly important by the learners themselves' and which may entail a redefinition of some aspect of the self. In particular, an individual may be transformed by a relationship that calls into question some of the assumptions underlying the way the individual conducts the personal relationship (Brookfield, 1987).

# A model of reflective practice for coaches

Reflective practices are consistent with the principles of transformative adult learning put forward by adult learning theorists. This section offers a theoretical model to help coaches shift underlying mental models and develop greater cognitive complexity in the course of their coaching. The changes that result from critical reflective practice enable practitioners to have a greater fluidity in responding to a variety of coaching contexts and situations. Such fluidity may be considered a form of 'judgement artistry' (Paterson et al, 2006) that mediates the science of theory and technique and the intuitive momentum of human relationships.

Reflective practice differs from simply 'thinking about what happened' insofar as it is characterized by intention, purpose and structure. Intention includes a determination to approach the process as a learning opportunity, with an open mind and curiosity about the opportunity to grow. The purpose of reflective practice is to facilitate one's own learning from experience. The structure of reflective practice includes a systematic approach to documenting experiences and a specific set of strategies for meaning-making. Such strategies may include identifying when and how to document experiences and who might be involved in the reflective process.

The model presented here focuses on helping coaches understand and develop a structured reflective practice which consists of three steps, each with an action and concomitant reflective processes. The first step of the process comprises research in action: participating in the coaching engagement and capturing relevant data from the engagement in ways that could serve as the basis for meaningful reflection. The reflective processes for this step consist of creating a mindset of curiosity and looking for ways to make meaning of the information. The second step consists of naming and reconfiguring one's own mental models of coaching. The processes in this step consist of dialogue with the self, applying critical and reflective judgement, and rebuilding the frame to encompass more complexity. The third step of the process comprises generating new experiments in action, taking a dialectical frame of mind into the next coaching engagement.

## Step 1: Research in action

Reflective practice is an intentional, systematic practice of thinking about thinking that integrates cognitive (analytical) processes and artistic (intuitive) processes (Schön, 1987.) At the heart of reflective practice is a retrospective analysis of a practitioner's choices and outcomes: the conscious or unconscious decision making that draws upon an often tacit base of knowledge that is drawn from formal and experiential learning and applied to the unique case of the moment. By documenting and analysing events, reflective practitioners explore their own problem-solving logic and related feelings to uncover nested paradoxes. A systematic approach to reflective practice identifies or creates parameters for research in action opportunities, creates a means of documentation (recording in written or verbal form), and defines the participant or participants in the reflection process. The latter may be limited to the individual practitioner (self-reflection) or may include reflective processing with a peer group, a mentor or supervisor.

Coaching conversations position the coach's technical expertise within the client's own unique system of meaning-making. Coaches represent themselves not as experts in the client's life but as expert in the techniques of being a coach. Such expertise requires the practitioner to deliver the best possible service for that client by making a conscious selection from the coach's repertoire and adjusting it in response to what has been learnt in working with that client. Such learning may result from intentional reflection on four types of 'research in action' that may occur in a coaching engagement.

Schön (1983) suggests that practitioners consciously or unconsciously engage in research in action. In framing a client's challenge, the coach focuses on some information to the exclusion of others, mentally labels events, interprets information and experiences, and holds dialogues. Frame analysis can help practitioners become aware of and judge their tacit frames: ie what they pay attention to, what they see as the goals, how they define their roles and set up expectations, and choices for processes and tools. Becoming aware of how they describe images, categorize events and reference other cases, precedents and exemplars, helps practitioners become more skilled in on-the-spot analysis of events. Analysing their methods of assessing client input and formulating overarching theories supports practitioners in building more responsive on-the-spot variations in response. Research on the process of reflection in action itself (observation and thinking about one's thinking) can surface tacit and habitual processes of mind and gain insight into the potential and limitations of such habits. Reflective practice provides coaches with a strategy for documenting these often intuitive experiments, undertaken in the moment with a client and overlooked as a potential catalyst for success or challenge in the engagement outcome.

## Step 2: Naming and reconfiguring mental models

The second step consists of naming and reconfiguring one's own mental models of coaching. The inner processes consist of dialogue with the self, applying critical and reflective judgement, and rebuilding the frame to encompass more complexity. A mental model is a complex frame of reference, a 'structure of assumptions and expectations through which we filter sense impressions. It involves affective and cognitive dimensions which shape and delimit perceptions, cognitions, feeling and dispositions' (Mezirow, 2000). Mental models are formed and shaped through a lifetime of experiences. Analogous to Schön's tacit knowledge frames, Mezirow's frame of reference has two dimensions: a habit of mind and a resulting point of view. Habits of mind include: sociolinguistic habits – cultural and language norms, customs and communication patterns; moral and ethical norms; preferences in learning styles and modalities; philosophical preferences; personality traits such as character, self-concept and other psychological dimensions; aesthetic values. Points of view comprise a 'clustering of meaning schemes' – expectations, beliefs, attitudes and judgements that serve as lenses for the interpretation of perceived events. The point of view may manifest as an espoused theory which 'is consistent with the integration of received, socialized knowledge into practice' (Brookfield, 1987). Self-directed learning may alter or counter espoused theory and 'foster the formation of new, unique and learner-specific ways of understanding' (Brookfield, 1987).

Understanding one's own mental model is especially relevant in coaching practice, which may be construed as an ill-structured problem. The structure of the problem is defined as 'the degree to which a problem can be described completely and the certainty with which a solution can be identified as true and correct' (King and Kitchener, 1994). An ill-structured problem cannot be completely described or resolved with a high degree of certainty; there is disagreement among experts as to the best solution. Coaching, with the variation of client, coach and context characteristics might be considered to meet this description.

Reflection can be considered as 'a series of thinking activities or differing levels of thinking activities to critically analyse, question and evaluate feelings and experiences, ultimately producing outcomes of new understandings and appreciations of the way we think and operate' (Rutter, 2006). As adults, our most significant learning experiences 'involve critical reflection – reassessing the way we have posed problems and reassessing our own orientation to perceiving, knowing, believing, feeling and acting' (Mezirow, 2000).

To step away from models that are rooted in received knowledge gained through formal education and indoctrination into the technical rules of a practice, one must accept that knowledge must be 'constructed into individual conclusions about ill-structured problems on the basis of information from a variety of sources (both objective and subjective) and is based on evaluations of evidence across contexts' (King and Kitchener, 1994). The fluid nature of reflective thinking demands not only that a solution to an ill-structured problem be 'evaluated in terms of what is most reasonable or probable according to the current evidence [but that] it is re-evaluated when relevant new evidence, perspectives or tools of inquiry become available' (King and Kitchener, 1994).

The reflective process is conducive to the development of professional artistry that involves a blend of practitioner qualities, practice skills and creative imagination processes. Such artistry is an integration of professional knowledge (both theoretical and practical) and personal experience. In all coaching engagements, the coach is one element of the interaction and change dynamic. In a reflective consideration of events, the coach must consider his or her own qualities (including spiritual, emotional, cognitive and physical characteristics); practice skills (which may include coaching specific competencies, interpersonal and relationship skills, analytical and communication skills); and creative imagination processes (ie the ability to anticipate outcomes and develop creative strategies for facilitating the desired outcomes) (Paterson *et al,* 2006).

## Step 3: Enacting the changes

The third step of the process comprises generating new experiments in action, taking a dialectical frame of mind into the next engagement. Stepping away from familiar patterns of thinking and behaving and into newly constructed concepts indicates that transformative learning is taking place. Transformative learning differs from informational learning in three key ways. The first is understanding that transformation comprises an irreversible paradigm shift. Transformative learning engenders an epistemological change, not merely a behavioural one. The practitioner experiences a fundamental change in the form or model from which meaning is constructed: the source of ideas and standards for what constitutes data, authority and validity. Transformative learning informs the whole life, requiring an understanding of the epistemological complexities of the current challenge and the ability to shift from the socialized mind to the self-authoring mind (Kegan, 2000).

Because such learning involves self-critical engagement, enactment requires 'awareness, empathy and control' (Mezirow, 2000). The process itself is cumulative and non-linear and has the potential to engender feelings of resistance, anger or shame. Such feelings can themselves be a source of transformative learning and, as such, warrant attention and reflection. Studies of adult learning demonstrate the degree to which critical reflection and affective learning are interdependent. 'Acquiring the ability to recognize, acknowledge and process feelings and emotions as integral aspects of learning from experience' is a prerequisite to critical reflection (Mezirow, 2000). Feelings may be both provocative – ie trigger reflective learning; and evocative – ie leading to greater self-awareness and change in meaning structure. Learning from experience entails attending to emotions that can direct attention towards the more fundamental bases of meaning-making and perspectives. Affective learning may lead to a great sense of confidence and self-worth, tolerance for ambiguity and acceptance of differences. This means there is value in attending to feelings that arise in the reflection process as well as feelings captured in the reflection log. In tapping into both analytical thinking and emotional experience, the reflective coach is able to create a more integrated, intuitive and fluid framing of coaching challenges, relationships and processes. However, there may also be the negative emotion of grieving the loss of old meaning structures and the challenges of internalizing new ones.

# The reflective coach model – processes and example

## Step 1: Research in action – capturing the data and making meaning

Documenting the learning opportunities in coaching entails the development of meta-awareness in the practice situation. One becomes a practitioner-researcher using the data of real-life experience to construct models or revise existing ones to fit each unique case (no two clients' contexts, relationships are alike). Data from real-life experiences may be captured and examined using a reflection journal. Having presented a theoretical overview of the reflective coaching practitioner model, in this section I offer an example of a reflective journal (see Table 2.1) along with recommendations for how a coach might adapt and use such a journal.

What should one document? There are several points at which the experience offers learning opportunities. Challenging events in particular provides a window on what is working and not working and may often serve as an effective tool for identifying the multiple dimensions of an engagement. A dilemma can offer insight into a clash between the practitioner's values and the necessity of accomplishing some external objective. The experience of uncertainty spotlights an area where we are uncertain about our work or what to do in a given situation. Positive experiences can also offer insight: breakthroughs can reveal the strategies that engender success and can instruct on an emotional level by viscerally highlighting conditions conducive to creativity. Significant learning can arise from situations of uncertainty and situations that vary from those laid out in prescriptive training models and 'best practices'.

Whether positive or stress-inducing, these critical incidents can be characterized as:

**TABLE 2.1** Sample of a reflective coach journal

| External Events | Internal Events | Meaning-Making | Frames/Reframes |
|---|---|---|---|
| (Situation: ongoing work on client's sense of being out of balance with work and home life; goal to 'have more time for wife and child'). | Reflecting on what we've already tried – schedule planning, using reminders. Think we need to investigate some behaviour modification – a 'just do it' approach to turn off technology at home. | Sticking pretty much to behaviours and questions to generate more options. What can he do differently? Notice a tendency toward a desire to consult and think I know what the issue is and how to solve it for him. | Maybe I assume coaching is about behaviour change? Assume that if the client wants to change he just can? Desire = action? |
| Client lists his work tasks and spill over to home life via e-mail, voice messages, Blackberry; says 'I want to turn it off'; leans forward in chair; voice sharp. | Ask – what would it take to turn it off? | | |
| Client seems agreeable to idea – nods head; says 'I could just turn off the signal at 7 pm when I get home instead of waiting until before bed.' | That seemed to work. When I taught this activity to a team last week, they found it helpful. Let's keep going with 'what would it take to … ask again' | Ok – I'm sticking with the 'keep asking what can you do' approach. Not sure we have got clear on the real issue. | What about pacing? Am I moving too quickly to get some solutions? What's driving me to do it this way? |
| Says 'But they need me to be available sometimes because something might come up.' | Here we go again! Say – what are your choices? Am thinking maybe a cognitive along with behavioural will help. | | |

**TABLE 2.1** continued

| External Events | Internal Events | Meaning-Making | Frames/Reframes |
|---|---|---|---|
| Client suggests some other choices – 'maybe' answering e-mails before leaving the office; 'could consider' shutting down Blackberry on the train ride home. | Not sure this is different. Sounds pretty tentative. Now what?<br><br>Long pause from me while I think about it. | Finally picked up on the repeating pattern – this approach isn't working. Not sure what to do now.<br><br>Shifting gears – and outside my comfort zone. | So maybe I've moved off a narrow facilitate solution-generating role. Where am I now? Who am I being here? Why do I seem to feel uncomfortable? What do I think the client is expecting of me here? |
| Says again 'I need to shut it off.' | Second time using that phrase. Maybe a clue. Ask – what keeps it 'on'? Feels weird – a little 'woo-woo'. | | |
| Client sighs. Long pause. Says – 'It's really about me – wanting to always be seen as the hardest working person in the office. I'm afraid if I turn off at night, my boss will think I'm slacking off, not committed. I really want to be considered for this upcoming opportunity ....' | Uh-oh! I wonder if we're going to get into some psycho stuff here? | Sitting on the horns of a dilemma – outside my comfort zone and still seeing some shift | What am I lacking? Why can't I do this more comfortably if it's working for him? |

1   a situation, event or experience that a person believes has had a significant impact on his or her development;

2   a clearly remembered event that is unexplained and was unanticipated;

3   a lived experience with a profound effect on the participants; or

4   a 'synchronistic event' that uncovers meaningful connections.

These are often the experiences that stop us in our tracks, either for celebration and recognition, head-scratching or a brief moment for recovery. In addition to such events, one may want to make note of experiences that resemble what Schön (1983) considers experiments in action. The most common of these among coaches is the exploratory experiment: seeking to find out what happens if one just lets a situation unfold by listening without interruption or inviting the client to tell a story without hearing it first from others. The second experiment is move-testing, a different kind of 'what if'. In this, the coach takes a specific action with an anticipated outcome in mind, eg what if I just reflect the positive? Would that help the client shift to a solution orientation? What if I invite the client to notice his or her non-verbal language right now? Would that help downshift the rising emotions? The third type of experiment is hypothesis testing. For example, a coach hypothesizes that the client's reluctance to give negative feedback is rooted in some pattern of family dynamics. The coach decides to test the hypothesis by asking the client to think about a time when he or she received praise from someone who was important to him or her. The resulting response would add useful information to the coach's interpretation of the client's challenge.

The data from a learning event should be captured as soon as possible following the event or through reconstruction of notes made during the event. Fundamentally, the raw material of inquiry is captured in stories: narratives of the event and dialogue, both with the other person and with the self. One makes meaning by looking at how the stories have been constructed – what was observed, how it is described, the character of the author and others. The stories captured for reflective learning must include some description of thoughts (eg interpretations, expectations, remembered information); feelings (eg curiosity, aversion, anticipation); and behaviours (what was said and done). Preferably, these narratives also identify the anticipated courses of action and expected response, along with the actual unfolding of the event.

Data may be collected on any of several facets of a coaching engagement. Contextual data include information that provides a portrait of the client, the coach and the coaching context. Contextual data might include demographic information (age, gender, position in the organization), assessment outcomes as well as process information (the how of initiating the coaching engagement, establishing agreements, conducting the sessions). Contextual material may also include descriptions of the organization, coaching goals and other relevant material. To the extent possible, 'the main idea is to "triangulate" or establish converging lines of evidence to make your findings as robust as possible' (Yin, 2006). In other words, what is captured in the journal represents and distinguishes, to the extent possible, both objective and subjective information. In Table 2.1, for example, the notes capture the client's verbatim dialogue, internal dialogue, body language, inferential judgements and contextual summaries.

Given different cognitive styles, professional experiences, education and training, it is reasonable to expect that different individuals will practise and reflect in different ways. One model of reflective learning (Thorpe, 2004) distinguishes reflectors from critical reflectors and suggests differences in the impact on practice and performance. Reflectors tend to reflect on the content of their data and on the processes indicated by the content: ie descriptions of actions, thoughts and feelings and how they did it. Critical reflectors examine the underlying premises of their actions, including assessments of the effectiveness of those actions and seeking alternative explanations and options for choice. In considering the documented event, reflectors attend to feelings, make associations and test informal or tacit hypotheses. Critical reflectors take the process a step further and examine the frame of the problem in context and identify learning or developmental opportunities. Critical reflectors 'show awareness of important and relevant aspects of self and situation – including feelings and thoughts concerning complex issues and dilemmas'. Further, they explore the parts and rationale for choices and can perceive their own underlying assumptions as well as the knowledge and experience grounding those assumptions (Rutter, 2006). Meaning-making invites the practitioner to take a step back from having an experience to holding up an experience to a questioning light. Looking at the document of the experience, the reflective practitioner can start to ask questions that surface links and patterns between actual and anticipated events, between thoughts, feelings, actions and reactions. One looks for clues to what worked and what didn't, or seeks to identify conditions that might have influenced the trajectory and outcomes.

The reflective practitioner may also look for patterns in making professional judgements. 'Judgement artistry' encompasses a practitioner's skill in making professional judgements at several levels. At the micro level, the practitioner may examine process decisions (what to do) or examine the accuracy or validity of decision-making protocols for process decisions. At a macro level, the practitioner examines output decision or conclusions: the effectiveness of diagnosis, intervention or action plan and the underlying assessment and decision protocols. At the meta level, practitioners evaluate their own reflective decision processes: awareness of the client's cues and changes; self-awareness and self-monitoring; communication effectiveness and challenges (Paterson *et al*, 2006). Through reference to the documentation of practice experience, one can begin to gauge the degree of artistry and identify patterns of opportunity as well as strengths. In the sample provided in Table 2.1, the coach notices a tendency to keep the client's focus on generating possible actions. The coach also notices herself sticking closely to her own comfort zone and some uncertainty about her knowledge base. The question of context in the form of expected outcomes and potential conflicts comes to the surface. Technical considerations of whether the session went according to the rules are put aside. Creating practice actions is deferred until there is a deeper understanding of the meaning behind the experience.

## Step 2: Naming and reconfiguring mental models

Surfacing mental models entails taking critical reflection to a next level. One is given the opportunity to revisit and judge the input (both what was attended to during the experience and what may have been overlooked); and to trace and evaluate the trajectory and pattern of events, including actions and reactions. Critical evaluation includes attending to knowledge, experience, values, roles, professional patterns and risks displayed in the documentation of the event. Essentially, critical reflectors are invited to seek answers to several questions: What did I expect? What's the implicit working hypothesis of how I thought this might unfold? What was confirmed? What was disconfirmed? What is the evidence?

Implicit mental models are, by their very nature, lurking beneath the surface of awareness. They are elusive and slippery characters whose shapes can only be guessed at by closely measuring the footprints left in the observation material. To bring the footprints into relief, the reflective coach may want to think about four dimensions: cognitive, affective, interpersonal and intrapersonal. Exploring the cognitive patterns entails asking a series of questions. What did I know (or think I knew) about the situation? Where did I learn that? What seems to be my theoretical or hypothetical stance on the situation and what is the impact? Investigating the affective dimension, the coach looks at his or her own emotional reactions and the possible interplay of feelings and thoughts. In the example, the coach notices a sense of discomfort about possibly treading into psychological territory and thinks it might be driving persistence along a behavioural path. The third dimension is the interpersonal one. What is the power dynamic in this coach-client relationship? What is the pattern of give and take? Does the journal present a dialogue between equals or is there subtle dominance or leading? The fourth dimension is the intrapersonal. What are the patterns of coach self-awareness and self-management? Is the coach internally aligned or experiencing inner conflict?

Critical thinking processes are person-specific, varying according to the individual's abilities, experiences, personality and culture. Critical thinking often has a highly emotional dimension. Even with a systematic and logical process of critical thinking, one's own mental models are not easily drawn to the surface. Insights may occur unexpectedly and only in the wake of repeated visits to the coaching experience. In order to accurately envision that transformation, it is helpful to document several events and follow the questioning process repeatedly. This creates a bigger container for the coach's concept of coaching, one that is more complex and multi-dimensional, able to encompass all that has preceded it and accommodate more as it is encountered. This ever-expanding mental model or frame of reference incorporates the coach's point of view about self, other and the nature of coaching work.

## Step 3: Enacting the changes

Recognizing the elusive and ephemeral nature of one's own frame for coaching, the reflective practitioner must, nonetheless, look to make the meaning-making meaningful by turning learning into action.

Mindful inquiry serves as a means of socializing an individual into a community of practice (Bentz and Shapiro, 1998). If we consider coaching as a postmodern practice, it is important to note that such fields face significant challenges. Not least of these is the absence of shared agreement over what constitutes valid knowledge, what the sources of valid knowledge are and the extent to which such knowledge may be challenged. While there is no evidence that the coaching field is experiencing a crisis of public confidence such as that which Schön (1983) suggests has taken place in other fields, we also lack a substantive and cogent body of evidence about core knowledge and best practices. It therefore falls to us as individual practitioners to consider how we might evaluate our own knowledge by considering these questions:

- Is what I've learnt in my coach training sufficient as the basis for a continually evolving professional practice? What are my learning edges?
- Are my self-assessment processes producing new insights and learning?
- Can I ethically and substantially fulfil the expectations I have created with my clients?

The result of consistent reflective practice may be a change in conceptual view; a new understanding of coaching phenomena; increased self-awareness; and integration of multiple learnt and experienced forms of knowledge. The reflective practitioner is seeking to 'produce and evaluate new understandings and perspectives, create and test out new and original solutions to meeting the client's unique needs; change practice methods and values' (Rutter, 2006). The 'connective strand' of professional artistry (Paterson *et al*, 2006) requires the practitioner to consider 'how present theory and practice will relate to future theory and practice, drawing on propositional knowledge'. Reflective practice is essential to the development of these connective strands in an individual's practice.

Work-related reasoning depends on the ability to 'dialectically analyse tensions and contradictions in existing systems and see how those contradictions might be evolved through developmental transformation' (Basseches, 1984). In a dialectical engagement, the coach revisits an experience and questions the patterns and preferences that emerged in the analysis. Specifically, the reflective coach looks to answer four questions:

1 What is the basis for this preference (familiarity, philosophical/values alignment, learnt habit, prior success, other)?

**2** What are the underlying assumptions of this pattern (ie executives have a behaviour change expectation in coaching; changing behaviours changes beliefs; changing thinking is unnecessary to change behaviour)?

**3** What conditions in coaching might undermine or run counter to the underlying assumptions?

**4** What does the coach need to change (internally or externally) to extend or diversify the mental model of coaching (eg honing specific skills)? Answers to this question generate specific cognitive or behavioural changes that a coach may test out in subsequent coaching engagements.

For the coach in the example, the dialectical frame in action might include a re-evaluation of the mental model of coaching purposes and boundaries that guides judgements and may limit the framing of a client's challenges and choice of coaching strategies.

# Conclusions

Reflective practice is a useful strategy for coaches who are seeking to build their practice. The strategy, in various forms, has long been a component of ongoing professional development in fields that are parallel to coaching. The steps of collecting data from real-world experience, applying critical reflection and formulating new perspectives helps coaches develop broader repertoires and customize the choice of strategies to client and context.

Coaches can capture meaningful data from pivotal moments in coaching or a sequence of coaching interactions. By critically examining descriptions and analysing patterns and themes, the coach is able to observe the impact of expectations and chosen coaching strategies. Understanding the potential and limitations of one's own mental models suggests useful and practical opportunities for the coach's growth.

## *References*

Askeland, M K (2009) A reflexive inquiry into the ideologies and theoretical assumptions of coaching, *Coaching: An International Journal of Theory, Research and Practice*, 1 (1) 65–75

Basseches, M (1984) *Dialectical Thinking and Adult Development*, Ablex, Norwood, NJ

Bentz, V M and Shapiro, J J (1998) *Mindful Inquiry in Social Research*, Sage, Thousand Oaks, CA

Brookfield, S D (1987) *Developing Critical Thinkers: Challenging adults to explore alternative ways of thinking and acting*, Jossey-Bass, San Francisco, CA

Kegan, R (2000) What 'form' transforms? A constructive-developmental approach to transformative learning, in (eds) J Mezirow and Associates, *Learning as Transformation: Critical perspectives on a theory in progress*, Jossey-Bass, San Francisco, CA

King, P M and Kitchener, K S (1994) *Developing Reflective Judgment*, Jossey-Bass, San Francisco, CA

Liljenstrand, A M and Nebeker, D M (2008) Coaching services: a look at coaches, clients and practices, *Consulting Psychology Journal: Practice and Research*, 60 (1) 57–77

Mezirow, J (2000) Learning to think like an adult: Core concepts in transformation theory, in (eds) J Mezirow and Associates, *Learning as Transformation: Critical perspectives on a theory in progress*, Jossey-Bass, San Francisco, CA

Paterson, M, Wilcox, S and Higgs, J (2006) Exploring dimensions of artistry in reflective practice, *Reflective Practice*, 7 (4) 455–68

Rutter, L (2006) Supportive reflective, practice-based learning and assessment for post-qualifying social work, *Reflective Practice*, 7 (4) 469–82

Schön, D A (1983) *The Reflective Practitioner: How professionals think in action*, Basic Books, New York

Schön, D A (1987) *Educating the Reflective Practitioner*, Jossey-Bass, San Francisco, CA

Svaleng, I L J and Grant, A M (2010) Lessons from Norwegian coaching industry's attempt to develop joint coaching standards: an ACCESS pathway to a mature coaching industry, *The Coaching Psychologist* 6 (1) 4–13

Thorpe, K (2004) Reflective learning journals: from concept to practice, *Reflective Practice*, 5 (3) 327–43

Yin, R K (2006) Case study method, in (eds) J L Green, G Camilli and P B Elmore, *Handbook of Complementary Methods in Education Research*, Lawrence Erlbaum Associates, Hilldale, NJ

# Action learning supervision for coaches

**ROY CHILDS, MARTIN WOODS, DAVID WILLCOCK
AND ANGY MAN**

## Introduction

This chapter is about making more high quality coaching available to a much wider community. This stems from a strong belief in the benefits of coaching and a desire to create/support initiatives that promote this aim. However, our experience is that coaching, certainly coaching in organizations, has been focused on high value individuals where the concept of 'value' usually has a salary connotation. While this is understandable and, in many ways, justifiable we believe that organizations would benefit from making coaching available to more people at different levels. However, a key barrier to this is cost. Coaching is usually conducted one-to-one, which means that it involves a high level of resourcing that is inevitably costly. While those of us who believe in coaching may well argue that the benefits exceed the costs, we have found that persuading people of this does not necessarily lead to a slackening of the purse strings. This suggests that our aim of increasing the community that can benefit from coaching is likely to be a long, hard battle. We have therefore promoted the concept of action learning supervision (ALS) as a way of accelerating our aim. Along the way we have discovered that this is not a second-best option – rather it is of clear value and should exist alongside the traditional approaches to supervision. Done in the right way we believe that this is a method for launching novice coaches into a community of practice that is low cost without sacrificing the aim of achieving high standards of professional standards.

# Background to supervision in coaching

The idea and practice of supervision has its roots in counselling and therapy. In these disciplines the practitioner may address many deep, long-term issues that involve a range of psychological and emotional levels. In such situations there is a danger that the practitioner becomes emotionally entangled with the client and so supervision is seen as a way of bringing some perspective and distance to the relationship. From the therapy and counselling perspective the purpose of supervision has been seen as threefold; this was summarized by Kadushin (1992) in his discussion concerning supervision in a social work context:

1  Education – to ensure the development and upgrading of knowledge, skill and attitude through the encouragement of reflection on and exploration of their work and providing ideas, tips, techniques and knowledge to the process.

2  Support – the practical and psychological support to carry through the responsibilities of the role. Coaching is a taxing process and the stresses and pressures of the work can affect coaching performance potentially, in extreme circumstances, leading to burnout. Here the supervisor's role is to support the coach in managing the pressures and supplying emotional support where needed.

3  Administrative/managerial – the promotion and maintenance of good standards of work and adherence to policies and good practice. Here the supervisor would provide support and guidance in the areas of good practice and values of being a coach. It would include the aspects of standards, ethics and boundaries.

Since coaching is a relatively new discipline/profession, it is useful to borrow from related professions. However, important questions need to be asked about what is genuinely relevant and how far the parallels provide an appropriate or inappropriate model for coaching. Such questions are complicated by the lack of agreement on the boundaries for coaching. Some suggest that it should be focused on performance issues and behaviour change only. Others argue that, even if the aim is performance and behaviour change, these are profoundly affected by deeper psychological, emotional and motivational issues and that these will inevitably occur in the course of a good coaching relationship.

These issues aside, few would argue that the core of supervision (as defined by Kadushin) can only be beneficial to coaching as a profession and the people it hopes will benefit from good practice. However, questions still remain. An important one is how much psychological background, training and knowledge are necessary or advisable for coaches and, more pointedly, for coach supervisors. Many of those advocating supervision from a counselling or therapeutic context generally see this as absolutely essential on the basis that such coaches should see the psychological and emotional dimension to performance issues earlier and with greater clarity than their (psychologically) untrained counterparts. They may also work to a different boundary and depth with their clients and therefore regard supervision as a psychological process. However, there are many coach/mentors who neither have a counselling/therapy background nor hold it necessary to be supervised by someone who has. Their work may be more strategic than behavioural and they may regard supervision more as a process of consultation. This highlights some of the debate concerning the form that supervision should take and some of the options (Salter, 2008).

# Background to action learning

Action learning, as the name suggests, is something that happens all the time. Whatever activity we are engaged in can provide an opportunity for learning. With children we see this happening at a phenomenal rate. As we get older, we are less likely to learn as quickly and so a more conscious approach is required. What is now called action learning was founded by Reg Revans, a Cambridge scientist, in the 1930s. He observed that his colleagues learnt a good deal from each other even if they were not of the same discipline. Simply by sharing problems, questioning each other and receiving each others' views and comments, all the scientists made useful contributions even if it was not their expertise! This moved the emphasis away from knowledge and expertise towards discovery and exploration. Subsequently, as director of education and training at the National Coal Board, he developed the approach that has now been carried across the globe and applied extensively within and across organizations in every sector. As long ago as 1985, an MBA based exclusively on action learning was started and in 1995 Revans hosted the first action learning conference in London. Revans noted that 'lasting behavioural change is more likely to follow the reinterpretation of past experience than the acquisition of fresh knowledge'. This shifts the emphasis of learning towards action.

Following action there is a need to reflect and consider what has happened, what worked, what could have been better and to then consider what could be done differently. At some point this leads to experimenting with new actions and the cycle can begin again – all of which is very reminiscent of Kolb's learning cycle. Revans (1982) summarized the process in terms of a simple formula:

Learning (L) = Programmed Knowledge (P) + Insightful questioning (Q)

This means that the essentials for Action Learning are:

1 An environment in which people are willing to share, admit mistakes and learn.
2 A process of enquiry – clearly fuelled by insightful questioning.
3 Periodic opportunities to practise and review that practice.
4 Access to resources (people, books or electronic information) that can fill knowledge gaps if required.

Action learning has parallels with a number of group processes such as group facilitation, group coaching, team coaching and peer coaching (in a group context). All of these are overlapping models and all can be useful for development. However, we wanted to position our approach to the action learning model because we wanted to de-emphasize the need for the 'wise and experienced' supervisor. Now this is not to devalue what wisdom and experience has to offer – which is a great deal – but there is not enough of it around and it can be expensive.

## Why use the action learning supervision approach?

One reason for ALS is not so much the cost of traditional supervision but the fact that it is not always effective. For example, one of the critics of supervision in therapy (Myler, 2007) makes the following points:

1 Most supervision is ineffective (which he claims from his personal experience and from anecdotal evidence).
2 Supervisors are themselves problematic (making the point that a good practitioner does not necessarily make a good supervisor).
3 It is a money-spinning exercise (the fact that it has become a requirement for qualification introduces motivations beyond 'noble support').

4 Most famous therapists were never supervised in the modern sense.

5 It is a power play that plays out a parent–child relationship.

6 It can be easily replaced by other methods (namely group/peer support).

Of course it can be easy to find examples of ineffective practice and this should not be used to condemn a practice that can be done well. However, it does show the weakness of relying on one approach that may not always achieve what is desired. We are not presenting ALS as an alternative to more traditional approaches. Ideally we would see it running alongside (ie 'as well as' rather than 'instead of'). However, it is important to note that we do not see ALS as a second-best option. We regard it as having equal standing because, in some ways, it is more in tune with the basic principles of coaching. This is because, no matter how it is dressed up, the traditional approach is founded on knowledge, wisdom and expertise (ie the common expectation is that it is like an apprenticeship with 'a more experienced colleague providing learning input, challenge and support to more junior colleagues'). ALS challenges this approach in two ways. First, it proposes a group process rather than the one-to-one dyadic relationship. Second, it honours the fundamental belief of all coaching – that the coachee already has the skills and answers to his or her most important questions. A criticism of traditional approaches to supervision has been conceptualized in terms of Berne's work in transactional analysis. Myler (2007) states that:

> As a supervisor you are acting as a Parent to the counsellor's Child ego state. This means that the supervisor is not acting as coach or mentor but as a superior who is often judgemental and parental in guidance. It does not matter whether the supervisor takes a critical parent's role or that of a nurturing parent – the power play is the same. The counsellor is submitting through experience of childhood to a parental symbiosis with the supervisor. This is unhealthy and restrictive and most counsellors will take the Adaptive Child's role in that they will submit to supervision as a way to make their Parent (supervisor) happy.

While Myler cannot claim that this is true for all supervision relationships it does advise us to be wary. It could also be implied that that ALS is more easily concordant with coaching's fundamental beliefs since it does not depend on the skills and experience of a more experienced supervisor (although this can still be available). Instead, it relies on creating a spirit of enquiry together with good questioning.

These are the fundamentals of the action learning approach from which the best learning can ensue.

# What is involved: setting up the parameters

As part of the training participants are invited to sign up to the principles for working in each of the groups. These are summarized below and are communicated prior to Module 1 and then revisited prior to the division into groups. Each trainee is asked to sign up to:

- Bringing real problems, questions and issues to the group.
- Being willing to share openly his or her experiences, mistakes, hopes and fears that arise from the process of coaching – recognizing that attention is given to the process, feelings and relationships as well as the content.
- A firm (signed) commitment to treating all information disclosed by the trainee coaches and information about their coachees as confidential – the only thing to be taken out of the group is the learning (this signed commitment includes the usual proviso concerning serious illegality or risk of harm).
- Taking full responsibility for him- or herself in terms of his or her own learning and development.
- Using 'I' language as far as possible.
- Giving equal attention and commitment to other's issues and learning as he or she does to his or her own – which means giving as well as receiving.

The role of the facilitator: each group has a facilitator who helps the group to form and to understand the process. In the early stages the facilitator manages the process, which means establishing the format and timing, enabling everyone to participate, ensuring that the questions build up coherently in terms of enquiry and clarification before offering ideas and solutions, checking that the questions are of most use to the presenter of the problem, and checking with the other participants about the usefulness of the process at each step.

# How it works

There is a nine-part sequence involved in a typical action learning session, as follows:

1 A group check-in where set members report briefly on what is happening in their life including any reflections or actions from the last meeting plus a brief description of what they would like to bring to the session.

2 The group decides who will present their issues and what time will be allowed to each.

3 The first person (the presenter) is chosen, who presents a problem, experience or issue without interruption. It can sometimes be useful for this to be summarized in a short sentence and written on a flipchart.

4 The group asks clarifying questions to ensure that the elements of the problem are fully articulated and understood. These questions should be asked slowly and encourage reflection since they are designed to help the presenter to come to a deeper understanding of the issue and are not opportunities for the group to offer advice, pass judgement or tell their own anecdotes. The presenter has a clear brief to only address the questions that he or she feels are appropriate, relevant or useful.

5 When sufficient understanding has been achieved and if it is appropriate, the problem can be acted out in a 'fish bowl' setting. This involves one or more members of the group playing the role of the characters involved. For example, one member can play the role of the presenter (as coach) and another of the presenters the coachee.

6 The presenter reflects, expands or reframes the problem and then formulates some options and actions.

7 The group assists the presenter to review these options and, if he or she desires, they can offer suggestions until such time as he or she is ready to make a resolution to take specific actions (no matter how small).

8 The group then reflects on the process and gives feedback on what has taken place. It is useful to capture some of the key moments and insights and to identify what was particularly useful. It can also help to identify which questions were particularly challenging and insightful.

9 The process is then repeated with the next presenter.

For this process to work, it is important that group members show genuine respect for the presenter and that they see their role as helping him or her to articulate and understand the problems and to explore the issues. As in all such situations the key skills are listening and questioning. It can be useful to analyse the questions that are asked and to reflect on whether there is scope for a greater range and variety to be used. In the early stages, the facilitator will play a major role in this and may, sometimes, intervene by asking the questioner to rephrase the question in a more open way. However, this is all aimed at modelling the process so that eventually the group participants will become skilled at doing this themselves. Some of the ways to think about the questions asked by the group are whether they helped the presenter to:

- clarify the situation, the options or the way forward – these are 'inquiry' questions;
- achieve a deeper insight – these are 'challenging' questions;
- consider new ideas and options – these are 'catalytic' questions;
- identify/release hidden emotions that are blocking the process – these are 'cathartic' questions.

## CASE STUDY 1   (David Willcock facilitator)

The key theme that emerged very early on was the development of good listening and questioning. Perhaps this was particularly evident because of the background of the people in this action learning group. All were very busy operational managers who had been selected for the programme to help the organization develop a coaching and mentoring capability. Their usual style (which had been the basis for their success in their career to date) was to work at a fast pace, giving advice and opinion and making quick decisions. Hence the expectation of their organizational role was to provide (rather than facilitate) solutions. This was in stark contrast to the needs of the coaching role they were hoping to take up. They needed to learn to appreciate the need for a slower pace and for different kinds of questions – ones that would encourage the coachee to reflect on the meaning and best course of action that would be true for him or her. However, the early group dynamics were characterized by their old habits – a fast pace, rapid conversations and the trading of views and opinions interspersed with leading questions. All were well intentioned, but the intellectual understanding of the coaching process and skills (acquired in the training modules) had yet to become natural. It quickly became apparent that the style they used in the action learning groups was habitual and was inevitably played out in their coach/coachee interactions. The facilitator's contribution helped them to reflect on how they were operating and what needed to change – namely to learn, listen and ask questions that were relevant to the presenting issue, rather than making judgements, giving advice based on their own experience and getting side-tracked with their own examples.

Thus the action learning group provided a context for learning from the parallel process – how their approach in the group mirrored how they worked with their coachees. All group members, to a greater or lesser extent, tended to slip into advice-giving with coachees early on in the programme, making suggestions about action or asking 'leading' questions. Working on this in the group helped them to experience the benefits of the coaching approach directly – asking the questions, providing space for the focal person to reflect, staying with the silence rather than filling it. Since the facilitator was able to demonstrate (role model) the appropriate behaviour they all learnt to recognize the appropriate approach and soon began to call each other to account, thus increasing the amount of listening and questioning in the group. Early on in the programme a 'time out' would often be called to review the group process, the impact it was having and the implications for coaching practice. Knowledge inputs were provided where relevant, such as a reinforcement of good listening and questioning and an explanation of the issues of power and control in the coaching relationship.

From the facilitator's perspective a key learning point was that, no matter how well defined your process or ground rules, the process is going to be 'lumpy' in the early stages. Patiently role modelling the process combined with group coaching and occasional 'expert' inputs gradually steered the action learning set towards a more sustainable self-managed process. Maintaining a light touch and a sense of humour also helped. The groups' development over the period of the programme can be likened to a shift in the locus of control, from the facilitator to the action learning group members and from them as coaches to their coachees. A key lesson that emerged over the period of the programme was summarized by one group member who said: 'Of all the actions agreed with my coachees, the only actions they committed to and followed through on were those they arrived at themselves. All the actions I suggested earlier in the programme were not followed through on. This is powerful learning for me.'

## CASE STUDY 2   (Martin Woods facilitator)

The background for this case study is an action learning group of five individuals who worked for a large local government authority. The participants were aiming to become internal coaches across a partnership of local authorities – this was part of the process for introducing a coaching culture within the authority. The trainee coaches had attended as a large group of 24 trainees but the action learning based supervision was in the smaller groups. One of the trainee's (Rose – name changed) main role within the authority was as a trainer and subsequently training manager. She was very enthusiastic about this role, which she enjoyed, but she saw the benefits of undertaking the coaching training and supervision to extend her skill set and effectiveness.

At the first session, the facilitator explained the process for action learning (see above) and the importance of bringing real coaching examples and issues to subsequent meetings. To facilitate this, the other four members agreed to use each other as coachees. In addition they agreed to seek out other coachees so that they could obtain sufficient practice in between meetings. The group took personal responsibility for arranging their own practice sessions and reviews and used the ALS sessions as a way of formally reviewing their progress and presenting questions on how to best learn and progress.

At the second ALS session Rose presented her issue, which was about how she could become more 'inquiring' since she recognized her tendency to 'fix'. She explained that, having been a trainer for many years as well as having a personality that tended towards being a real action-based problem solver, she couldn't stop herself from suggesting ways to resolve her coachee's issues. She recognized that the coaching process was different – requiring her to help the coachee identify his or her own way forward. She was finding this hard to do.

Rose then summarized her 'issue' as 'turning problem solving into enquiry'. The group then began to ask her questions about her last coaching session. This enabled her to identify specific examples of when she had slipped into problem-solving rather than enquiring. The process required the facilitator to act as 'referee' by 'blowing the whistle' when the group moved towards closed questions or trying to give advice. Once Rose had a clear picture of what she did and how she did it she was asked what she felt would be the best way forward. She decided to 'try doing it differently' by practising in front of the group. This meant choosing one of the members to play the role of her coachee. During the role play the facilitator called some 'time-outs' which allowed a review of progress at various points.

Rose was surprised by how often she unconsciously stepped into 'fixing' things. Interestingly, during the time-outs, the group also demonstrated the same tendency – ie suggesting how she could have phrased her question rather than asking her how she might have phrased it differently. This was an extremely useful example of the 'parallel process' whereby Rose's own tendencies were being played out by the group. She was also able to give feedback to the group about how, when they showed genuine curiosity (enquiring rather than giving advice), she found herself relaxing and being able to be more reflective, thoughtful and experimental. She stated how she felt more in control, more respected and more willing to trust her own thinking and conclusions. In other words, the coaching process was being enacted.

Naturally, Rose was not immediately able to make all the necessary changes but over a period of two or three ALS sessions it became clear that her practice was improving dramatically. This became really clear to the group when, at a later meeting, Rose facilitated the learning of another group member. In a 'fish bowl' coaching process she managed to pursue an issue with a group member right through to a quality outcome (without intervention or time-outs). The 'coachee' had not expected to make such progress and this was the point at which both Rose and the group realized the progress she had made. Subsequently Rose has presented a very competent portfolio of coaching evidence to the coaching assessment team, resulting in her obtaining her recognized coaching qualification with flying colours.

The successes in this action learning group can be summarized as follows:

- *Trust:* the development of openness and trust between members was very evident – from some hesitant beginnings to some very open declarations of fears, uncertainties and vulnerabilities that the group respected and supported. The group became able to discuss almost anything without fear of judgement.

- *Responsibility:* there can be a propensity for the group facilitator to take an expert/parental role. The process allows a rapid shift from being facilitator-led to self-managing – and this group took early responsibility for managing their own time and learning. After the second ALS they began running sessions without the facilitator (which were necessarily restricted due to costs).

- *Diversity of process:* the process is flexible enough to appeal to all learning styles – visual (the group members see each other in action in co-coaching scenarios played out in the ALS sessions), auditory (group members hear examples of good and bad practice) and kinaesthetic (group members have the opportunity to try out new ways of working and responding to what 'effective' feels like).

- *Diversity of inputs:* the process encourages non-experts to contribute. It is very powerful to see how even the most naive question can produce great learning.

- *Learning through action:* the focus is on learning not judgement. This gives trainee coaches an opportunity to experiment live. It also gives them a rare opportunity to see others in action. This not only gives a rich source of ideas about questioning and styles through observation, but it also provides real practice in a safe environment.

# Why is ALS useful: what are the benefits of this approach?

As we mentioned at the start of this chapter, one of the key benefits of an ALS set approach is its low cost. Using external coaches or supervisors can be expensive. By teaching people ALS skills and role modelling these with the group, the process skills are built in preparation for 'going alone', which makes for a very efficient model. Thus, although efficiency and cost were the initial drivers for this approach, the benefits appear to be much wider. They include:

- A process that allows multiple relationships and perspectives to become part of the learning process.

- The development of relationships that extend the informal network of communication, which has impact beyond the work on the coaching development – an antidote to the isolation that is sometimes felt by those primarily engaged in coaching in organizations.

- A tone and approach that is empowering since all group members contribute and new trainees learn that they have valuable perspectives that are helpful to others even when they are not 'experts'.

- Moving from a culture of 'training' to one of 'learning by doing' with the opportunity to take risks in a safe environment and hence allowing people to experiment and 'stretch' with different approaches and behaviours.

- Moving responsibility for learning from the 'teacher' to the 'learner' and the avoidance of 'social loafing' since all members are actively involved.

- A forum where people can feel listened to and where feelings and emotions can be expressed and explored.

- A self-sustaining process – group members can continue to meet and support even when funding dries up.

- Creating a community of practice that allows the ideas and principles to be more widely shared and promoted within the organization than tends to happen with individually focused interventions.

Our experience of ALS is that it can work very well – and that it has advantages over individual supervision. We recognize that some people who have experienced individual supervision may doubt that they would learn as much in a group situation; this is usually because they have concerns about developing the high level of trust that is necessary for a group to operate with the degrees of openness and challenge that characterizes the best ALS groups. Perhaps this means that ALS is not the right approach for some groups. However, our experience is that the people who want to become coaches have a strong orientation towards openness, learning and support.

# Conclusion

Traditional approaches to supervision can be highly effective – but not in all situations at all times. We know that the purpose of supervision should be to develop competence, capability and learning in an environment that opens people up for this opportunity rather than closes it down. The word 'supervision' can have connotations of one-way traffic, of the 'right-wrong' world of the expert. Given some of the limitations and criticisms it is useful to have alternative approaches. In the same way as there is a need for both individual therapy and group therapy, there is value in individual supervision and group supervision. For those interested in group supervision, the approach adopted here, stimulated by the action learning approach, has merit as a tool since it fits closely with the coaching ethos.

## References

Kadushin, A (1992) What's wrong, what's right with social work supervision, *The Clinical Supervisor*, 10 (1) 3–19

Myler, S (2007) Supervision for Therapists – A Critique, **http://ezinearticles. com/?Supervision-for-Therapists--A-Critique&id=561830**, accessed 5 July 2010

Revans, R W (1982) *The Origin and Growth of Action Learning*, Chartwell-Bratt, Brickley, UK

Salter, T (2008) *International Journal of Evidence Based Coaching and Mentoring*, Special, 2, November (**www.business.brookes.ac.uk/research/areas/ coaching&mentoring**)

# The Gestalt supervision model

**MARION GILLIE**

## Introduction

There is a growing interest in the application of Gestalt principles to coaching, with an increasing number of articles (Gillie, 2009; Siminovitch and Van Eron, 2006; Simon, 2009) including a special edition of the *International Gestalt Journal* specifically on coaching (Magerman and Leahy, 2009). However, at the time of writing there is nothing in the literature on the application of Gestalt theory to *coach* supervision, only to clinical supervision. Siminovitch and Van Eron (2006) say that Gestalt coaching 'offers a safe arena where vulnerability, strong emotions, and failure can play themselves out in the service of learning and growth'. I agree with this description and I believe it is particularly true of Gestalt-oriented supervision, where supervisees can feel especially vulnerable as they put their practice 'on the line' in front of a fellow professional.

The exact genesis of the theory and practice of Gestalt is difficult to pinpoint accurately. Frederick 'Fritz' Perls (a psychoanalyst trained in Berlin, Frankfurt and Vienna), his wife Laura and his co-author Paul Goodman are generally recognized as the originators of Gestalt therapy as we know it, and the practice of Gestalt integrates a great many influences. In this chapter I show how the core principles of Gestalt can form a coherent model for coach supervision and can complement other supervision models. I offer examples of supervisor–supervisee dialogue, all of which have been taken from my own practice.

# The core principles of Gestalt

Coach supervision has evolved out of the practice of clinical supervision. Resnick and Estrup (2000: 125) believe that clinical supervision requires a theoretical frame of reference that can be articulated and which enables the supervisor to account for his or her practice and interventions. I believe this to be equally true of coach supervision. Such a frame needs to include the supervisor's theoretical stance on:

- the nature of human functioning;
- the process of human growth and change;
- a methodology of intervening that is consistent with these core principles.

## *The nature of human functioning*

The supervisor supports coaches in their personal growth and professional development so, therefore, needs an understanding of basic behaviour and functioning of the human being, ie what facilitates growth and what interrupts development and learning.

The Gestalt theory of human functioning grew from the work of Gestalt psychologists who studied how people organize experience to make sense of their world. Perls became interested in the research on human perception, which concluded that we seem to be 'hard wired' to see wholes, and when data are missing we strive to make meaning by filling in the gaps (switch off a familiar piece of music before the end of the 'phrase' and who doesn't complete it silently in their head?) As you look at another person you don't see an arm, then a leg, etc, you see another human being, and this whole is the *Gestalt* (the rough translation of 'Gestalt' being shape, form or pattern). Perls applied this notion to the emotional and intra-personal realms, concluding that when important needs are not met and the 'Gestalt' remains incomplete, energy remains invested in the ongoing attempt to finish 'unfinished business'.

One key influence was the work of Kurt Koffka (1935) who described the process by which we organize our visual perception as that of *figure and ground*. Unless people are in thick fog, where the visual field is a blur, people focus on one thing at a time (the figure) and everything else is the ground against which that figure appears. Attention then moves on and that figure dissolves into the background as a new figure emerges. As I look around a crowded room, I don't see all of the people and all of the room at once; I differentiate (and thereby make sense of my world) by focusing on one person or thing at a time. Another example:

> As I am typing my thoughts about this chapter (current figure), I begin to notice that I'm feeling chilly, but I don't want to stop writing. However, the sensation of cold (new figure) becomes such that I can no longer concentrate on my writing, and need to take action and find a jacket. Now warm again (the need is met) I begin to notice that I am hungry (new figure) and so on ….

Over the decades this process has been developed from the purely psycho-biological into a theory that describes the process by which we interact with our environment (including the world of other people) to meet our emotional, psychological and social needs. Figure 4.1 shows the Gestalt *Continuum of Experience*[1] (eg, Melnick and Nevis, 2005) which emphasizes the continuous flow which, if uninterrupted, happens effortlessly all of the time. It is what Perls referred to as *self-regulation*, and 'a measure of psychological health and well-being is how you move (or not) with grace through this never-ending flow' (Gillie, 2009: 34).

Of course it's not that simple. Healthy self-regulation requires the person to, a) notice the sensations as they arise that indicate a need is forming, b) accurately identify that need, c) know what action will satisfy that need and, d) have the capability and resourcefulness to take the appropriate action. Anyone who has ever eaten a bar of chocolate to cheer themselves up, or had too many alcoholic drinks to 'drown their sorrows' will know that this process can become all messed up. Thus a critical aspect of the Gestalt supervisor's role is to help supervisees identify their *real* need (we call this 'the *figure of interest*'), explore what action would be appropriate, and find out what they need to do to mobilize to act.

---

Jane comes to a supervision session saying that she has good news; against all odds, her coaching contract with a local authority has been extended for another year. She has worked hard to negotiate this. Her tone is flat, her shoulders are slumped, and she looks glum. When I ask her how she feels about this, she tells me that it is great, because it will be an enormous help financially when she is making other changes in her life. She looks down at her feet as she says this and sounds far from great. I invite her to exaggerate her posture and tone, and to say the words again ('It's great …'). She tries this for a moment, then stamps her foot on the floor, raises her head and shouts 'It's not bloody great at all …'.

**FIGURE 4.1** The continuum of experience

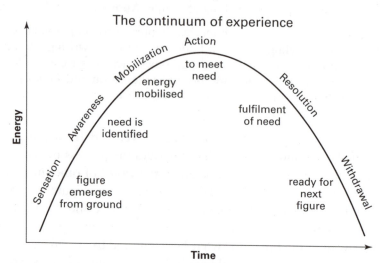

We discover that she really doesn't enjoy the work there any more, but she feels trapped and believes that she 'should stay there for the sake of the money'. In this illustration, the 'presented issue' (her good news) is clearly *not* the real figure of interest. The Gestalt continuum of experience tells me that the supervisee's level of energy (as manifest in body, tone, etc) is a big clue as to how genuinely 'interested' the person is, because when the real figure of interest (need) is identified, energy *always* swells, and then you know that you are working on something that matters. In this example, the supervisor is helping the supervisee become clearer about her own needs, and on another level, is developing the supervisee's capability to do this with her own clients.

## Meaning-making

Perls was deeply interested in how people create meaning and 'make sense' of their world. He studied Zen Buddhism, existential philosophy and the 'phenomenological method', all of which contributed to Gestalt's focus on understanding the person's immediate lived experience, from moment to moment in the 'here and now'. He became fascinated by the fact that every individual exists within a highly complex context that is totally unique to him or her, and which shapes his or her view of the world. Further, he recognized that it is impossible to make any sense of a person's lived experience without some understanding of this context.

He drew on Kurt Lewin's field theory (Lewin, 1951), which calls the totality of a person's context his or her 'phenomenological field', and includes his or her immediate situation, personal history, thoughts, feelings, conscious and unconscious beliefs, anxieties and fears, memories of past experiences, hopes and aspirations. In any situation what stands out for us, what we notice, what we hear, what we assume (ie what becomes *'figural'*) is a function of many things that are unique to us.

In the above example, as Jane tells me her 'good news', it would have been very easy for me to move quickly into congratulating her, to hear the words, remember previous conversations about this contract and, as a result, impose my meaning on her situation. My context and Jane's are different. I am aware of the tough year Jane has had and of my desire for her to find success. However, even though this is my fifth session with the same supervisee, the here and now context is new each time. While Jane would have been thrilled about this contract four months ago, her context has changed and I need to set aside my preconceived ideas of what it is like in her shoes. I need to help her find *her* meaning, which I do by helping the real figure of interest to emerge.

## The wider field

While individuals brings to supervision their unique phenomenological field, everything is part of a wider field, which includes ethnicity (supervisor, supervisee, end client) culture (organizational, country), society (historical and current prevailing perspectives on gender, sexual orientation and class) and the economic and political climate, to name a few. While nobody could be expected to be consciously aware of all aspects of this wider field, Gestalt nevertheless holds that all parts are interrelated and to be understood; a person must be seen within his or her wider context.

Peter is coaching a young Asian woman who has just been promoted to a senior role in an investment bank. Peter talks of his frustration with his client's reluctance to assert her own needs. We explore their relationship (what she evokes in him, what parallel might there be with this and her impact on her colleagues). We explore his 'process', ie the *'shoulds'* that he holds about the behaviour of senior leaders ('she's a senior manager now, she ought to be able to speak her mind …'). It suddenly occurs to me that the wider cultural issues are simply not in my supervisee's awareness … what are the acceptable ways of being in her culture of origin? What are the rules she may hold about how assertive a women from her culture can be?

This session illustrates how a Gestalt perspective can complement the Seven-eyed Model (Hawkins, 2006), indeed our supervision focus moves from the coaching relationship (Mode 3) to Peter's own process (Mode 4) onto the wider context (Mode 7). It enabled Peter to acknowledge his blind spot about this 'lens', stretch his thinking and enhance his practice as a coach.

## The process of human growth and change

### The paradoxical theory of change

Every model of coach supervision needs a coherent theory of how change takes place and how supervision supports this process. Gestalt's approach to change grew out of Perls' fundamental conflict with the psychiatric and psychological establishments of his day, whose methods were rooted in a model that, to put it crudely, aimed to change people judged to be in need of 'fixing'.

Perls observed that trying to force change, even when the change is desired, simply sets up (not necessarily consciously) resistance to that change. Arnold Beisser first documented his understanding of Perls' stance when he described the paradoxical theory of change: 'change occurs when one becomes what one is, not when he tries to become what he is not' (Beisser, 1970: 77). Perls' experience showed him that change does occur, however, in an emergent, organic way, when his clients engaged in a process of exploring and *staying with what is*, which in turn enabled them to discover their real needs, which in turn facilitated the process of healthy self-regulation (as outlined above). People who are trying to 'push change', particularly those trying to meet some externally imposed standard (real or imagined) are inevitably caught between two positions *how it should be* and *how it really is*, without fully identifying with either. Anyone who has tried to lose weight/give up smoking/start exercise because someone else applies pressure (parent, partner, doctor, society) will be familiar with the rebellion–remorse cycle ('To hell with it, I'll just have one more' followed by 'I've blown it again'). This is the pattern that Perls named the top-dog/under-dog dichotomy (Perls, 1969). Beisser's premise is that 'one must stand in one place in order to have firm footing to move, and that it is difficult or impossible to move without that footing' (p 77). Without that firm footing the swing between 'I should … I won't' is inevitable and, paradoxically, once a person can stand *fully* in the place that is reality, then the energy that gets diverted into rebellion is released and mobilized towards something which is a *genuine choice*. Remember Jane in the case above.

> Jane tells me that she is happy yet her whole body is telling me something different. I work with her to really stay with, in fact to exaggerate, her body's message (which I imagine is her real position). As she does this, her skin tone reddens, she stamps her foot and shouts (indeed there is a tremendous release of energy). I invite her to shout once again 'It's not bloody great at all …', and then she says, 'Yes this is absolutely right, I really *don't* want to work there any more', she looks very grounded as she says this, and it is clear to me that she is fully acknowledging her truth. As her burst of energy subsides, we are able to engage in a conversation about what her options are, what feels possible and how to handle the pressure on her from her partner.

## Change through relationship

Gestalt also holds that change happens through *relationship*. The importance of the quality of the relationship between supervisor/ supervisee is not exclusive to Gestalt of course (eg De Haan, 2008), but Gestalt does bring a perspective, which is quite different from conventional wisdom. To Perls, the 'self' is not a semi-fixed entity that endures over time. Instead 'self' is a process, always in flux and totally contextual; it is a function of what gets evoked in the interaction between individuals under the unique set of circumstances of that particular interaction (Perls, 1978). Simply put, the 'me' that I experience when I am with my boss is likely to be different in some respect from the 'me' that I experience when I am with my best friend. The implication of this for supervision is that you, as supervisor, are a critical aspect of the supervisee's experience and how you 'show up' will inform (not necessarily consciously) what the supervisee chooses to reveal. Two aspects of the way you work as a Gestalt supervisor are critical: your *presence* and your ability to engage in *dialogue*.

Presence is much more than how 'professional' you are as a supervisor. It includes how 'grounded' you are in yourself and your work, how able you are to 'contact' the client, even when they are difficult to reach. It is the ability to *be in the here and now*, ie to tune into what is going on within yourself (your reactions to your supervisees, what they evoke in you, what images come to mind, what sensations are stimulated) as you are impacted by them, and to disclose some of this in order to 'make contact'.

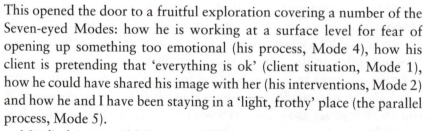

I am listening to Peter talk about his client who has returned to work after a miscarriage and is struggling as a new partner in a professional services firm. Peter talks in a jolly, light, cheerful manner and I notice that I am struggling to stay present. Suddenly the image of a bird comes to mind. I see it skimming along the top of the hedgerow, never really coming to land anywhere. I share this image with Peter, owning that it is *my* image, and ask if it has any meaning for either him or his relationship with his client.

I trust that because this vivid image has arisen within the interaction between me and my supervisee it is reasonable to assume that it has some relevance to the supervisee's situation and is worth checking out. You do this of course in the service of *his or her* awareness and part of the process is to find out what impact your disclosure has had on him or her.

Peter is thoughtful for a while, then looks at me and says that he feels a bit embarrassed about an image that he has had a couple of times when working with this client, of a pint of thick stout, black beneath the surface but frothy and white on top. He looks at me intently, and I notice how much more engaged I feel.

This opened the door to a fruitful exploration covering a number of the Seven-eyed Modes: how he is working at a surface level for fear of opening up something too emotional (his process, Mode 4), how his client is pretending that 'everything is ok' (client situation, Mode 1), how he could have shared his image with her (his interventions, Mode 2) and how he and I have been staying in a 'light, frothy' place (the parallel process, Mode 5).

My disclosure enabled Peter and me to *make contact*, ie relate in a different way, to move from 'skimming the surface' to something more helpful to him and to us. This is the Gestalt notion of 'dialogue', which has its roots in Buber's (1970) existential philosophy that differentiates between 'I-thou' interaction (two people engaging in an open, mutually respectful way without attempting to impose their will on the other) and 'I-it' interactions in which one or both attempt to shape the other towards some desired outcome. Genuine, moving contact cannot be made to happen. It flows from the supervisor's willingness to be him- or herself without any attachment to what might happen in the encounter. This means that as a Gestalt supervisor, I am particularly attentive to the quality of the relationship between the two of us. Even when I step into the role of educator or challenger of ethical practice, the overarching spirit in which I work is one of dialogue, with mutuality of respect and directness of contact at its heart. I never lose sight of the fact that I may have greater 'expertise' in psychological theory and more years' experience than my supervisees, but they are the experts on their own experience.

In this section, I have outlined the core theoretical principles of the Gestalt approach. The next section offers a clear methodology for intervening which flows from those principles.

## Working with Gestalt in supervision

Whether inviting the supervisee to stay with 'what is' (paradoxical theory of change) or disclosing your own feelings, observations, images, etc (presence and dialogue) the overarching rationale is to support the process of self-regulation, the healthy flow through the continuum of experience. In his original writing, Perls maintained that the route to healthy self-regulation is self-awareness and believed that awareness *per se* – by and of itself – can bring growth, because when we know and understand how we limit ourselves, we open up choice (Perls, 1969). He later acknowledged that awareness alone could be a slow method of achieving change, and developed the idea of active experimentation as a creative way of accelerating growth (Perls, 1973). By experimentation he meant encouraging clients to try something out in the session to see what new awareness or new learning it might elicit.

This section explores the many ways that the Gestalt supervisor might work to raise the awareness of the supervisees and mobilize them towards appropriate action, using the complementary methodologies of phenomenological exploration and active experimentation.[2]

## *Phenomenological exploration*

This wonderful term simply means working with the *'in the moment' data* that the supervisee brings into the room, without any interpretation, comment or judgement from the supervisor. Typically, the supervisor pays close attention to the supervisee's movements, breathing pattern, changes in skin tone (red patches, going pale, etc) and tracks patterns that emerge over time. The supervisor would then share these observations and invite the supervisee to note his or her own 'here and now' reactions, which might be sensations, feelings, images or thoughts, eg:

> Supervisor: 'I notice that every time you talk about coaching in that organization, you look down and shake your head *(the supervisor would then mirror the movement as a way of focusing on the phenomenon rather than offering a verbal interpretation)*. As you think of the organization again, and maybe try that movement again, what do you become aware of ...?'

With every move closer to the supervisee's actual experience, he or she becomes increasingly aware of the intensity of the feeling, which will lead to greater clarity about the real needs in the situation. Furthermore, if the supervisee can *stay* with his or her 'stuckness' and experience it fully, often by exaggerating it, it will usually either dissolve or transform, freeing the supervisee up to move forward. By working with the phenomenological data you support a journey of discovery.

> Ralph is new to running his own coaching business, having been an internal coach for many years. He has just started coaching a very senior woman in a pharmaceuticals firm. He is giving me a detailed description of their second session, in which he felt stuck. He keeps shuffling his feet and rubbing his hand up and down his arm as he speaks.

Nothing stands out in his lengthy account, which is bland with no clear figure of interest, but his body appears to have information of which he seems unaware. I invite him to move away from 'talking about' into 're-experiencing', as a way of moving closer to his actual experience:

> **Supervisor:** 'Imagine that you are back there, in that session with her in front of you ... take a long look at her, what do you notice? How does she look ... her tone of voice ... what do you notice about your own reactions, feelings, sensations, thoughts ...?'
>
> **Ralph:** 'I feel tense. I can feel my stomach muscles tighten ....'
>
> **Supervisor:** 'As you speak I am aware that I am holding my breath, and I see you wrap your arms across your body. What happens if you exaggerate that movement?'
>
> **Ralph:** (lets out a long breath) 'Yeah, I was holding my breath too ... (tightens his arms) ... I think I'm trying to hold myself together ... (stays with the movement). Yes, definitely, I realize that I am trying to protect myself.'

The supervisee was stuck in an early phase of the cycle of experience; he was not aware enough of his needs in the situation. My first supervision task was to help him to clarify the *real* figure of interest. By re-creating the 'in the moment' experience with his client and then staying with (and even exaggerating) the sensations evoked, Ralph could access a greater awareness of what this client elicits and a very clear figure emerges (his need to protect himself) which opens the door to the next step, which is what this means for him in terms of his work with this client.

Once this level of awareness has been reached, many supervisees will naturally clarify what they intend to do next. In Ralph's case, he decided to disclose his insight to his client, given that she may evoke similar reactions in others in her organization and it would give her useful data.

## Active experimentation

There are occasions, however, when despite his or her level of awareness, the supervisee is stuck because he or she feels unable to act ('Yes, I could do that, but ...'). Here the supervisee is blocked at the mobilization phase of the continuum of experience and active experimentation can help the supervisee mobilize energy into appropriate action. Had Ralph been stuck at this point, I might have invited him to 'try out' what he'd like to say to her, or suggested he put himself in her shoes (more on this methodology later). There are always many options, and the Gestalt supervisor is guided by his or her knowledge of the supervisee, 'grades' the suggestion according to how much challenge is appropriate, and always seeks genuine consent to try the experiment.

## Active experimentation through metaphor

Ideas for experiments will flow naturally from the material presented by the supervisee, if you allow yourself to relax and 'be present'. However, for supervisors who are new to Gestalt (or believe they lack creativity in crafting experiments) a fruitful route to identifying possible experiments is through metaphor. As a Gestalt supervisor I pay close attention to the metaphors and images used by the supervisee, and allow possibilities to float through my mind. For instance, when Ralph first used the word 'stuck' I pictured him physically 'stuck' eg in the chair, or standing unable to move. Recently another supervisee described her contract with one organization as being in a 'straitjacket' from which she wanted to 'break free' but didn't know how. I happened to have a very thick scarf with me, and after contracting to do so, I wrapped the scarf around her, trapping her arms by her side, and invited her to 'break free'. She started with little energy, but as my grip tightened, she began to mobilize. As she wrestled and struggled I asked her to articulate what was happening. Eventually she leapt out of my grasp shouting 'I won't put up with this any more!' We were then able to explore how she might mobilize her energy towards re-contracting with this organization.

People use metaphor much more frequently than is noticed. Sometimes the metaphor is simply a well-established colloquial phrase (eg 'I was on thin ice', 'he's out of his depth'), and sometimes it can be the doorway to completely new awareness. However, all too often we hear a metaphor and assume that it means the same to the supervisee as it does to us.

---

June is coaching Mark, an intelligent, creative director from a media company. She feels slightly stuck about how best to work with him. She tells me that working with him 'is a bit like struggling up hill, where you can't get a grip because of the small stones'. In a misplaced attempt at empathy I tell her that this sounds tough (my interpretation). 'Oh no! It's really exhilarating … like climbing a challenging, steep hillside!' I acknowledge my assumption (I'd forgotten that she is a hiker) and ask if she is willing to explore the metaphor. I invite her to imagine the hill track and where she is on it.

**June:**  '… about halfway up. Mark is near the top'.

**Supervisor:** 'What happens if you stand and look around, what do you see, experience? Try it out if you'd like to.'

**June:** 'I look up and see Mark, and can feel my feet slide a bit on the loose stones … it's scary (she stands up and imitates the movement), hard to get my balance.'

**Supervisor:** 'Ok, so if you stay where you are, what happens?'

**June:** 'Hmmm, I can stand still for a moment and get my balance back. It feels good, I feel much stronger.'

**Supervisor:** 'So what happens if you look back to the top?'

**June:** 'I am picturing myself walking up a mountain track, it is getting steeper.'

**Supervisor:** 'Do want to try it out?'

**June:** (takes a couple of steps) 'Yes, I *know* that it's what I want to do, I can do it. I can imagine the view from the top, it's really rewarding!'

**Supervisor:** 'What's the "it" you know you want, can do and will be rewarding?'

**June:** 'I can get to the top.'

**Supervisor:** 'And Mark?'

**June:** (long pause) 'It fits. He certainly challenges me, and I do feel on a slippery slope sometimes. But I can see that I haven't been challenging *him* as much as I need to. If I pause, slow myself down, I can stay grounded, and then we can both get to the top.'

By working with her metaphor as she develops the theme, she arrives at a new awareness of what she needs to do in her work with him. Of course Gestalt is not the only approach to use metaphor, but it does have a particular way of engaging supervisees with the metaphor, bringing them as close as possible to their experience in the here and now, which evokes a level of awareness that goes beyond the cognitive.

## Active experimentation with the classic two chairs/empty chair approach

When many people think of 'Gestalt' it is this way of working that often comes to mind. The two-chair/empty chair approach is particularly useful when you hear 'duality' of some kind in the supervisee's story. This might take the form of the supervisee facing a dilemma ('On the one hand I could …, but on the other hand …'). Or you might hear your supervisee engaging in an internal battle with different aspects of themselves. This often takes the form of a critical 'Top-dog' that tells the supervisee how he or she *should* be and how inadequate he or she is, and a hopeless, stuck side that passively resists, which Perls (1969) called the 'under-dog'.

In both cases, neither side of the duality is fully owned, and the supervisee remains stuck as they oscillate between the two horns of the dilemma or the two inner voices, and energy is trapped in the constant movement between the two positions. Mobilization comes when each side is brought fully into awareness (separation) then brought into contact with each other (integration):

Alan is debating whether to leave a well-paid, secure role as internal consultant to set up his own business. I hear him going round in circles. This is a classic dilemma where there is no easy or obvious answer. I offer Alan two chairs, one for each option, and suggest he sits in each in turn and talks about the benefits. This physical separation supports the untangling of the thoughts and emotions that accompany a genuine dilemma. I watch carefully for what happens to Alan's energy as he speaks. As he talks of his current role, his tone is fairly flat, except when he talks about his wonderful colleagues. As he switches seats, he becomes much more animated.

In my experience, supervisees usually have more energy for one option than the other, which is outside their awareness but which shows through in their body language. My task is to help Alan become aware consciously of what he 'unconsciously' knows. I share my observation and invite Alan to revisit the two chairs and try exaggerating his energy as he does so, flatter for one option and animated for the other. Alan realizes that he has already made his decision. We are then able to move into a discussion about next steps, in particular about how he can support his need for social contact.

This way of working is also very useful when the supervisee is experiencing some difficulty in his or her relationship with another person. There are many variations depending on the situation:

- Supervisees place the other person (eg their client) on the 'empty chair' and experiments with what they would really like to say (you could go further: ask the supervisee to exaggerate, be outrageous, be 'super coach', etc).

- Supervisees swap chairs and speak as the client, eg how does the client respond to the supervisee's statement? The supervisee could speak as the client: what do they want from the coach?
- Invite supervisees to stand away from the two chairs and to imagine watching the coach–client exchange. What do they see? If they were to give the coach (themself) advice, what would it be?

This can be quite a challenging experiment for supervisees who are new to this way of working, so it is important that you clarify your suggestion beforehand so that they can give genuine consent or can genuinely decline. However, it is extraordinary the insight someone can get by stepping into the other's shoes.

Finally, whatever experiments you work with it is important that you have plenty of time in the session to help them make sense of their experience and help them clarify what choices they want to make about their situation going forward.

## Active experimenting working with the whole system

Supervision is a valuable place for coaches to explore the complex systemic and boundary issues that arise when working within an organization (Mode 7 of the Seven-eyed Model). Coaches have many relationships to juggle, eg with their coachee, the coachee's boss, other senior sponsors, with HR, possibly with other coachees in the same sub-system, etc. By inviting your supervisee to bring the system into the room, you can use active experimentation to support exploration of these complexities.

There are many ways of doing this. If I am working in an environment that is 'artefact rich' I ask my supervisee to select a range of objects to represent themself, the client, the boss, other relevant individuals or sub-systems, etc. However, if such interesting material isn't available, I might invite my supervisee to represent each person/sub-group with a picture or image. This opens up a range of possible experiments depending on the issue at hand.

You could explore what each person in the system evokes in your supervisee. In my office I have a bowl of stones collected from all over the world. One supervisee selected a stone to represent each person in his system:

Supervisor: 'Take each stone and describe the person it represents in terms of that stone.'

Supervisee: 'Yes, this is definitely Nigel, very sharp edges and a dark side!'

It is amazing what someone can project onto a piece of granite. You have many options now: one would be to ask the supervisee to speak as each person, using the words elicited by the object, eg the supervisee above might speak as 'Nigel', 'I have a sharp edge, I have a dark side', which could lead to an interesting conversation about, a) how Nigel might feel in the system, b) what of himself the supervisee sees in Nigel.

You might ask the supervisee to give each object/picture a voice. What would it be saying if it could speak? This can reveal insights about how the supervisee sees others in the system and how others might see each other.

When the issue seems to be tricky relationships you might ask the supervisee to place each object, image or picture in relationship one with another, where the distance between them could be strength of relationship, degree of trust, who is closest to whom, etc. From there, you could invite your supervisee to stand in each location, and to speak from that place in terms of what it feels like to be there, how he or she perceives the rest of the system as he or she looks around, what needs he or she has, etc. While it is important to hold in mind that you are not working with the real system but with the projections of the supervisee onto the system, I have found it a creative way of exploring the wider systemic issues.

# Gestalt supervision vs Gestalt therapy

Supervision clearly plays a key role in the *professional* development of the coach, and in my experience this cannot be separated from his or her *personal* journey. Achieving excellence in coaching requires a high level of self-awareness, the ability of the coaches to reflect on their 'process' (both when they are effective and when they are less so, ie, their biases, how they 'get stuck', how they get 'hooked' by the client or client's material, etc). In turn this requires the supervisor to work in ways that facilitate this level of exploration.

Gestalt supervision is particularly well placed to do this. However, given that that Gestalt approaches originate in Gestalt therapy and the human body is such a gateway to the supervisee's emotions, the Gestalt-oriented supervisor needs to pay particular attention to the boundary between supervision and therapy. I am aware that my Gestalt orientation predisposes me to work in certain ways, it biases me towards Hawkins' Modes 4, 5 and 6 (the supervisee's process, the supervisor–supervisee relationship and the supervisor's process, respectively). Experienced coaches will frequently seek out a psychotherapeutically trained supervisor for this very reason. I am clear in the contracting process about how I work, the background that I bring and that we will use the 'here and now' information about our co-created relationship to explore how the supervisees 'shape' (albeit out of conscious awareness) their relationships with their coaching clients. Like other clinically trained supervisors, I am able to educate my supervisees about psychological dynamics of the coach–coachee relationship. However, as Gestalt frames 'healthy functioning' as the natural flow of energy from need identification to need satisfaction, Gestalt supervisors don't engage in 'pathologizing' the end client (eg 'he sounds somewhat narcissistic/borderline/paranoid, etc'). Instead they encourage their supervisees to take an optimistic stance and view their clients as 'doing the best they can under the circumstances' (the field conditions). Supervisors also help their supervisees explore how they, in turn, can support their own clients in investigating how they limit themselves through their fixed Gestalts.

There is no doubt that as a Gestalt-oriented supervisor I do work with the emotional world of my supervisees and I know that my interventions can be experienced as 'therapeutic', if not in intent then in impact. As I have said elsewhere about Gestalt coaching (Gillie and Shackleton, 2009) it is vital that the Gestalt supervisor knows how to 'anchor' the outcomes of the work within the supervisee's developmental journey by inviting him or her to reflect on what new awareness the experiment brings and what meaning it has in the context of the work with his or her end client. Finally, the Gestalt supervisor, especially if clinically trained, needs to pay attention to when the work is beginning to focus on the personality structure of the supervisee and would be more helpfully taken into the supervisee's personal therapy.

# Conclusions

Gestalt provides a rich and coherent model for coach supervision. It offers a clear theoretical stance on the following:

1 The nature of human functioning: the *continuum of experience* offers an excellent compass for orientation through a supervision session, where the supervisee's energy is, what's in/not in awareness, how energy is/isn't being mobilized towards action, etc.

2 The process of human growth and change: *the paradoxical theory of change* that encourages the supervisee to fully embrace who he or she *is* and not try to be something he or she is not; and change through relationship, bringing the supervisor's own process through *presence* into the relationship and engaging in *dialogue*, where the supervisor and supervisee are fully present and meet in the spirit of genuine enquiry with no attachment to a particular outcome.

3 The methodology of intervening: *phenomenological exploration*, working with the 'in the moment' *data* as a way of raising awareness; and *active experimentation*, encouraging the supervisee to try something out in the session as a creative way of bringing new awareness and mobilizing energy for action.

Finally, a Gestalt orientation is very much 'a way of being' rather than a set of techniques. In practice, it is an endless process of awareness, choice and action as you continuously move your attention between your supervisee (his or her story, tone and movement) and your own internal response to what you see and hear. It becomes a way of life.

## Notes

1 Originally named the Gestalt Cycle of Experience by the faculty of the Gestalt Institute of Cleveland, it was developed into the Gestalt Continuum of Experience by the Gestalt International Study Centre, Cape Cod. This representation shows the relationship between the stage in the continuum and the level of energy exhibited by the individual (or system). Both the Cleveland and the GISC models use the term 'contact' where I use 'resolution'. Both refer to the point at which the need is met to whatever extent it can be. This could be a real 'ah ha' moment of new insight, or it could be the point at which one is able to move on from whatever is holding one's interest; in either case it represents the moment at which the Gestalt is completed.

**2** I like the term 'experiment' and use it with my supervisees. It conveys the spirit of 'trying something on for size', with no attachment to any particular outcome.

## References

Beisser, A R (1970) The paradoxical theory of change, in (eds) J Fagan and I L Shepherd, *Gestalt Therapy Now,* pp 77–80, Science and Behaviour Books, Palo Alto, CA, available via **www.gestalt.org/arnie.htm**

Buber, M (1970) *I and Thou,* Scribner's Sons, New York

De Haan, E (2008) *Relational Coaching: Journeys towards mastering one-to-one learning,* Wiley and Son, Chichester

Gillie, M (2009) Coaching approaches derived from Gestalt, in (eds) D Megginson and D Clutterbuck, *Techniques in Coaching and Mentoring, Volume 2,* Elsevier, Oxford

Gillie, M and Shackleton, M (2009) Gestalt coaching or Gestalt therapy? Ethical and professional considerations on entering the emotional world of the coaching client, *International Gestalt Journal,* 32 (1)

Hawkins, P (2006) Seven-eyed model of supervision, in (ed) J Passmore, *Excellence in Coaching,* Kogan Page, London

Koffka, K (1935) *The Principles of Gestalt Psychology,* Brace and World, Princeton, NJ

Lewin, K (1951) *Field Theory in Social Science,* University of Chicago Press, Chicago, IL

Magerman, M H and Leahy, M J (eds) (2009) The lone ranger is dying: Gestalt coaching as support and challenge, *International Gestalt Journal,* 32, 1, Spring, 173–96

Melnick, J and Nevis, S (2005) Gestalt methodology, in (eds) A Woldt and S Toman, *Gestalt Therapy: History, theory and practice,* pp 101–14, Sage, Thousand Oaks, CA

Perls, F S (1969) *Gestalt Therapy Verbatim,* Real People Press, Utah

Perls, F S (1973) *The Gestalt Approach and Eye Witness to Therapy,* Science and Behavior Books, Palo Alto, CA (republished by Bantam Books in 1976)

Perls, F S (1978) Finding self through Gestalt therapy, *Gestalt Journal,* 1 (1) 54–73

Resnick, R and Estrup, L (2000) Supervision, a collaborative endeavour, *Gestalt Review,* 4 (2) 121–37

Siminovitch, D and Van Eron, A M (2006) The pragmatics of magic. The work of Gestalt coaching, *OD Practitioner,* 38 (1) 50–55

Simon, S N (2009) Applying Gestalt Theory to Coaching, *Gestalt Review,* 13 (3) 230–39.

# Self-supervision using a peer group model

**BARBARA MOYES**

## Introduction

**C**oaches and clients can self-coach (eg Ellison, 2009), but can supervisors self-supervise? Hawkins and Shohet (1998) have advocated the need for supervisors in the helping professions to develop a healthy internal supervisor, but apart from Lahad (2000), who describes a self-supervision technique drawn from art therapies in his work with mental health professionals, self-supervision for coaching supervisors remains a largely under-explored practice.

Discussing the aims of supervision, Hawkins and Schwenk (2006) argue that supervision tries to help coaches develop their internal supervisor and become better reflective practitioners. It does this by providing a space for coaches to process what they have absorbed from their clients and their clients' systems, and enables coaches to remain objective.

Coaches are increasingly turning to supervisors to help them do this. But how can coaches develop their internal supervisors? This chapter explores how supervisors can develop their supervisory practice themselves through drawing on the Gestalt model of inquiry. This is not intended as a replacement for supervision with a supervisor, but it is suggested as a way of increasing self-awareness and capability, which can provide food for thought for personal reflection, or for sharing with a supervisor in a supervision session.

The chapter begins with a brief consideration of what supervision is trying to do. It then describes the key elements of the Gestalt inquiry approach. It shows how supervisors can use this approach to self-supervise when planning and reviewing group supervision. The chapter ends by critiquing the model and the value it offers to practising supervisors in terms of enhancing their self-awareness, reflective capacity and practice.

# Coaching supervision

Supervision has a long history in the therapeutic professions, but is still fairly new in coaching (Moyes, 2009). Hawkins and Smith (2006: 142) say that coaching supervision provides 'a protected space in which the coach can reflect on particular client situations and relationships, the reactivity and patterns they invoke for them, and by transforming these live in supervision, can profoundly benefit the client'. Bluckert (2006) fleshes this out a little more:

> Firstly, (supervision) is a time and space to reflect on one's work either with a senior colleague, in a led group, or with peers. The purpose of that reflection is to make greater sense of difficult and complex work situations and to gain more clarity going forward. Secondly, it is an opportunity to receive support both practical, in the form of ideas and suggestions and emotional, in the sense of sharing issues, and when appropriate reassurance. Thirdly, supervision can be a place for ongoing learning and professional development.

The question regarding supervision's function has been debated for several decades. Kadushin (1976), writing about social work supervision, has been a particularly influential voice in this debate. He identified three functions of social work supervision: educational, supportive and managerial. Two of the leading thinkers in the field of coaching supervision, Hawkins and Bluckert, former social workers themselves, have been influenced by Kadushin (Bluckert, 2006; Hawkins, 2006). Indeed, Hawkins' and Smith's (2006) schemata only slightly adapts Kadushin's; see Table 5.1.

The most popular model taught to coaching supervisors is the Seven-eyed Model, which Hawkins and Smith (2006) developed from the therapeutic model Hawkins and Shohet (1998) had developed earlier for members of the caring professions.

There is no agreed model of self-supervision in coaching. The model described in this chapter draws on Barber's thinking and experience as a research-practitioner using a Gestalt inquiry approach. He describes a

**TABLE 5.1** The functions of supervision

| Kadushin | Hawkins | Hawkins' Definition |
|---|---|---|
| Educational | Developmental | Skills development through reflection on work with client |
| Supportive | Resourcing | Understanding how the emotions stemming from the client contact affect the coach |
| Managerial | Qualitative | Quality control, spotting coach's blind spots, ensuring standards and ethics are maintained and that the organization's agenda is not lost |

research-practitioner as someone who performs inquiry as part of their professional duties, citing teachers, trainers, therapists, counsellors, managers, and 'indeed all who facilitate qualitative social inquiry as part of their job' (Barber, 2006: 6). This approach uses a structured process, based on reflection, self-examination and research, to make sense of what is going on. It therefore seems to me to provide a good basis for self-supervision in that it facilitates self-examination in order to improve one's capability as a supervisor. This equates to Barber's definition of supervision as summed up in the simple statement: 'At root, supervision concerns the facilitation of self-examination' (2006: 99). The next section discusses the theoretical underpinning of the model.

# Gestalt – a brief review

Gestalt and its background are fully discussed in Chapter 4. Barber sums up the Gestalt approach as working 'primarily with direct perception and what a person is sensing, feeling and projecting out upon the world, rather than what they are thinking or interpreting' (Barber, 2006: 2). Gestalt aims to raise awareness, and in so doing, enable people to change by:

- moving towards a greater awareness of self – body, feelings, environment;
- learning to own these feelings, instead of projecting them onto others;

- becoming aware of their needs and developing skills to satisfy themselves, without violating others;
- supporting themselves, rather than expecting the environment to do this for them (Zinker, 1978).

Gestalt uses all the senses and focuses on the 'here and now', attending to everything and dismissing nothing, as everything has meaning. An important Gestalt principle is that a person can only be understood as part of his or her environment.

Satisfaction comes only through closure of each interaction. The quality of the Gestalt relationship is more important in effecting change than the methodology. The goal in Gestalt is to make the best contact you can with another person so that you complete the interaction as fully as possible (Leary-Jones, 2007). This is also important for supervisors to bear in mind. Using self-supervision to understand what went on in a group supervision session can help the supervisor achieve closure.

# Self-supervision using the Gestalt inquiry model

Adopting the Gestalt inquiry model (Barber, 2006) means that the supervisor's primary concern is with what is being experienced, felt, seen and heard. Theory and interpretation are important, but are secondary to the felt experience. Supervisors are trying to catch the Gestalt, the patterns that emerge in the group. In keeping with the research practitioner role, they develop hypotheses based on the patterns they perceive and what they experience. They then reflect on these hypotheses, test them and draw conclusions. This process enables supervisors to move towards the state Zinker (1978) described: 'greater self-awareness', 'owning one's experiences rather than projecting them on to group members' and 'better quality practice'. The model is based on a series of questions that supervisors ask themselves at different stages of the group supervision cycle.

There are three sets of questions. The first set makes clear what models inform the supervisors' practice and their preferences, and are asked at the outset, before the first session with the group. The second set is also posed before the first group session. The questions help raise the supervisors' awareness about their skills and experience, and aspects of their relationship with the group. The third set of questions focuses on the group itself.

## The first set of questions: getting started in self-supervision

There are three questions supervisors ask themselves at this stage (Barber, 2006). First, what models and theories inform their practice? For example, do they systematically follow a model such as the Seven-eyed Model (Hawkins and Smith, 2006), or do they prefer to use creative supervision techniques such as cards, stones and toys (Lahad, 2000)? There is a range of theories drawn from a variety of fields that can inform supervisory practice: psychodynamic, cognitive/behavioural, Gestalt, positive psychology, systemic, neuro-linguistic programming are just some of the approaches supervisors might draw on (Peltier, 2010). The important issue is for supervisors to be aware of the way their models and theories affect how they see and interpret things – and what they might miss as a result.

Allied to this is the second question. This refers to the kind of information supervisors prefer to pay attention to. Do they prefer to attend to specific information and facts to find out what is actually happening? The Myers Briggs Type Inventory (MBTI) (2000) describes people who do this as having a Sensing (S) preference. Supervisors with this preference are therefore likely to be good observers of what is going on around them. They are attuned to factual and concrete information and like information to be precise. They notice details and remember specifics, and focus on the practical realities of situations.

However, other supervisors might prefer to attend to patterns and inter-relationships between facts, rather than the facts themselves. In MBTI terms (2000), people who do this are described as having an Intuitive (N) preference. They are interested in themes and connections, and their focus tends to be on the 'big picture' and possibilities, on what might be, rather than the S preference of focusing on what is.

Third, how do supervisors interpret information and reach decisions? Do they do this through empathizing with the people involved, stepping into their shoes and seeing the world through their eyes? Or do they prefer to make decisions from a detached standpoint, by analysing the logical consequences of a choice or action? In Myers Briggs' terms, this equates to a preference for making decisions based respectively on feeling (F), or thinking (T).

Supervisors with an F preference are likely to prefer to make decisions from an involved standpoint, empathizing and placing themselves inside a situation, and being guided by personal values and convictions. Supervisors with a T preference, on the other hand, tend to apply objective criteria, looking for flaws in logic, and using a cause and effect model in making decisions. They like to apply consistent principles in dealing with people, rather than treating each person as a unique individual, as a supervisor with an F preference prefers to do.

These questions begin the process of self-supervision by raising awareness of what supervisors are bringing to group supervision at the outset, and how they are likely to operate as a result. Reflecting on these questions can remind supervisors of some of their key preferred ways of working, and their biases. For example, supervisors with an S preference are likely to prefer to trust their experience, whereas supervisors with an N preference are more likely to trust inspiration and their intuition.

The process of self-supervision can also suggest areas where supervisors' typical repertoire falls short, thus alerting them to the potential need to adopt other approaches if difficulties occur later during the life of the group. Supervisors with an N preference, for instance, may need consciously to remind themselves to pay sufficient attention to facts or details (what do we know and how do we know it?), and the practical aspect of the situation under discussion. Supervisors with an S preference may sometimes find it helpful to think about what ideas or theories might be brought to bear during supervision, or what new approaches might be taken. Supervisors with an F preference may remind themselves to think about the pros and cons and logical consequences of the situation, and the need to take a tough stance at times (why aren't you following through now?), whereas supervisors with a T preference may use empathy to gain understanding of what supervisees and clients like, dislike and feel. Such examination can therefore play a part in helping supervisors avoid potential blind spots and enhance their practice.

## The second set of questions: the supervisor's relationship with the group

Having reflected on what informs their practice and their preferred ways of working, it is then helpful for supervisors to focus on their relationship with the group they are about to start working with.

## Skills and experience

Supervisors need to be clear what skills and qualities they bring to the group. This includes training and practical experience of areas such as business, change management, organization development, psychology and sport. This constitutes the supervisors' professional credibility. How confident they are that their skills and experience match the group's expectations – and how they might check this? Following on from this, if confidence is lacking, what internal 'interference' (Gallwey, 1979) might get in the way of the supervisor working optimally with this group, and how might the supervisor manage this interference?

## Feelings about the group

Second, supervisors need to try to surface any bias and transference that might be clouding their vision. How do they feel about the participants in the supervisory group? What are their expectations of the group? Supervisors typically take on a wide variety of roles during supervision (Moyes, 2007). When thinking about the group, what relationship do they find themselves taking towards it – for example, are they feeling and acting like a teacher, helper, parent, rescuer, artist, magician, or sage?

## The supervisors' motivation

Third, what are their motivations for supervising this group? How high profile is this piece of work? How important is it in terms of their career or reputation? Who will notice how well the group performs? How much might they learn from taking on this piece of work? How obliged do they feel to take it on? The consistent focus on the supervisor during the self-supervision process means that Gestalt's emphasis on using how the researcher/supervisor experiences the situation is there right from the start.

## Devil's advocate

Fourth, is there someone who can act as devil's advocate to 'rattle their blind spot', as Barber puts it? This is part of the role a formal supervisor can play, but it could equally be played by a trusted colleague or friend. This prompt to think about personal bias right at the beginning is particularly useful in helping reduce subsequent distortion.

## Contracting

Finally, what type of contract would be appropriate in terms of the group's needs? Good contracting ensures that supervisor and group members share the same idea of the purpose of the meetings, and that respective roles and responsibilities are made explicit (Hay, 2007). A clear contract at the outset can help prevent or manage problems that might arise later on.

It is usual to work out the contract with the group. One method is for the supervisor to prepare a list of issues the group needs to address together before the first session, and then let the group decide the order in which to address them. I have found this works well where group members value a degree of flexibility and dislike a prescriptive approach. Issues include practicalities such as frequency and duration of meetings; boundary issues such as what confidentiality means for this group, and the boundary of the relationship in terms of therapy; the format and methodological approach the group would like the sessions to take; and the context within which it is operating. The latter includes the organization – the coaches might all be working in, or for, one organization – and the ethical framework within which the group is operating.

Finally, it is important to discuss and agree accountabilities, and the sort of working alliance the group wants to have. One group I supervised developed their initial thinking about their working alliance as follows:

- What does success look like? We are all open, we can be ourselves, relaxed, excited, supportive atmosphere, becoming more challenging as time goes by, not blaming or condemnatory, everyone feeling valued. Everyone participates, we all learn and develop.

- 'What I fear happening in supervision is ….' It doesn't deliver value – it falls apart, gets boring, not challenging or informative enough, jargon gets in the way.

- How do we evaluate? Fairly formally after three or four sessions; informally in the last five minutes of each session to review how the meeting has gone. Our criteria are:

  - have we tried new things with clients – have we increased our confidence to do so?

  - 'unsticking' stuck cases;

  - increased professional development;

  - managing anxieties about 'doing it right'.

## The third set of questions: the supervisors' perceptions of the group

In thinking about the group, the first question to answer is, how have these people come together? What is their relationship? How well do they know each other? Then, what is unique about this group? For example, if group members are from the same organization, is the culture of this group different from that of other groups in the organization? If it is, what are the implications?

Second, what are the stated goals of the group – and what might be the hidden, unstated goals. How much disparity is there between these? Gaining clarity about this can help identify potential problem areas. What are the current influences on behaviour? How far are the unstated goals exerting an influence; is there a dominant member in the group who influences the rest; or perhaps the wider organizational culture is influencing group behaviour.

Finally, I have found it illuminating to ask myself what is the group in the process of becoming (see Table 5.2). What is the group creating? Thinking of this in terms of an image has helped me surface intuitive hunches about the group's functioning that have helped shed light on what is going on in the group. Gaining clarity about this can also sound a warning about potential problem areas.

## The fourth set of questions: monitoring performance

Questions during and after the supervision session focus on evaluation and quality control. This includes asking how what went on differed from what was expected; how judgements were formed and acted on; and what coping strategies were chosen and implemented (Barber, 2006). Supervisors might reflect upon the advantages and disadvantages of their approach and ask themselves how they could approach things differently next time to improve their practice. A question I have found particularly useful is, what am I blind to or excluding at this time? This is where the devil's advocate can play a crucial role. If the supervisor is struggling with knotty problems with the group, this powerful question can shed helpful light.

**TABLE 5.2** Questions about the supervisor's perceptions of the group

| | |
|---|---|
| **1** | How is the group organized – how have these members come together and what is their relationship? |
| **2** | What is unique about the group? |
| **3** | What current influences are affecting members' behaviour? |
| **4** | What are the stated goals of the group? |
| **5** | What are the hidden, unstated goals of the group? |
| **6** | What is the group in the process of becoming? |

# Group supervision

This section describes how I used these questions to self-supervise when supervising a small group of internal coaches.

The supervisor's role in group supervision is complex. The central skills of facilitating reflective supervision are similar to one-to-one supervision. But in addition, supervisors have to facilitate the responses of the group, link these back to the case under discussion, and manage the group contract and organizational boundaries. They also have to be aware of and manage the group dynamics: 'It is essential the group leader ensures group dynamics do not proceed unacknowledged and find ways of bringing the dynamics into awareness so that they can be attended to and learnt from, without taking over the focus of the group' (Hawkins and Smith, 2006: 180).

Stoltenberg and Delworth (1987), discussing group supervision with counsellors and therapists, suggest that the greatest difficulty with group supervision is how to meet the diverse needs of members at different levels and with individual concerns. The supervisor's role in group supervision is therefore a demanding one.

## CASE STUDY Working through the first and second set of questions

Several years ago I supervised a group of coaches in a small company that was just starting to use internal coaches. This case study describes the initial meeting. The group failed to continue. I think that it is particularly valuable to examine experiences that fail because it throws the learning into sharp relief. This case study shows how using self-supervision helped me understand what was going on below the surface in the group, reach some conclusions as to why the group did not continue, and learn from my mistakes.

In working through the first and second set of questions before meeting with the group for the first time I surfaced the following issues:

- *My skills and preferred ways of working.* The model that underpins my work is psychodynamic, and my Myers Briggs preferences are N and F. Although I was experienced in one-to-one supervision I had not supervised a group before. I could not be sure that my skills and experience matched the group's expectations. This felt uncomfortable, and I began to wonder if I had bitten off more than I could chew.

- *My feelings about the group.* I expected it would not be an easy group to work with, and I did not feel confident about doing so. I recognized that there was therefore considerable 'interference' in my head at the outset (Gallwey, 1979).

- *My motivation.* My motivation for the group was high. I felt it was important in terms of my professional credibility and reputation.

- *Devil's advocate.* I did not give this as much thought as I later realized I should, and did not appoint a devil's advocate.

- *Contracting.* I identified three possible formats for our sessions, and decided to leave the choice to the group. In hindsight this was a mistake, and reflected my lack of assertiveness and confidence.

### The group supervision session

When the group met I was dismayed to discover that three of the four members were joining the meeting by video conference. They felt very distant. Only Claire was in the same room as me.

The aim of the meeting was to agree how we would work together. To get a sense of them as coaches, I asked them about their coaching and training, but apart from Claire, members were not forthcoming. The others enthused about coaching, saying how great it was just to listen and let people come up with their own solutions. I felt this was an idealized picture of coaching, and challenged it.

Claire mentioned the encounter group that had recently begun on her course. She had found it uncomfortable, and did not understand what it was getting at. She had been the one to open up, and had cried, leaving her feeling embarrassed and determined not to open up again. She described how she sometimes felt 'not there' when coaching, although the feedback was always more positive than she expected.

I wondered if she might be feeling this way to protect herself. I pointed out that a similar pattern was happening in this group, with Claire opening up and the others sitting back and letting her. I decided to return to this later with Claire on her own. On reflection, another approach I might have taken was to ask the others if they could relate to this issue. This would have treated the individual issue as a more universal theme, and an issue of the system as a whole (Kepner, 1980), but I suspect that it might have been a risky strategy with this group at this early stage.

When I asked what they wanted to get out of supervision I felt the protection theme surfaced again. One said she already had some external support and just wanted to focus on the organizational perspective. Another said she was familiar with the model we had said we would use, and had already developed the coaching skills she needed. I was aware of feeling quite frustrated. When I asked which of the three formats I had identified they wanted to use in supervision, the group was unable to agree on one. They wanted a bit of everything.

At the end of the session, members responded positively, and said they wanted to continue, but I felt sceptical about this.

## *Working through the third set of questions*

### My perceptions of the group

The group knew each other well. They had come together because they were some of the few people in the organization who were undertaking coaching training. They were acting according to best practice in requesting supervision, but I was unsure if there were unstated goals, and if so, what they were. The group was unique in that it was the first of its kind in that organization. The group supervision type of meeting was far removed from the usual formal meetings conducted there. What I failed to answer fully was the question about how current influences affected group behaviour, and in particular, members' desire or ability to be open.

### How are people and events organized here?

Although I knew the group members beforehand, we did not have a strong relationship.

## What influences of the present field explain current behaviour

The stage of the group was an important influence. I allowed the fact that we knew one another already as individuals to minimize the reality that as a group we were still in the first, inclusion phase (Katzenbach and Smith, 1993), when members are asking whether they will be accepted and belong, or be rejected. These concerns apply to supervisors as well as to group members. Will contributions be seen as valid and insightful, or as trite and unhelpful? A key goal in Gestalt is to make the best contact you can with other people so that the interaction can be achieved as fully as possible (Leary-Jones, 2007). Focusing more on trying to help the members feel they belonged to the group (Kepner, 1980) might have achieved a better contact between them and me.

Group dynamics were a powerful influence on behaviour. The explicit aim had been task focused on contractual issues, but at times the group dynamics took precedence and I struggled to retain the focus on the task. Bion's (1968) theories about group dynamics helped me develop a hypothesis to make sense of what had been going on. Bion's thesis is that the task any group is trying to achieve is threatened by collective forces within the group, and that these forces are not random, but are unconsciously organized in certain configurations or emotional states. These configurations are, 1) fight/flight, 2) dependency and, 3) pairing (Karterud, 1989). The group behaves as if one of these basic assumptions is held in common by all the members, and this influences any rational work it is trying to do. In my view, Liz, Paul and Janet were in flight.

Bion also argues that each member's dependency needs are split off and projected onto one person. In this case I thought this was Claire. The sense I picked up was of her vulnerability. I wanted to protect her, because it felt to me as if she couldn't protect herself (the counter-transference). Bion says this 'dependent leader' is often the 'least intuitive member', which might accord with her not understanding why she got upset. The group expects the formal leader to take care of this person – which is exactly what I did, by taking further exploration of her situation out of the group and into a subsequent one-to-one session. In doing so, I was acting out of my need to protect and rescue, and be rescued by, Claire. In retrospect I felt that Claire had not only been protecting the other group members, but me as well. This last realization helped me become more aware of my own needs and own my own experiences rather than projecting them onto the group members (Zinker, 1978).

## What is unique about the current situation?

This was a totally different type of meeting from the ones normally held in the organization. As surveys had shown, the culture in this organization was one of lack of trust, and this may well have influenced group members' behaviour – as stated earlier, a Gestalt principle is that a person can only be understood as part of his or her environment.

It was therefore perhaps not surprising that I felt protection was the main theme. Three members protected themselves by using the video-conference facility, by not opening up, and by presenting an idealized picture of coaching. In addition to trying to protect Claire, I too had tried to protect myself by suggesting that another colleague might join the group, because I knew she would be supportive of me.

## Stated and unstated goals

The unstated goal of self-protection was at significant variance to the stated goal of initiating supervision to enhance members' coaching practice.

## What is in the process of becoming?

Thinking of the group as a family, the image that came to my mind was that we were in danger of becoming still-born. This was suggestive of my degree of pessimism, and turned out to be right. The group did not meet again.

## What was I blind to, or excluding at this time?

A chance comment from a mutual colleague shed light on this. She told me I would never get anywhere with one of the members because it was hard for her to trust me. In this way my colleague unknowingly acted as my devil's advocate and exposed what I was blind to. My usual experience is that people trust me, and so I had excluded the possibility that someone might not.

# Conclusion

The self-supervision model described in this chapter provides a process that supervisors offering group supervision can use to reflect on their own practice. The model focuses on the 'here and now' and encourages supervisors to pay attention to different sensory input. Asking a series of questions before and after each group session prompts supervisors to reflect on what they are bringing to the group, sharpens their perception of and feelings towards the group, and helps make sense of what has happened during the group supervision session.

A real strength is the model's systematic approach, which makes it hard for supervisors to ignore issues. A common argument for the need to have an external supervisor is the difficulty most people have in being aware of their blind spots and the need for an objective person to help them do this. The self-supervision model addresses this through its focus on bias, on what is being excluded, and the use of a devil's advocate. It is particularly helpful in enabling supervisors to own their feelings and their part in any perceived failure in the group's functioning, rather than projecting them onto the group members. This, in turn, enables supervisors to achieve closure, learn from their experience, and move on.

How far does the self-supervision model address the three functions of supervision mentioned earlier? It is certainly developmental, in that it encourages reflection on the work with the group. It fulfils the resourcing function in its focus on understanding how the emotions stemming from contact with the group affect the supervisor. And it meets some of the qualitative function through the way it addresses the supervisor's blind spots. It is less focused on the organization's agenda, but supervisors could fill this gap by including additional appropriate questions. Finally, as a research-based model, it has the potential to contribute to the currently small body of research into coaching supervision.

## References

Barber, P (2006) *Becoming a Practitioner Researcher: A Gestalt approach to holistic inquiry*, Middlesex University Press, London

Bion, W (1968) *Experience in Groups*, Tavistock, London

Bluckert, P (2006) Retrieved from **www.peter.bluckert.com** on 3 February 2010

Ellison, R (2009) Talk to the ego, *Coaching at Work*, 4 (1) 48–9

Gallwey, T (1979) *The Inner Game of Golf*, Pan Books, London

Hawkins, P (2006) Coaching supervision, in (ed) J Passmore, *Excellence in Coaching*, Kogan Page, London

Hawkins, P and Schwenk, G (2006) CIPD research, presented at the CIPD annual Coaching at Work Conference, 12 September, London

Hawkins, P and Shohet, R (1998) *Supervision in the Helping Professions*, Open University Press, Buckingham

Hawkins, P and Smith, N (2006) *Coaching, Mentoring and Organizational Consultancy, Supervision and Development*, Open University Press, Buckingham

Hay, J (2007) *Reflective Practice and Supervision for Coaches,* Open University Press, Buckingham

Kadushin, A (1976) *Supervision in Social Work,* Columbia University Press, New York

Karterud, S (1989) A study of Bion's basic assumption groups, *Human Relations,* 42 (4) 313–35

Katzenbach, J and Smith D (1993) *The Wisdom of Teams,* Harper Business Essentials, New York

Kepner, E (1980) Gestalt group process, in (eds) B Feder and R Rowell, *Beyond the Hot Seat: Gestalt approaches to groups,* Brunner/Mazel, New York

Lahad, M (2000) *Creative Supervision,* Jessica Kingsley, London

Leary-Jones, J (2007) Feeling groovy, *Coaching at Work,* 2 (5) 24–32

Moyes, B (2007) Supervision matters. What goes on in coaching supervision?, Unpublished Master's dissertation, Portsmouth University

Moyes, B (2009) Literature review of coaching supervision, *International Coaching Psychology Review,* 4 (2) 160–171

Myers Briggs, I (2000) *Introduction to Type,* OPP, Oxford

Peltier, B (2010) *The Psychology of Executive Coaching: Theory and application,* Routledge, New York

Stoltenberg, C and Delworth, U (1987) *Supervising Counsellors and Therapists: A developmental approach,* Jossey-Bass, San Francisco, CA

Zinker, J (1978) *Creative Process in Gestalt Therapy,* Brunner Mazel, New York

# Narrative supervision – the experiential field and the 'imaginal'

## 06

**SUE CONGRAM**

## Introduction

The coach brings his or her work to supervision in order to learn how to do it better (Carroll and Gilbert, 2005). It is a place to reflect, and to learn how to reflect, on the finer more subtle characteristics of the work. Coaches present to the supervisor their questions, puzzles, curiosities, issues about their work with their clients and their wider coaching practice, using the supervisor as a sounding board. Where the supervisor can make a strong contact, this relationship has the potential to do much more than touch the surface of the coach's work. It can be a space for deep learning and insight. I will describe two methods I use to reach this space, how they affect the supervisor, the coach and the coach's client, and how they interweave together.

The first method builds on the 'narrative', the story that the coach brings to supervision, using this as a vehicle for learning. I develop the idea that the deeper issues in the coaching relationship lie not so much in what is visible and what is said in the story, but in what is not seen or said. The supervisor can then bring the unspoken and unknown into the coach's awareness so his or her story can grow and illuminate the work he or she is doing.

The second method is the 'experiential field'. Here the supervisor and coach tap into the different, often unseen layers of practice. I will also describe that part I call the 'imaginal', which is the totality of the imagined, the imaginary and images. Needless to say, trust is at the heart of the relationship between supervisor and coach: without trust supervision in this in-depth way does not work.

# Working with narrative in supervision

Why narrative? We are by nature storytellers, our lives are filled with telling and listening to stories that recount the incidents that we have experienced. Narrative stories are based on fact, rather than story-telling which is intentionally fictional. Told and re-told in different ways to different people, what might appear as fact may carry a great deal of fiction, but its intention is not fictional. The truth of a narrative story lies not in its accuracy but in its meaning (Gabriel, 2000), and meaning comes through what is not said as much as what is said.

Narrative exists in all societies and cultures; it is a universal quality that is deeply rooted in our human structures, it is critical to child development, family bonding and learning, it helps people through difficult times and to celebrate joyful experiences, it is central to knowledge development, communication, cultures, cross-cultural communication and the survival of communities. Narrative is a competence that we are not taught: it is handed down through the generations and across cultural borders. We all naturally and unknowingly engage in narrative every day: 'our definition as human beings is very much bound up with the stories we tell about our own lives and the world in which we live ... the gift of narrative is so pervasive and universal that there are those who strongly suggest that narrative is a "deep structure", a human capacity genetically hard wired' (Brooks, 1985: 3)

We tell each other mini-narratives about everyday incidents all the time. It is so common that we do not even notice:

'I got caught in traffic and arrived late at my meeting. My boss was not happy, I knew by the look on her face that I was on my way out.'
'The party was great fun, it was the hottest day of the year. We ended up having this massive water fight.'
'Who do you think I bumped into today when I went into town?' (Although this is asking a question it also tells a little story of a surprise meeting in town.)

'I was tele-coaching and the line went dead. My client was in the middle of telling me about a serious difficulty with her boss, she was in tears. I could not re-connect on the phone. I imagined that she must have felt stranded. I felt helpless.'

We do not need a lot of language to conjure up images and imaginings about life.

Narrative stories particularly rely on personal experience, a story that only the teller can tell. That's what makes it a narrative story in contrast to a fictional story, and that's why narrative lends itself so well to supervision. An attribute of the telling is that of creative licence; in everyday life we elaborate, embellish, refine, modify, tell it imaginatively, sometimes poetically, often persuasively. We are also factual, historical and speculative, as we tell and re-tell the stories that are meaningful to us. It is then that willing listeners witness and validate what we say. These qualities in the telling become fruits for supervision and a way of accessing 'the narrative beneath the surface narrative' (Case, 2007) where a deeper learning can be found. Narrative stories carry a quality of wholeness.

You might ask, isn't supervision really about addressing accountability, ethical practice and maintaining good standards? These standards of practice are infused throughout the coaching relationship, they are not always explicit, more often than not they are hidden, more subtle than we imagine. Cognitive work alone will not uncover the deeper aspects of coaching practice. For example, let's take choice-making in coaching. At every point along the way the coach is making small choices whether to go this way or that, whether to respond to this or that, in the coaching relationship. This choice-making is often out of awareness. There are always many perspectives and many paths to take. Good coaching means that the coach becomes aware of the choices he or she is making and the rationale, intuition or embodied response behind those choices. Yet there will be times when a coach gets caught by the dynamics of transference and counter-transference in the coaching relationship. As unconscious processes, these dynamics can stop a coach from fully seeing and hearing the client, as was the case here:

A coach was telling me about a client that had got angry with her. She reacted, and started believing the things that he was saying about her to be true. 'Who did she think she was, coming in here "coaching" when they had all been over-working for weeks to make sure the business didn't collapse!' The coach lost her footing, took it personally, got defensive, became stuck.

Such situations need teasing out. Different coaching methods bring a number of options that could be used. One may be to consider whether the management of the organization was listening to its staff through this crisis, that anger towards the management had been aimed at the coach. That may or may not have been the case; however, my interest in the supervision was much more to do with the processes in the coach's relationship with her client. As the coach re-told the narrative there was a point where her voice became high pitched. Why did she do this ? On raising her awareness of this she commented that she had felt belittled at that point, but believed that she had regained her ground at the time. I suspected she had temporarily embodied the projection, convinced that she was 'in the wrong' and this came through in the telling of the narrative. On further discussion she realized that a residue of the projection had remained, showing up in the voice change that I had noticed.

Coaches engage in a natural form of communication, telling their story about their experience with clients, and through this narrative the supervisor and coach are able to reflect on both the story that is told and the story as it is told. For the 'field aware' supervisor, the story that is told is usefully held in 'soft listening', that is, where the narrative is not the main focus. The story as it is told is where the supervisor can best serve the coach, for a coach is less likely to be aware of how he or she tells the story.

There are also advantages of working in this way for the supervisor. It prevents getting caught in content and problem solving. It avoids passing judgement on the coach, the coach's client or the client system. It also deepens the work beyond superficial learning, giving insight to coaches about how they are affected by, and relate to their work.

# Experiential field

Life is experience in constant flow. Even when we talk about the past or anticipate the future, what we experience is only ever in the present. In supervision and in coaching that is our greatest gift. In the 1940s social scientist Kurt Lewin (1951) took that a step further. He described a person's engagement in life as an 'experiential field' or a 'psychological field'; when people meet, this experiential field is co-created. With an overriding title of 'field theory', Lewin further proposed that fields carry their own self-regulating principles. My own study of experiential fields

**FIGURE 6.1** Supervisor–coach relationship

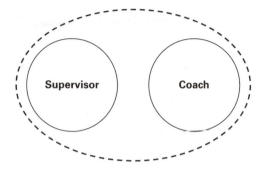

has brought me to realize the extent that the imagination, the imagined and images contribute to the co-creation of experience. Later in this chapter I introduce this concept of the imaginal, describing its value to supervision. In this section I describe experiential fields in terms of supervision and coaching, highlighting some of the core principles.

## The supervisor–coach relationship

The first of these co-created fields is the supervisor–coach relationship; see Figure 6.1.

Within this experiential field is a relational dynamic between two people. It includes how supervisor and coach perceive each other, the levels of trust between them, the power relationship that they establish, the hidden aspects of both people and how they make meaning of their world, and their cultural perspectives. The dynamics of this field are also affected by the room and space in which they are working, how they are sitting. I am a strong believer in creating a supervision space that is pleasing for my clients to walk into. It affects the work. However, what we see from a field perspective is a context that is much more than the physical environment. This context contains layers of the hidden psychological world – personal, relational, social and cultural.

This field is rich in information – known and unknown. The co-created field between the supervisor and coach and what is brought into that field (narrative stories, memories, feelings, body responses) are in fact all there is to work within a supervision session. Working with narrative will bring creativity to the field; other traditional approaches may bring more intellectualization to the field.

**FIGURE 6.2** Coach–client relationship

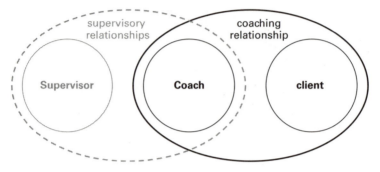

There is yet another 'experiential field' that enters supervision. That is the co-created field between the coach and his or her client (see Figure 6.2), which is brought to supervision through the narrative stories.

Although this experiential field is not directly present in supervision, the resonances, vibrations, colours, textures and emotions of the coach–client relationships come into supervision through the narratives. Furthermore, the supervisor and coach are able to step back and examine these relationships. The principles of field theory (and that part of the field I call the imaginal, which I will discuss shortly) can be considered from this position.

A third experiential field exists that affects the coach–client work. This is the client's relationship with his or her work or family system (see Figure 6.3).

Again the resonances of this experiential field bring colour to the coaching work and fragments of this may well find their way into supervision. From a supervisor's perspective this third experiential field may seem distant, where only a far-off view can be taken. Nevertheless these fields are themselves interconnected, part of a greater whole, where a pebble dropped in one field will send ripples to the others. The example that I used earlier suggested that the anger aimed at the coach might have been displaced anger that was felt towards the client's management. That would be an example of an experiential field outside of coaching that is entering the experiential field of the coaching. If the coach then takes this to supervision as a feeling that she is 'a waste of time, hopeless, not fit to be a coach', the ripples are felt in supervision. The narrative holds this deeper reality, and points towards what isn't spoken.

**FIGURE 6.3** Client workplace or family system

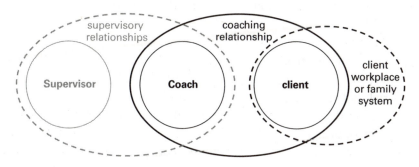

## *Principles of experiential fields*

The beauty of experiential fields exists in their core principles, the underlying rules of engaging with life that influence and shape people's interactions with the social and physical world. In supervision these principles equip a supervisor and coach to make creative leaps. I will briefly describe five core principles (O'Neill and Gaffney, 2008; Parlett, 1991) and explain how this happens:

1 change;
2 whole;
3 organization;
4 contemporaneity;
5 singularity.

### 1. The principle of change

The supervisor–coach relationship is not static, but always shifting and changing as trust builds, perceptions change and learning grows. It is also worth noting that memory changes and stories change as they are told and re-told. A coach may narrate two or three different versions of the same coaching session; each version has its own validity, each carries potential for learning.

When change is seriously considered, what is then brought to the attention of the supervisor is the paradoxical nature of change (Beisser, 1970). O'Neill and Gaffney (2008) describe this as 'being in control by being out of control. It's a matter of letting things happen rather than making things happen.' What a supervisor notices may or may not be significant or agreed to by the coach, but bringing attention to it enables the coach to reflect, question and expand the point raised.

## 2. The principle of wholes

All aspects of the field are connected and create a whole. What is experienced is determined by the whole field, not isolated parts. Working from this holistic perspective can be paradoxical. Paying attention to detail within the narrative as it is told, reflecting this back to the coach, is one way of bringing insight. As human beings we naturally fill gaps in what we perceive, with what we 'think' is there, rather than question what is really there. Reflecting back what we notice that seems odd or unusual brings this gap-filling into question.

What this means in supervision is giving attention to the 'possible relevance' (Parlett, 1991) of detail that may seem insignificant or unrelated to the presenting narrative. The slight shift in voice that I referred to in the example earlier was worth exploring, to find in that case that it held significant relevance to the work. We cannot assume relevance: we have to ask a question to find out. The point is that we all too often ignore the very thing that is crying out to be noticed, and in supervision the pointers towards that are often many.

## 3. The principle of organization

The current situation organizes itself around dominant themes – these may be explicit or implicit. A simple example of this is the difference between supervision as a hierarchical structure and supervision as a working alliance. The relationship between supervisor and coach will be quite different in these two arrangements, as will the learning that takes place. Being open to this principle enables a supervisor to make better informed choices and notice the micro shifts that are taking place in the supervision session.

This principle of organization also brings with it patterns that form and reform. Narrative stories reveal patterns, repetitions, conversations and conflicts that become caught around a theme. Patterns also, of course, form around the dynamics of transference and counter-transference in each of the relationship pairs I described.

## 4. The principle of contemporaneity

Although a word that is not in common usage, 'contemporaneity' is quite simple. It means that only that which exists in the current time and current situation explains current behaviour. What exists in the present does not and cannot explain behaviour in the past. This principle is particularly relevant when attending to narrative. The event as it happened in the past is not what concerns us now because those actual 'field' conditions no longer exist (Parlett, 1991), the narrative is a memory of the past, what is told and how it is told then becomes the focus of the supervisor's attention – how that memory is coming into and affecting the present.

### 5. The principle of singularity

The point with singularity is that every situation is to be seen in its uniqueness. Our tendency towards generalizations and a wish to predict, or box people into defined categories, acts against us. We fail to see the uniqueness of situations; instead we 'act as though we know the answer'. The result is that people do not feel seen or heard, instead they might feel that a 'standard answer' or 'label' is being provided. Each time a coach repeats a narrative it is worth considering it as new and unique, offering new perspectives for supervisor and coach to consider, to question, to explore.

These five principles are not the only principles at the heart of field theory, but they are core principles, and stand well for anyone beginning to work in this way for the first time.

# The imaginal

The experiential field is filled with a rich supply of creative material. The imagined, the imaginary and images are always present in some form. Working with this imaginal world is where creative leaps in coaching practice can be achieved.

## The imagined

When we tell narrative stories and draw on our memory, we do not and cannot paint the whole picture for the listener because we do not have it ourselves. We tell others about the past in a narrative summary, not the full story because we do not have it. We miss out a lot of detail. Both teller and listener fill the gaps through their imagination as the story is being told, often without question. We know this from the psychology of perception, which has shown that we see things in wholes, not in fragmented parts, even though what is put in front of us are fragments of

**FIGURE 6.4** Line drawings

the whole. The line drawings in Figure 6.4 demonstrate this. In each case a complete image appears even though the lines are broken – we see the whole image and not just broken lines or shapes.

The same occurs in how we make meaning. Where there are gaps in information our human tendency is to fill them in. During the course of life and relating, this naturally occurring phenomenon does not bode well for relationships because 'filling the gaps' can only be achieved through our own life experiences and knowledge base. That is all that we have, unless of course we ask. So the experiential field in supervision is an ongoing ever-changing process of gap filling and making meaning, hidden by assumptions and projections. To see the gaps, and question them, takes awareness, effort and a quizzical mind – this is the task of both supervisor and coach.

> Having talked through his client case in supervision, the coach sat back in his seat looking bewildered. I commented on this, asking him if that's what he was experiencing. 'No,' he said, 'on the contrary, I've suddenly realized what I missed. It was there in front of me all the time, I just didn't see it.'

Narrating the client work in supervision, having someone listen and to witness the work, often reveals the gaps in a different way. It's like standing back after completing a painting: you see the emerging picture from a new perspective.

There is something else very significant that takes place in supervision, and that is 'what is imagined' by the supervisor. Like reading fiction, as the narrative story is told the supervisor inevitably creates imaginary glimpses of the settings, the people involved, what people might look like and so on, almost without realizing it. Next time you supervise a coach, pay attention to this, notice how you build a picture in your mind of the coach's case work. Ideally this process happens without judgement or prejudice. This is where stereotyping has its advantages: it supports the imagined and works very well as long as it is treated as a temporary, inaccurate platform that emerges from the field between you and the coach.

## The imaginary and imaginative

Life today is dominated by theory, knowledge, structures, models and numbers. We are not educated to be imaginative. Our ability to imagine is often seen as a resource to call on when we want to be creative. In truth we use this ability as a natural aspect of engaging with life. What does not exist in the here and now requires imagination. Furthermore, what *does* exist in the here and now also requires imagination because all is not visible. We cannot tell what people are thinking or feeling unless they say. Our imagination is always on call, a deeply integrated part of our lives. However, this process is flawed, often conjuring up 'imaginings of what exists' in a way that we believe to be true, when in fact it is all or partly false. We add in imaginary extras, we tell narrative stories with inflections that emphasize this and de-emphasize that. We re-shape the past in order to meet our needs in the present. We are highly imaginative beings. So in each and every experiential field there exists an ocean of imagination – a plentiful basket for any supervision session. The secret is how to use it intentionally.

When I am working in supervision (and in coaching), imagination comes out of the situation in-the-moment, with a strong sense of purpose for the work. I tend to draw on resources around me to help bring the coach to the edge of his or her work, to see things in a different way. I might use objects in the room, simple art materials, pictures, or draw on hobbies, pastimes and tools of their trade.

> The coach's client was a plumber who seemed stuck, unable to move forward in his life. The coach was interested in trying something new but felt it was hard to be creative with the engineering mind of a plumber who was definitely not interested in using art materials. After some imaginative thinking the coach came up with the idea that she might suggest to her client that he bring his plumber's toolbox along to the next session. This she then encouraged him to use, to visually articulate problems in his private life – this brought new meaning and insight.

I will generally challenge coaches on the use of structured exercises in coaching and question why they see them as useful. Occasionally I am convinced, often I am not. What usually happens is that the coach had found the exercise useful when he or she first came across it, so thought that the client might benefit from it also. I challenge this approach in coaching because it is based on the coach's agenda not the client's. Far better that the coach connects well with the client and is imaginative, creative, even inventive, in a way that will bring deeper awareness and insight to the client, based on deep listening and understanding of the client's issues.

## *The image*

Finally we come to image and with that come metaphor and symbols. Our everyday language is filled with metaphor (Lakoff and Johnson, 1980) and images; much of the time we are not aware of this. Image has a particular role to play in supervision, which depends on the approach of the supervisor. Whereas a structured way of working fashions supervision according to the supervisor's model, a more open exploration of the dynamics in the situation is where the supervisor 'trusts in the innate process of growth and development' (Case, 2007) and is more open to this approach. The freedom to work with images brings supervision alive and has the potential to deepen meaning for the coach. The following example demonstrates this:

> As the coach was re-telling his story he described a point in the session as being 'like a cold fog'. He had quickly skipped over it, as though it had little to contribute. I could easily have missed it. He had not mentioned this earlier, it was new. After he had finished re-telling his story I asked him what he had noticed telling it again. He did not return to the fog image, so I reminded him of it. The image set off an explosion of feelings that led to new insight into the work.

What it means for you as a supervisor is to pay attention to images that stand out for you from the coach's narrative, and bring them into a reflective conversation with the coach, without feeling the need to understand what they mean.

# Developing an imaginative supervision conversation

Within these multi-layered experiential fields exists the potential for deep, insightful and challenging learning. There are a few things that supervisor and coach can do to bring the imagined, imagination and images more fully into the experiential field of their work together. In this section I provide a few examples. I encourage you to come up with your own ideas. The possibilities are limitless. The key is to keep the purpose of co-creative learning in mind.

## *Finding the underlying narrative*

Story-telling brings with it drama, or the teller might unconsciously bring drama in through the way he or she tells it. This often goes unnoticed: people tend to concentrate on the content, barely taking in this other process taking place – the lifting or deepening of the voice, speeding up and slowing down, different emphases and inflections, all indicate another process, an underlying narrative. Drama is where the conflict is, where new learning can be achieved. You could say that the coach already knows what he or she needs to learn simply by the fact that he or she brings drama into the narrative.

So there is great benefit to be gained simply by reflecting back to the coach these points in the telling, where you notice shifts in the way the narrative is told. Picking up on the possible relevance of something, which may not appear significant, but bringing it to the attention of the coach offers a choice that might not have been there before. The example that I used earlier when the coach raised her voice was precisely that, ultimately bringing deep insight.

Other indicators of underlying narrative include metaphor, images and symbols within the story. Asking for some explanation of these can destroy meaning, when our aim is to expand meaning. Reflecting metaphors, images and symbols back to the coach invites a response. In my example of 'cold fog' I had said, 'I noticed your description of … as "like cold fog".' Such a simple reflection enables the unknown to unfold.

Finding the underlying narrative in itself requires imagination. It can feel safe for a supervisor to stick to his or her known models and modes of working, a narrative approach does not exclude that. However, what it invites is a flow of imagination to enter the field of your work with the coach.

## Re-telling the narrative in a different way

Whatever the coach brings to supervision can be told and re-told, each time bringing with it new information, new images and a different way of telling it. To invite the coach to 'tell it again', is an easy step. The skill of the supervisor is to notice shifts and changes in the telling and re-telling and the shifts in his or her relationship with the coach as it is re-told (contemporaneity). The supervisor steps aside from content, keeping the content to soft listening, not blanking it out completely but listening to the underlying story and reflecting this back to the coach; this underlying story the coach is unlikely to hear on his or her own.

The supervisor might also suggest to the coach that he or she tells the story in a different way. There are many ways of doing this, depending on the purpose. For example:

- from a perspective of the client's boss;
- from the coach's most admired role model;
- from a perspective of a 'fly on the wall';
- to re-tell the narrative again in a positive way;
- to re-tell it in a way that he or she would have liked it to be, or liked it to end.

Change is paradoxical. By amplifying 'what is', hearing the detail, connecting with emotional responses, getting to know the narrative more, new learning comes through.

## Writing down the narrative

Case (2007: 95) describes how she invites supervisees to write down their narrative stories of client work. The point is that 'the process of writing and setting space aside starts a process of reflection'; it is also a good memory recall process where the act of writing brings in more detail. In my own experience I have noticed many times that having completed my narrative writing, I might go back to it some hours later having remembered more. This is a process of self-supervision, a useful practice for a professional supervisor. Writing down the narrative enables coaches to take the whole of their experience into the supervisory space.

The coach then takes this writing to supervision and reads it out. The supervisor may also request a written copy. Through the reading, further detail is remembered raising questions as to why it might have been forgotten. Again, this process provides as much to the coach about what is missing, as it does about what exists (wholes). Coach and supervisor can also go through the text piece by piece, throwing light on transference and counter-transference, moments of self-deception, unnoticed confluence, within the coach–client relationship. By taking into account feelings that emerge as the text is worked through, these coaching disturbances often reveal themselves.

There is another benefit gained by writing down the narrative in this way and that is through the images that come to mind. Stories contain images, and through telling the narrative story in supervision more images are formed. Case (2007: 96) writes, 'it is in these additional images that our understanding of the client hovers on the edge of awareness'. There is a richness that builds, which otherwise could not happen. Images often say a great deal more than the literal word, providing a focus for creative exploration in supervision. Recalled images, emerging images, feelings, expanding the detail, noticing what is absent, fact versus fiction, are all part of this process. The format looks like this:

- Writing down the narrative of the client work, soon after the coaching session.
- Self-supervision, through reflection, connecting the work to theory, constructive assessment of the work.
- Further recall, adding details to the written narrative and new images coming up.
- Conscious reflection with the supervisor.
- Creative process in supervision.
- Intuition, new feelings, images, insights that arrive for the coach through the process.

# Conclusion

I have described an approach for supervision that is quite different from the more traditional analytical approaches. Both approaches are helpful, and they address different aspects of a coach's work. This approach, with the narrative and the experiential field methods, engage supervision in a very personal way respecting what is happening in the constant change and flow of the coach's work. Rather than analysing historical events, these methods deal with what those events precipitate in the present, into the moment of supervision. The narrative story, for the supervisor, is therefore more important in what it reveals at the point of telling. The revelations are less in the content and much more in the manner of telling.

The experiential field for the supervisor is important in revealing the relationships between supervisor and coach, between coach and client, and the field of a client. Of course the content is important, but the way the actors relate to each other is often a greater guide to success of any coaching.

Starting to use these open and exploratory methods may seem daunting at first. However, this disappears as the relationship between coach and supervisor begins to develop. The close contact and trust in the relationship allows the use of images, imaginings and the imagined to throw light on the coach's work. Once you try, you will find these open methods take you and the coach into many new avenues towards understanding the work and the skills of the coach being supervised.

## *References*

Beisser, A R (1970) The paradoxical theory of change, in (eds) J Fagan and I L Shepherd, *Gestalt Therapy Now* (pp 88–92), Penguin, Aylesbury

Brooks, P (1985) *Reading for the Plot,* Random House, New York

Carroll, M and Gilbert, M (2005) *On Being a Supervisee: Creating learning partnerships,* Vukani, London

Case, C (2007) Imagery in supervision, in (eds) J Schaverien and C Case, *Supervision of Art Psychotherapy: A theoretical and practical handbook* (pp 95–115), Routledge, London

Gabriel, Y (2000) *Storytelling in Organizations: Facts, fictions, and fantasies,* Oxford University Press, Oxford

Lakoff, G and Johnson, M (1980) *Metaphors We Live by,* University of Chicago Press, Chicago, IL

Lewin, K (1951) *Kurt Lewin: Field theory in the social sciences, selected theoretical papers,* Tavistock, London

O'Neill, B and Gaffney, S (2008) Field theoretical strategy, in *Handbook for Theory, Research, and Practice in Gestalt Therapy* (pp 228–56), Cambridge Scholars Publishing, Newcastle

Parlett, M (1991) Reflections on field theory, *British Gestalt Journal*, 1 (2) 63–81

# Non-directive supervision of coaching

## 07

**BOB THOMSON**

## Introduction

In this chapter I'd like to explore the notion of non-directive supervision of coaching. I begin by looking at a range of behaviours that a coach or supervisor might use that lie along a continuum from directive to non-directive. I then offer a definition of coaching supervision based on a definition of primarily non-directive coaching, and look at some of the ideas of Carl Rogers that underpin a non-directive approach. I go on to consider the purpose of supervision, look at supervision as an adult:adult relationship, and ask if supervision is more than just coaching the coach. I then look at the idea of the internal supervisor, and consider how a coach might use interpersonal process recall or keeping a journal in developing his or her internal supervisor. Finally, I share some questions for the reader to reflect upon.

At the outset let me say that I believe that it is impossible to be totally non-directive as a coach or supervisor. As the client speaks, your face or your body language can reveal your reaction, either conscious or unconscious. When you ask a question or play back to clients what you understand of their world, you are inevitably selective in choosing your words, even if your words are originally their words. And when you choose not to respond, you are being selective.

However, it is possible to be more or less non-directive. In my own practice, I think I am directive about the structure but not the content of the conversation. I believe part of my responsibility as a coach or supervisor is to manage the conversation in the interests of the client.

Within a session I am continually making judgements about things like offering a summary, phrasing a crisp, open question, letting a silence run or not, proposing an exercise, and so on. I may introduce a model or framework – for example, the idea of parent, adult and child ego states – to help a client reflect upon his or her situation. However, I believe that I am non-directive about the content of the session. While I may ask clients to draw a picture, I leave it up to them what they put into their drawing. If I ask a question, I try to ask a genuinely open question – without any attachment to the answer – rather than one that contains a suggestion or a desirable answer. I do occasionally offer a suggestion, hopefully making it explicit to the client that I am doing so. In my experience, what seems to me a suitable way forward is more often than not met with a response giving a reason why the client doesn't think it will work.

# Directive and non-directive behaviours

In a coaching or supervision conversation you are continually faced with choices about what to do next and how to respond. What question should I ask now? How do I deal with this silence? The session seems to be going nowhere, so what should I do? And so on. There are a host of possible responses, and choosing which response is an art rather than a science. A vital notion to bear in mind when you say or do anything is your intention. When you ask a question, give advice or offer a summary, what is your intention at that point?

In practising as a coach or supervisor, you implicitly or explicitly make choices all the time about how directive or non-directive to be. It is useful to be clear in your own mind about your position on being directive or non-directive, which helps you in choosing what to do next in a session or in managing the relationship.

Here is a list of 10 behaviours that you might engage in during a coaching or supervision session; I've simply listed them alphabetically. As you read these you may reflect on where each sits on the directive to non-directive spectrum:

1 Asking questions that raise awareness.

2 Giving advice.

3 Giving feedback.

4 Instructing.

**5** Listening to understand.

**6** Making suggestions.

**7** Offering guidance.

**8** Paraphrasing.

**9** Reflecting back.

**10** Summarizing.

The list highlights that there is a range of different behaviours you might engage in as a coach or mentor. It also raises the fundamental question of how directive or non-directive you wish to be in your practice. This applies at two levels. At one level, you are continually making choices about what to say or do next within a session. At a more fundamental level, you are making a choice about how you view your clients and the approach you take in helping them. Figure 7.1 offers one answer to the task of arranging the behaviours along the directive to non-directive spectrum. Behaviours such as instructing, giving advice and offering feedback are at the directive end, while listening, questioning and reflecting back are at the non-directive end.

The figure also suggests that when you are operating in a more directive style you are more likely to be looking to solve someone's problem for them or to push them towards a solution that you have in mind. On the other hand, when working non-directively your role is to help the other person to find his or her own solutions or to pull the ideas from him or her.

## A definition of coaching supervision

My own working definition of coaching runs as follows:

> Coaching occurs through a series of conversations in which one person uses their ability to listen, to ask questions and to play back what they have heard to create a relationship of rapport and trust that enables the other to clarify what matters to them and to work out what to do to achieve their aspirations. (Thomson, 2009)

I would highlight two aspects of this definition. First, it views coaching as a relationship, and suggests that an effective coaching relationship is one based on rapport and trust. Second, it emphasizes my view that the role of the non-directive coach is to help clients to articulate their goals and how they will set about achieving them.

**FIGURE 7.1** Directive and non-directive coaching behaviours

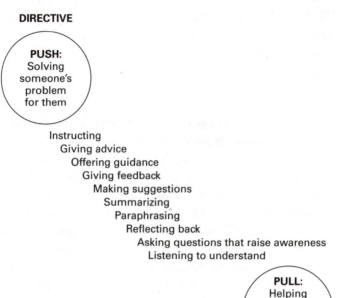

DIRECTIVE

**PUSH:**
Solving
someone's
problem
for them

Instructing
Giving advice
Offering guidance
Giving feedback
Making suggestions
Summarizing
Paraphrasing
Reflecting back
Asking questions that raise awareness
Listening to understand

**PULL:**
Helping
someone
solve their
own
problem

**NON-DIRECTIVE**

Here is a definition of coaching supervision that builds on this definition of coaching:

> Coaching supervision is a relationship of rapport and trust in which the supervisor assists coaches to reflect upon their practice in order, on the one hand, to develop their capability and enhance their effectiveness as a coach and, on the other, to process their emotional responses to their work with clients.

The definition can be compared with that of Peter Bluckert, which adds explicitly the idea that supervision is in part about protecting the client:

> Supervision sessions are a place for the coach to reflect on the work they are undertaking, with another more experienced coach. It has the dual purpose of supporting the continued learning and development of the coach, as well as giving a degree of protection to the person being coached. (Quoted in Hawkins and Smith, 2006)

Hawkins and Smith (2006) define supervision as follows:

> The process by which a coach/mentor/consultant with the help of a supervisor, who is not working directly with the client, can attend to understanding better both the client system and themselves as part of the client-coach/mentor system, and transform their work.

This definition is somewhat different to mine, with an emphasis on systems thinking and on transformational change where the supervisee experiences a 'felt shift' within the session.

In their review of some definitions of supervision, Tudor and Worrall (2004) quote a definition from Christian and Kitto that they regard as 'entirely congruent with the notion of facilitation within the person-centred approach'; supervision:

> denotes a role, not a person. The supervisor's job is to show that the questions the worker has brought can be thought about, and maybe to show ways in which they can be thought about. Supervision is a process whereby one person enables another to think better. (Christian and Kitto, 1987)

I really like this idea that supervision – and coaching too, I suggest – is about helping people to think better.

In my own definition of supervision above I am viewing supervision as being first and foremost a relationship. I am also indicating two purposes of supervision: first, to develop capability and enhance effectiveness and, second, to work through the emotional impact of the role on the coach. We shall look later in the chapter at a third possible purpose – to provide quality control – that is not included in my definition. The definition also emphasizes the importance of learning by reflecting on experience and practice. In my view:

> Deep and sustained learning – becoming able to do something you couldn't do before – only comes through experience. Experience on its own, however, is not enough. Experience needs to be reflected upon and made sense of to create knowledge, and this knowledge deepens when it is applied in fresh situations. The process can be viewed as a learning cycle (Thomson, 2006); see Figure 7.2.

The notion that supervision provides a space for the coach to reflect on and develop their practice is reflected in this extract from Hawkins (2006):

> In workshops you can learn models and develop competencies, but these do not by themselves produce an excellent coach. Supervision provides the reflective container for the trainee to turn his or her competencies into capabilities and to develop his or her personal and coaching capacities.

**FIGURE 7.2** The coaching learning cycle

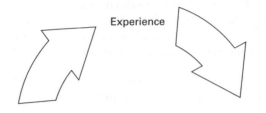

Experience

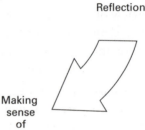

Performing differently

Reflection

Making
sense
of

# The influence of Carl Rogers

The ideas and philosophy of Carl Rogers and his person-centred approach to psychotherapy, counselling and education are one of the cornerstones of my practice. I don't think the importance of his ideas is adequately recognized in the coaching literature.

A long time ago I read a sentence written by Rogers that profoundly affects my approach to development, coaching and supervision. It is a sentence whose meaning and implications I am still thinking about more than two decades later. In *On Becoming a Person,* he wrote: 'It seems to me that anything that can be taught to another is relatively inconsequential, and has little or no influence on behavior' (Rogers, 1961). He added, 'That sounds so ridiculous I can't help but question it at the same time that I present it.'

In an article published a year before his death, 'Client-centered/ Person-centered Approach to Therapy', Rogers states briefly his central hypothesis:

> It is that the individual has within himself or herself vast resources for self-understanding, for altering his or her self-concept, attitudes, and self-directed behavior – and that these resources can be tapped if only a definable climate of facilitative psychological attitudes can be provided. (Rogers, 1987)

The person-centred approach is 'built on a basic trust in the person'. It depends on 'the actualizing tendency present in every living organism – the tendency to grow, to develop, to realize its full potential'.

In the article Rogers describes three conditions that are both necessary and sufficient to create an effective therapeutic relationship. To provide Rogers' 'definable climate of facilitative psychological attitudes', the facilitator needs to have and to demonstrate to the other person three things:

1 *Congruence:* being genuine, being real, sharing feelings and attitudes, not hiding behind a façade.

2 *Unconditional positive regard:* non-judgmental acceptance and valuing of the other, in a total not conditional way.

3 *Empathy:* understanding the other's feelings and experience, and also communicating that understanding.

It is essential that the facilitator not only possesses these qualities but also that the client to some extent perceives their congruence, unconditional positive regard and empathic understanding of them.

Rogers actually states that there are six conditions that are necessary and sufficient for therapeutic change. As well as the three conditions listed above and the fourth condition that the client perceives them in the facilitator, Rogers states two other conditions that are required to support a client's change and growth – that the two people are in psychological contact with one another, and that the client is experiencing some incongruence or discrepancy. I am assuming that in coaching and supervision the helper and the client are indeed in contact with one another. I am assuming too that the client has come to coaching or supervision with some degree of desire to change, grow or become more effective.

Supervision isn't the same as therapy or psychological change. In their book *Freedom to Practise: Person-centred approaches to supervision,* Tudor and Worrall consider the six conditions and argue that the two conditions I have omitted are 'not strictly necessary for the process of supervision'. They write that:

a supervisee's experience of being empathically understood and unconditionally accepted is perhaps the single most important factor in effective supervision, and we retain in our thinking about supervision the idea that a supervisee will benefit to the degree that he feels fully received. (Tudor and Worrall, 2004)

These ideas have some profound implications for the supervision of coaching. First, if you agree with the premise that things that can be taught have little or no influence on behaviour, then there isn't much that a supervisor can usefully teach a coach. Even as I write these words, I am aware of how challenging, perhaps disturbing, they are. As you read them, you may be asking yourself, how can I operate as a supervisor if there is no place for me to teach anything of consequence?

One idea that may help to clarify what is possible here comes from some words of Galileo: 'You cannot teach people anything. You can only help them to discover it within themselves.' One of the roles of the supervisor, therefore, is to help coaches to discover things within themselves – by facilitating their reflection on their practice, not by teaching or telling them.

A second implication of Rogers' ideas is that supervisors need consistently to demonstrate to the coach their empathic understanding, their non-judgmental acceptance and their genuineness. The relationship offered in this way provides a container within which coaches can tap into their own resources to make sense of their world and their work, which in turn may lead to shifts in their attitudes, behaviours and sense of self. There are indeed rich prizes. The role of the supervisor is to facilitate this kind of learning by the coach. But the supervisor can't control this, can't force it to happen. Rather he or she needs to trust the coach and trust the process.

## The functions of coaching supervision

Hawkins and Smith (2006) define three main functions of supervision: developmental, resourcing and qualitative:

1 The developmental function is about developing the skills, understanding and capacities of the supervisee, through reflection on their practice.
2 The resourcing function is about helping the supervisee to become aware of and deal with their reactions to the emotional intensity of their work with clients.
3 The qualitative function provides quality control of the work of the supervisee, ensuring that the work is appropriate and ethical.

How do these three functions of supervision correlate to the definition of coaching supervision offered above and the nature of a supervision relationship based on demonstrating to the client Rogers' three core conditions?

I think the developmental function maps directly. My definition says that the purpose of supervision is to enhance the capability and effectiveness of the coach, through reflection on his or her practice. The resourcing function is also explicit in my definition. While I certainly agree that helping coaches to process their emotional reaction to their work with clients is a valid and useful aspect of coaching supervision, I suspect that the emotional intensity of a coaching relationship is generally less than occurs in therapy, counselling or social work. Perhaps my assertion here reflects my affinity with a humanistic rather than a psychoanalytic approach to coaching.

However, I think that the qualitative function sits awkwardly with a non-directive approach to supervision. Let me emphasize that I do agree that coaching work should be appropriate and ethical. However, if supervisors take on a responsibility to ensure the quality of the coach's work and to monitor the coach's compliance with a relevant code of practice, then I think their acceptance necessarily becomes judgmental and their positive regard becomes conditional. And coaches are aware that their supervisor is making judgements about their competence and their practice. This is likely to limit the degree of rapport and trust that is established in the relationship.

In *Freedom to Practise* Tudor and Worrall write that the belief which a person-centred supervisor has in the self-actualizing tendency within people:

> helps free supervisors to hold a high level of trust in the work that their supervisees are doing, and in the capacity of their supervisees' clients to make the most of and take the best from that work. It follows from this that supervisors do not normally need to assess, monitor or police the work of their supervisees, and can instead devote their attention to helping supervisees explore their own thoughts and feelings about their work. (Tudor and Worrall, 2004)

They later comment that it is undesirable for a line manager to act as a supervisor, in part:

> because it is hard for a line manager, with accountability and ultimately with authority for hiring and firing, to offer genuinely and unconditionally much of the formative or restorative functions to their supervisee/worker, and for that supervisee to receive them. (Tudor and Worrall, 2004)

Note that the *formative* and *restorative* functions are similar to the *developmental* and *resourcing* functions, respectively, described at the beginning of this section.

Let me stress that I agree that there is a legitimate place for judgement of competence and for confronting or reporting unethical practice. However, this creates a different relationship and a different way of working in a supervision session. The supervisor who is also the line manager of a team of counsellors, the senior social worker who is judging whether a novice social worker is fit to qualify or practise, or the teacher who is deciding whether a student on a coaching programme is to be accredited do indeed have a qualitative function within their remit. They inevitably have to balance their quality assurance role with the importance of creating an effective supervisory relationship – and this is likely to hinder them in working non-directively. There is nothing wrong with that, but it is useful to be clear about it.

## Coaching on coaching

O'Neill (2000) also recognized the importance of coaching for the coach. She writes that, 'One of the best ways that coaches can stay effective in their role is to receive coaching themselves.' After 20 years of experience as an executive coach continuing to have a coach herself, she reckons that 'using a coach … [is] a smart investment'.

One of the questions I have been wrestling with in my practice as a supervisor is, to what extent – if any – is coaching supervision different from coaching on coaching? A common answer to this question would make two points. First, in supervision there is always a third party – the coach's client or clients – in the room during a supervision conversation. There might also be other parties, such as the client's organization, in the room too. Second, as we have just been discussing, the supervisor has a quality assurance responsibility to see that the coach is working ethically. This extends to the notion that the supervisor has a responsibility to the coaching profession, ensuring good practice within the profession.

I am not convinced by these arguments. In regard to the first point, I'm not sure that the presence, as it were, of a third party in the room makes supervision different from coaching. In many coaching conversations – for example, about managing a difficult team member, creating a more effective working relationship with a boss, or behaving more assertively in meetings – there are other parties in the room. And helping a coaching client to manage a highly stressful working environment has similarities to helping a coach to deal with the emotional intensity of his or her work.

In response to the second point, in the previous section I have indicated why I think that the qualitative function of supervision does not fit with a non-directive approach to supervision. Moreover, in a coaching relationship the coach, in my view, has a responsibility to consider how to respond or act if, for instance, a client is doing things that are dangerous or illegal. There may be times – albeit very infrequently – when being judgmental and non-acceptant are more important than the coaching relationship. In this sense, the coach has a responsibility to a wider constituency that is not dissimilar to the supervisor's responsibility to the coaching profession.

Hence, my thinking at present is that when the supervisor does not have an explicit responsibility for quality assurance then supervision using a non-directive approach is no different from coaching on coaching. It is only when the supervisor does have this qualitative role that supervision is more than coaching on coaching.

## Supervision as an adult:adult relationship

In this section I'd like to return briefly to the nature of the relationship that is at the heart of a non-directive approach to supervision. I see the relationship, in transactional analysis terms, as an adult:adult interaction. And I think there is a danger – particularly when there is a quality assurance aspect – that it can at times become a parent:child relationship.

The very word 'supervisor' is to some extent problematic, suggesting that the supervisor is in some sense superior. The thesaurus in my word processing package offers me two suggestions when I look up supervision – management or care. Under 'management' it then lists direction, administration, regulation, command, control. Under 'care' it lists custody, guardianship, protection, charge, guidance. The former is suggestive of a critical parent role, while the latter hints at more of a nurturing parent. In either case, the risk is that when one party comes from a parent stance it may prompt a child response in the other.

Reflecting on the times when as a coach I have mistakenly been drawn into making suggestions or offering solutions, I can identify a couple of situations when I sometimes catch myself doing this. One is when time is limited and I might push for a quick solution – which I don't consider good practice. I described a second circumstance as follows:

> Another situation when I occasionally catch myself offering suggestions or solutions is when I regard the client in some way as less competent. I sometimes realize that I have done this several times with a particular client. I then wonder if I am in some sense interacting as a Parent – perhaps a Nurturing Parent – and regarding the Client as being in some type of Child ego state. So, I need to consider what is going on that makes me behave in this way with this individual when my usual style is to operate in an Adult:Adult way, being predominantly non-directive and leaving the client to work out their own way forward. (Thomson, 2009)

As a non-directive supervisor, my preference is also to operate in an adult:adult way, inviting the coach to work out his or her own way forward. I don't see my role as being to direct, regulate, control, protect or guide. But, how do you see your role as supervisor?

## Developing your internal supervisor

Through the experience of supervision and reflection on their practice, coaches can develop over time the ability to tune into their thoughts and feelings in order to become more deeply aware of what is going on in the moment within a session or to critically appraise a session after it has ended. They develop the ability to self-supervise, as it were – though not as a replacement for ongoing supervision.

Casement (1985) introduced the idea of the internal supervisor. Casement was originally a social worker who then became a psychoanalyst. In his book he reflects deeply and honestly on his practice, particularly on the mistakes he made in his work. By listening closely and without preconception to what his patients were communicating to him at many diverse levels, he was able to learn what they needed from him and how, in turn, he needed to respond. Although he draws mainly on examples from psychoanalysis, he invites readers from other caring professions to relate the ideas to their own spheres of work.

He points out that support from a supervisor can offer hindsight on earlier sessions and foresight in relation to future sessions. However, therapists – and coaches and supervisors – also need insight within a session. He writes, 'As a counterbalance to the many pressures upon a therapist in a session, I have found it useful to think in terms of an internal supervisor.'

An important aspect of the internal supervisor is what Casement calls 'trial identification'. He writes that, 'This can also be thought of as related to empathy in seeking to understand a patient.' He uses trial identification in a number of ways;

- thinking or feeling into the experience being described by the patient;
- putting himself in the shoes of someone being referred to by the patient;
- imagining how a patient might hear a possible comment from the analyst;
- reflecting on how the patient has in fact responded to a comment from the analyst.

The internal supervisor enables the analyst to 'be in two places at once, in the patient's shoes and in one's own simultaneously'.

Casement illustrates the use of an internal supervisor with a case study from his early experience as a social worker. The case centres on Teddy, a 24-year-old 'catatonic schizophrenic' being treated at home where he lived with a very protective mother who led him by the hand into each session like 'a toddler being taken to play-school'. Teddy had started to give monosyllabic answers to questions, and this was how he behaved in his early sessions with Casement.

Casement writes, 'I imagined myself in his place, wondering what it might be like having a social worker intermittently firing questions at me like that. It soon struck me how persecutory that could be.' At their next session, Casement had moved the chairs around so they were nearly parallel rather than face-to-face. He explained why he had done this, and went on to say how he had been thinking about how Teddy might feel when he was here. He offered some thoughts about how he imagined what it might be like to be in Teddy's place with lots of questions coming at him. He said that he'd failed to recognize that Teddy might be keeping up a wall of silence to keep Casement at a safe distance. On hearing this, Teddy turned to him and replied:

It's funny you put it like that. I have often thought of myself as hiding under a man-hole cover, in a drain, with people trying to find me – and sewage down below. I'm not afraid of drains. It's people that smell. They make it difficult for me to breathe. My mother suffocates me. She treats me like a little boy. I am really a man inside, you know. She doesn't realize that. (Casement, 1985)

Casement's work with Teddy 'still had far to go' but this was the start of progress. Teddy persuaded his mother to let him come on his own to the sessions, which he began to use 'spontaneously'. In the second year of treatment he found a job in a toy shop where 'he could relate to parents and children on his own terms'.

Casement offers this case study as an illustration of internal supervision, and it vividly describes the use of trial identification. However, I think it also illustrates the power of Rogers' necessary and sufficient conditions. Casement demonstrates – and Teddy experiences – his genuineness, his empathic understanding and his unconditional positive regard. This of course is my analysis of the work and I have no idea if Casement would use these terms to describe how he worked with Teddy.

Casement later warns of a risk 'if the work of the internal supervisor is allowed to become too active and conscious during a session'. This can create an interference which gets in the way of working effectively with the client.

Casement suggests a number of stages in the development of an analyst's internal supervisor, with similar stages for those in other helping professions. He writes that, 'What I am calling the internal supervisor has origins that derive from before the experience of supervision and its development continues far beyond it.' The development of an internal supervisor might include the following stages, with of course some movement backwards and forwards:

1  the analyst's own experience of being a patient in analysis;
2  the early stages of training as an analyst where initially 'students rely a good deal upon the advice and comments offered by the supervisor';
3  developing the capacity to reflect spontaneously within a session, which is balanced with thinking internalized from the supervisor;
4  the move to autonomous functioning through dialogue between external supervisor and internal supervisor;
5  an autonomous internal supervisor that forms after the analyst has formally qualified;
6  further growth if the analyst has the opportunity to supervise others;
7  renewed reflection, since an analyst should always be in a state of becoming that is never completed.

Translated into the journey of someone learning how to coach well, a comparable set of stages might read as:

1 the experience of being coached (which might run in parallel with the stages below);
2 working in pairs or trios in workshops – or with practise clients – to learn about things like listening, asking open questions and using the GROW model;
3 beginning to use these skills and models flexibly in response to what is happening within a session;
4 the ability to balance critical reflection on practice with the views of a supervisor;
5 the development of greater skill, confidence and fluency – and the ability to use the internal supervisor – through extensive practice as a coach;
6 a deeper level of capability embracing lessons learnt from acting as a supervisor to other coaches;
7 the never-ending journey of reflection and learning to become a more capable coach.

# Interpersonal process recall

One method for reflecting on your practice that can contribute to the development of your internal supervisor is a technique known as interpersonal process recall, often simply called IPR (Kagan, 1980). IPR is a technique to help a coach or other professional to look back – through the use of video or audio tape – at a session with a client in order to recall what was going on for them at various points in the conversation. Through recall, the coach can become more aware of what he or she was thinking and feeling during the session, and can recognize things that he or she might have but didn't say or do. He or she may also become aware of some of the unconscious factors or interpersonal dynamics that influenced his or her behaviour in the session.

The technique was developed by Norman Kagan and his colleagues at Michigan State University in the 1960s. In Kagan's view, individuals can, on the one hand, derive great joy from being with others and, on the other, experience feelings of fear or helplessness when with others. The latter feelings are a result of early childhood experiences as a small person in a big person's world. This leads to an approach-avoidance syndrome where the individual seeks a safe psychological distance from others. This may be manifested in a coaching session as the coach behaving 'diplomatically' by missing messages from the client. IPR can help the coach to recognize the dynamics of the coaching relationship or conversation that they missed in the original session, possibly because they were behaving diplomatically.

Coming from a client-centred perspective, Kagan reckoned that, 'The individual knows best about the meaning of their own experience.' Allen (2004) argues that IPR is based on the notions that:

- People are intrinsically motivated to learn.
- People will only learn what they are ready to learn.
- People remember best what they discover for themselves.
- If you push, frighten or attack people, they will only learn how to keep you off their backs.

IPR thus sits very comfortably alongside a non-directive approach to supervision. In IPR, the coach rather than the supervisor is the authority on what was going on for the coach during the taped coaching session. The job of the supervisor within an IPR session is to offer a safe, supportive relationship that leaves the coach free to reflect and thereby to become less fearful and more skilled in their practice.

Here is one way in which an IPR session might be run:

1 Prior to the session, a coaching conversation between the coach and a client is taped, using video or audio tape.
2 This is played back between the coach and another, who is often called an 'inquirer' in IPR.
3 The coach, not the inquirer, pauses the tape when he or she recalls something that was going on for him or her at that point in the coaching conversation.
4 The coach speaks about the thoughts or feelings he or she had at that time.
5 The inquirer asks open questions to facilitate the coach's discovery process.

Note that the role of the inquirer is not to teach, offer opinions or pass judgements. Rather, the role of the inquirer is first and foremost to provide a safe place where the coach can deepen his or her understanding and acceptance of themselves, and thereby enhance his or her ability to coach others well.

It is important in an IPR session that the pause button is controlled by the coach, not the inquirer. As a participant on a programme to develop supervision skills, I have experienced the feeling of frustration when the pause button was taken over by the inquirer who proceeded to give me unsolicited and not especially useful feedback on my body language. It is generally the case that there is far more contained within a coaching session than can be processed, so the coach may wish to focus on particular sections of the tape or aspects of their coaching practice.

Using IPR can be very helpful in developing your internal supervisor. Allen (2004) writes that: 'my experience of the IPR method can be a helpful guide in processing a session for myself. I have the experience of knowing how to access stuff going on in me. Often that is all that is needed'. While IPR can play a useful part in supervision, complementing other supervision sessions, it is not by itself a substitute for appropriate supervision.

## Keeping a journal

One very simple and inexpensive way of reflecting on your experience that can help to refine your practice and develop your internal supervisor is to keep a journal. By a journal I don't mean a diary that records events. Rather, a journal is a place where you can take some time to reflect upon your practice as a coach or supervisor. In recalling individual sessions or in reflecting more generally about your thoughts and feelings, your hopes and concerns, you can explore what is going on for you in your work. Madeline McGill, an executive coach, writes:

> A journal is a place where we can be ourselves – where we do not have to pose – where we can remember and reflect on significant thoughts and events and so re-integrate them into the panorama of life … It is a means of talking and listening to ourselves – a way of 'speaking our thoughts' – of having a dialogue with ourselves (personal communication).

A journal is clearly a very personal thing, and keeping a journal will not appeal to everyone. There is no one style or format. It may be in a notebook or on a personal computer. It may contain drawings or quotations or pieces of poetry. It is not a work of literature, and you don't need to record your thoughts in perfect prose.

One way of working with a journal is to capture some headlines – a summary of what happened and how you felt – and then, when you are ready and have more time, to reflect more closely on what lies behind the headlines. Reflecting on what happened and your thoughts and feelings will help you to learn from your experiences as a coach or supervisor. Over time patterns may emerge, and you may understand more deeply the meaning of events and appreciate more clearly your own motives and feelings and behaviour. This in turn helps to develop your internal supervisor.

# Conclusion

I find that writing about coaching or supervision helps me to examine my practice and my views. In this chapter I have tried to offer some insights into my own practice using a non-directive approach as well as ways in which it is possible to develop our own internal supervisor to guide our own practice day to day.

## *References*

Allen, P (2004)The use of interpersonal process recall (IPR) in person-centred supervision, in (eds) K Tudor and M Worrall, *Freedom to Practise, Person-centred Approaches to Supervision,* PCCS Books, Ross-on-Wye

Casement, P (1985) *On Learning from the Patient,* Tavistock, London

Christian, C and Kitto, J (1987) *The Theory and Practice of Supervision,* YMCA National College, London

Hawkins, P (2006) Coaching supervision, in (ed) J Passmore, *Excellence in Coaching,* Kogan Page, London

Hawkins, P and Smith, N (2006) *Coaching, Mentoring and Organizational Consultancy,* Open University Press, Buckingham

Kagan, N (1980) Influencing human interaction: Eighteen years with IPR, in (ed) A Hess, *Psychotherapy Supervision: Theory, research and practice,* Wiley, New York

O'Neill, M B (2000) *Executive Coaching with Backbone and Heart,* Wiley, San Francisco, CA

Rogers, C (1961) *On Becoming a Person,* Houghton Mifflin, Boston, MA

Rogers, C (1987) Client-centered/person-centered approach to therapy, in (eds) I Kutash and A Wolf, *Psychotherapist's Casebook,* Jossey-Bass, San Francisco, CA

Thomson, B (2006) *Growing People,* Chandos, Oxford

Thomson, B (2009) *Don't Just Do Something, Sit There,* Chandos, Oxford

Tudor, K and Worrall, M (eds) (2004) *Freedom to Practise, Person-centred Approaches to Supervision,* PCCS Books, Ross-on-Wye

# Presence in coaching supervision

**ELAINE PATTERSON**

## Introduction

The word 'presence' in coaching supervision is frequently used. But what do we mean by it? How does 'presence' enrich supervision? Is 'presence' more about the supervisor 'being' than 'doing'? What does this mean for how supervisors supervise and how supervisees experience supervision?

In this chapter I will argue that presence is not a 'nice to have' or 'designer luxury'. Rather presence sits at the very heart of our ability as coach supervisors to work with what is in new, fresh and exciting ways with our supervisees; and in turn supports the supervisees' development as reflective practitioners to both enrich their practices and extend their market offer.

This chapter opens up the debate; seeks some definitions in a very new and emergent field; explores what 'presence' can potentially offer to the role and tasks of supervision; explores what 'presence' and the 'absence of presence' mean for supervisory practice; and offers some practical hints and tips for how supervisors can enhance their own 'presence' across all aspects of their work.

## Towards a definition of 'presence'

What do we mean by the term 'presence' in coaching and coaching supervision? Attempted definitions risk abstraction, dilution and wooliness. However, for us to understand the concept as practitioners we need to attempt to define what we mean.

A survey of the literature shows how the term 'presence' has been defined in a variety of ways. For example, *The English Oxford Dictionary* (6th edition, 1976) defines presence as '1. Being present (your presence is requested; ...) 2. Person or thing that is present 3. ~ presence of mind, calmness and self command' and evokes a sense of being 'here' in the 'now'.

The term has also been defined in coaching as the 'ability to be fully conscious and create spontaneous relationship with the client, employing a style which is open, flexible and confident' (ICF website, 2010) and is seen as one of the core coaching competencies. This evokes a sense of intention, attention and responsiveness. Silsbee (2010) has suggested presence is 'a state of awareness, in the moment, [which is] characterized by the felt experience of timeliness, connectedness, and a larger truth'. This adds the dimension of presence as a 'state of being' that makes possible wider connections in us and in others.

There is nothing new about people's ability to be 'present' with each other. We have all experienced moments of wonderful connection with another person where we feel that we have been truly heard. But what is new for us in the coaching supervision profession is how we can adapt and extend this everyday definition of 'presence' and how we can intentionally cultivate the very deliberate act and practice of 'being present' to enhance the effectiveness of coaching supervisory practice. This is what we will now explore.

## What is shaping our understanding of 'presence' in coaching supervision?

A range of work is now influencing our understanding of the importance of presence in coaching supervision. This includes the work of writers such as Tolle, Csikszentmihalyi and Scharmer, all of whom have written about this concept or parallel states.

Tolle (2005) has argued that today's problems are rooted in the mind; in our egos and by our inability to experience the present moment in the here and now 'behind or beyond our physical body, shifting emotions and chattering mind'. He suggests that peace and happiness rest in discovering our 'natural state of felt oneness with Being; a state of connectedness with something immeasurable and indestructible; of finding our true nature beyond name and form and the inability to find this connectedness gives the illusion of separation'.

Csikszentmihalyi (2002) is best known for his work on flow. Flow is a 'state of happiness ... of joy, creativity and total involvement'. Flow occurs when individuals are totally engaged in the here and now, are at one with the present experience or task, and are freed from the constraints of temporal time, which opens the door to new perspectives, implicit possibilities and hidden potential.

The Dalai Lama (Lama and Cutler, 1998) too has drawn attention to parallel themes to presence. He argues that the purpose of human existence is to seek happiness, and that this can be achieved by a 'training of the mind', by connecting through our shared humanity, and by acting with compassion, generosity and kindness. This strips happiness of its complexity and Western hype and returns us to the quintessential essence of how being present with ourselves, with others, with our experiences, brings us back to ourselves.

Scharmer (2007) developed Theory U – the theory of 'presencing' that shows how people can move beyond their habitual thought patterns to observing and really seeing and sensing, and to letting go and creating something new and different by working with what he describes as 'an open mind, an open heart and an open will'.

What these references – alongside many others – help to indicate is that many writers and researchers across a wide range of different disciplines, traditions and continents are exploring states of being. Such work is helping us to think more carefully about the nature of human existence and states of being that enhance effectiveness in different activities.

It is easy to confuse 'mindful awareness' with 'presence'. The distinction is subtle but important. Where mindfulness is defined as a total awareness of what is happening in the moment, it is a precondition for the state of presence but does not of itself guarantee presence, which is a wider, deeper and more encompassing state of bringing the whole self and being – and all of who we are – to the work. Taking this further it could be argued that the precondition of mindfulness could be defined as the solitary, personal and individual awareness that we bring to ourselves, to others and to our experiences, whereas the state of presence in coaching supervision is a wider embodiment of a mindfulness in action but which occurs because of the connection that has been co-created between the supervisor and supervisee within their relationship and learning partnership.

Given this body of work I would define presence as follows:

Presence is an alive and freeing state of generous, compassionate and mindful awareness in our being – which is felt and experienced – in the here and now in the relationship with another; and which opens our hearts, minds and bodies to a wider reality and joyful field of connectedness, possibility and potential.

A quick self-assessment will help you to appreciate the extent to which you embody this state of presence in your supervision and in your life as a whole; see Table 8.1.

**TABLE 8.1** Presence – self-assessment

| Quality | Extent applied in your supervision practice? 0 – 10 | Extent applied across all aspects of your life? 0 – 10 |
|---|---|---|
| Feeling free and alive? | | |
| Feeling generous? | | |
| Feeling compassionate? | | |
| Feeling mindfully aware? | | |
| Feeling present? | | |
| Open to a bigger picture? | | |
| Open to a wider sense of connection? | | |
| Open to a wider sense of possibility and potential? | | |
| Feeling joyful? | | |

# Learning to become present: a few simple exercises

Presence is accessible to us all. At its most fundamental it is about escaping our constant stream of mind chatter and getting back into a non-judgmental focus on the here and now. Presence is the gateway to a different level of conscious awareness which comes from being attuned to the wider field. One way to explore this is through undertaking two exercises: Grounding, centring and breathing exercise; and Into our hearts exercise. Try them and see what happens.

## 1. Grounding, centring and breathing exercise**·

How each of us gets into presence is very personal, but one of the most common ways is to get out of our heads and into our bodies. Meditation and breathing exercises have the great ability to help us to slow down, clear our minds and create space (see Marianetti and Passmore, 2009; Passmore and Marianetti, 2007).

---

**1** Grounding: Become very aware of where the ground touches your body. Bring this into your attention and awareness. Now feel the ground behind your feet.

**2** Centring: Now bring all your awareness to the trunk of your body. Be the centre of your body …. Let the trunk straighten and feel its strength.

**3** Breathing: Now bring you awareness to your breath, letting your breath breathe you. Notice the rise and fall of your breath in your chest.

---

## 2. Into our hearts exercise

The purpose of this exercise is to relax and expand our hearts – the centre for our humanity, kindness, compassion and love.

1  Find something that never fails to both inspire and move you and in some way expresses your best self … Use it as your talisman. This could be a work of art, a piece of music, a poem, an image, a quote, a photograph, a memory of a special time, friends, family, mentors, acts of kindness.
2  Develop a practice of reconnecting with it whenever you feel your heart and yourself closing down or contracting in some way. Allow it to communicate back to you abundance, generosity, fun and curiosity.
3  Take it with you to sessions in your memory, your bag or your pocket.

# Towards a definition of 'coaching supervision'

The coaching profession is still exploring the nature of coaching supervision and what it means in practice. This book is part of that process. A working definition is: Coaching supervision provides a safe and disciplined creative space for reflective inquiry into all of the dimensions of a supervisees work.

Supervision provides a unique space for 'super-vision'; the space for inquiry, for curiosity, for critical reflection of practice in a safe and supportive environment. This is best achieved when supervisors are both being and bringing all of who they are – their state of presence – to the supervision work and to the supervisory relationship. As Beisser (1970) observes: 'Change occurs only when we become all of who we are.'

Coaching supervision is learning through dialogue: it is an experiential conversation-based learning partnership working through the supervisees' stories of their practice to clear blocks, obstacles or anxieties that might be hindering them in their coaching relationships. Presence essentially pushes the 'pause' button, freeing us from current perceived constraints, habitual thought patterns, histories, what could or should be, to explore what can be and what is possible. Presence offers the possibility of working transformationally to explore the bigger picture behind the detail of individual cases.

Coaching supervision is a relationship. The work occurs in the relationship and through the conversation. Where this has been created between the supervisor and the supervisee in an open and equal learning partnership where both parties are learning and are on the edge of their learning, new generative learning is free to emerge.

The focus is on the supervisee; it is centred on the supervisee's practice and whatever impacts on that practice, and using the learning that has been created in the supervisory conversation to improve his or her future work. In this way it is possible to attend to the four core tasks of coaching supervision, which are:

1 Assuring professionalism, integrity and ethical practice of the supervisee.
2 The personal and professional learning and development of the supervisee.
3 The rest, refuelling and restoration of the supervisee.
4 Celebrating and honouring the work of the supervisee.

Presence holds and contains all of the relationship dynamics that are expressed in the huge complexity of the supervisees' practice and the systems fields in which they are working, shown in Figure 8.1.

# Bringing together the two definitions

With this working definition it becomes clear that 'the presence of presence' sits at the heart of effective supervisory practice. This is because 'who we are as supervisors is how we coach supervisees' (Murdoch, 2010).

We are more than a jumble of our thoughts, feelings, emotions and behaviours, our histories and shapers. Our values and philosophies influence how we behave. Presence can help us explore these aspects of who we are to deepen our understanding and put these aspects of ourselves in service of the supervisee. Becoming 'all of who we are' as supervisors helps supervisees to also 'become all of who they are in order to best serve the needs of their own clients'. This is absolutely fundamental because in coaching and coaching supervision it is the coach or the supervisor who is the primary instrument or tool, and it is the use of our whole authentic self in supervision that provides the oil to the supervisory wheel.

'Who we are' is cultivated by the ability of supervisors to be present with themselves in order to be fully present with their supervisees in the supervisory relationship. And our ability to be present with ourself and

**FIGURE 8.1** The Coaching Supervision Academy's full spectrum model

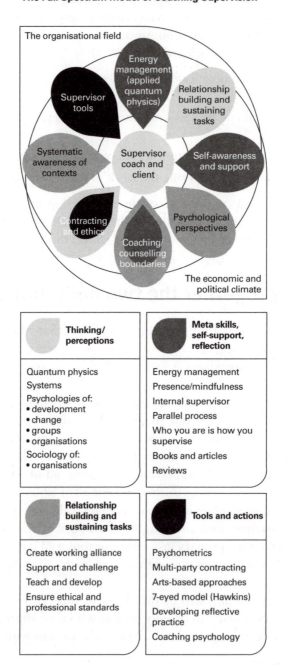

The Full Spectrum Model of Coaching Supervision

with others goes the heart of our shared humanity; of what it is to be human and what it is to be in relationship with another human being.

For supervisors this requires huge commitment, courage and compassion extended to both themselves and to their supervisees. It is about us working on the level of our humanity in a genuine learning partnership instead of being exclusively technically and expert driven. Coaching supervision is therefore a distinct practice that requires an understanding of presence alongside a robust knowledge base that includes psychological dimensions of human development, learning theory, change theory, organizational psychology, interpersonal dynamics and systems perspectives. To use an analogy, tools and techniques offer us the flexibility, and the bandwidth and presence offer us the radar to pick up the signals that are just out of awareness and that want to emerge.

## How presence unlocks reflective learning and supports the development of the reflective practitioner

Presence therefore sits at the very heart of our ability as coach supervisors to work with what is in new, fresh and exciting ways with our supervisees, and in turn support their development as reflective practitioners.

The act of 'being present' is essentially about supporting change through reflective inquiry, learning from that reflective inquiry and thereby supporting the whole of the learning cycle through compassionate appreciative inquiry. For supervision to be really effective supervisors need to be intentionally present to be able to both present to the experience and to be able to stand back to observe and notice all that is occurring. They need to be able to move between subject and the object, allowing themselves to be impacted while remaining the wise compassionate observer. Presence provides the spaciousness to truly support the supervisees in their learning.

Presence supports the supervisee's natural learning processes and how people best learn because it is working with – and not against – what is understood about how people best learn and develop; that people learn best with the right level of right support and challenge; they need hope; they are innately resourceful and curious; they have a natural and innate capacity to learn, unlearn and relearn by laying down new neural pathways; that the universe is full of latent possibility and potential (Lucas, 2003; Parsloe and Leedham, 2009). This supports the supervisee's ability to reflect on action as well as in action where the former is after the experience and the latter in during the experience.

Presence supports the development of the supervisee as reflective practitioner because presence is able to offer an invitation of a welcome inquiry without the voice of judgement, the voice of the internal critic, the voice of cynicism, the voice of fear and the voice of comparison, all of which distance, separate and isolate us. Presence helps the supervisee become a more reflective practitioner because it supports him or her in becoming more aware and to then reflect on the content of that awareness. It is like opening the door into a bigger more elastic space that shifts us into holding ambiguity and paradox. Presence also helps us to let go of habitual and linear thought patterns and to allow us to work with what wants to emerge.

Presence in supervision enables the supervisees to process events into experiences, into new awareness and insights, into new realizations and then learning. This holding space enables the supervisees to work openly with their own drives, agenda, triggers, assumptions, blind spots, shadow sides, habits and patterns as the supervisor is working with acceptance and tolerance while being able to access a wider field of possibility to share. This can clear underlying anxieties and fears that might be sitting on the edge of the supervisees' awareness and could be sabotaging their work with their clients.

The development of our ability to reflect without harshness – or rather with compassion towards ourselves and others – deepens our ability to learn from our practice. It helps us to keep moving, to stay fresh and open. McCongagill (2000) notes that reflective practitioners bring the following qualities to their work:

- An awareness of their own filters for making meaning.
- Awareness of their own assumptions, methods and tools.
- A commitment to an inquiring stance towards their own effectiveness.
- An ability to regard each new client as a fresh challenge and where models *et al* are in continual evolution.

Presence helps the supervisee to build his or her own internal supervisor: a supervisor who is tuned into the whole range of mind, heart and body experience and information during each coaching moment. The development of a supervisee's own internal supervisor helps the supervisee to enhance his or her ability to reflect in the coaching moment and to be open to all that is going on within and around. This means that coaching is no longer a surface layer of being strictly task- or totally outcome-focused but is getting at the real underlying issues that might be blocking flow, performance, impact or effectiveness. Presence enables both the supervisor and the supervisee to listen and pay attention at different levels and in different dimensions. This is because presence enables supervisees to work with self-awareness, to be fully centred, and open to a lot of intuitive, cognitive and psychological information that they notice and pick up through their senses and from which choices can be made about what to use, hold, file away or discard. This facilitates a shift from subject to object; from observer to observed; and from foreground to background.

Presence offers the supervisee the possibility of generative and transformational learning because it offers access to a wider consciousness. It frees us from our thoughts and through this to a world of lightness, play, joy and fun. Stepping into presence offers permission to let go of knowing and of being in control; to move into experimental and creative spaces to free blocks and obstacles. This requires humility, honesty and courage to be able to sit on the edge of our learning and our experience. This links to a wider truth that change happens when we become all of who we are (Beisser, 2000). From here the analytical mind has its place in checking, testing and analysing but comes in as a crucial support system rather than dominating everything it encounters.

A whole toolbox is opened up with the creative exploration of a range of exercises including, for example: breathing exercises; meditation exercises; visualization exercises; the use of inspiring images and quotations; Gestalt chair work; the magic box; and third party perspectives.

Presence offers the opportunity for fun and enjoyment; for lightness and humour; to creatively blend approaches that help to shift perspectives, opportunities, challenges and threats. Stepping into presence enables the supervisor to work from the place of the wise compassionate observer, from a place of curiosity and inquiry and move out of and away from his or her ego. This way of working can really help the supervisee to shift away from the guilt or shame often associated when new awareness and new learning arise and to reconnect with his or her own natural resourcefulness, creativity and learning.

Presence offers the potential for role modelling and richer work because both the supervisor and the supervisee are learning to access what they are feeling and sensing. This creates a stronger heartfelt experience of real authenticity, which in itself can be transformational.

# Developing an enhanced or new set of qualities

The 'ability to be present' therefore requires the profession to develop and agree a core set of qualities that need to include the following qualities.

## Coaching supervisor qualities

- Being able to meet, greet and work with experience and all that is occurring in the supervisory moment – in the now – with openness, intelligence and creativity.

- Being able to create the space and to truly be with the supervisee without knowing answers so that the supervisee can learn to be fully present with his or her own experiences.

- Being truly open to what might need or want to emerge in the supervisory session.

- Being able to work from the intelligence of the heart as well as the body and the mind.

The importance of this for a supervisor's personal and professional development cannot be overestimated because the quality of any intervention depends on the inner state of the intervener. We are our own most powerful tool. This is also reinforced by de Haan's research (2008), which has shown that the overriding key to success in any coaching relationship (which by implication can be extended to the supervisory relationship) rests in the quality of the relationship and not in the particular school or body of knowledge that the coach was trained in. There is also plenty of anecdotal evidence among supervisors and supervisees that supervisees will only work as deeply as they feel safe and where that safety has been defined as the sense of the supervisor's own grounding and personal development work.

# Learning to recognize when you are working in or out of presence

It is the supervisor's responsibility to create the safe environment for presence to flourish and for the work to take place. Four key structural processes can help with establishing intention. These are:

1 Contracting for the supervisory relationship and learning partnership.
2 Contracting at the start of each session.
3 Using Scharmer's Theory U to understand session process.
4 Self-assessment and feedback.

The keys to successful contracting are the four Cs: clarity, courtesy, commitment and communication if a successful learning partnership is to be created within which the formal tasks for supervision are to be attended to. This is, in essence, both a formal and psychological contracting process and is key to creating the container or safe space for inquiry, discovery and exploration. Requesting feedback – and providing the supervisee with the option to terminate the working arrangement at any time – is a critical element to building trust.

Each session also requires upfront contracting to attend to that session's agenda within the wider contracted framework. This can best be achieved by following a simple process of:

- Welcoming and connecting: extending a gesture of presence towards each other (for example a moment of silence; a pause before starting the work; or some shared meditation together).
- Extending an invitation: for example by asking, 'How would you like to use our time together …?' or 'What do you want to look at today …?' or 'What is your question …?'
- Clarifying intention: for example by asking, 'And what would you like by the end of the session …?'
- Ensuring what will best serve: for example by asking, 'How do you want me to be with you …?'

Moving into the actual supervision work:

- Closure: for example by focusing on the learning points by asking, 'So what have you learnt today …?'
- Disconnecting: by honouring the work and closing down.

The work of Scharmer (2007) provides a rigorous framework for understanding presence at work in a supervisory session. Scharmer uses the term 'presencing', which he defines as a blend of the words 'presence' and 'sensing'. He suggests it is a heightened state of attention that allows individuals and groups to shift the inner place from which they work.

Scharmer describes the process as a 'U' where it is possible for us to learn to shift our inner attention from habitual downloading (at the top left hand corner of the U) to a state of presencing (at the bottom of the U), which then creates new possibilities and solutions (emerging at the top right hand of the U) in seven distinct movements. These are from stopping, suspending and really starting to listen; to noticing and seeing with fresh eyes and with an open mind; to sensing the whole from our hearts; to presencing and connecting to a wider essential truth or source – a letting go to let come – to reframe, sense new possibilities and act from the emerging whole; to formulating; to experimenting to performing. These are shown in Figure 8.2, adapted from Scharmer (2007).

**FIGURE 8.2** Theory U

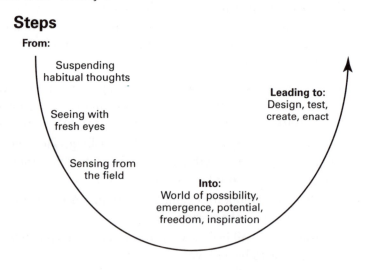

The supervisor's own self-assessment and the supervisee's feedback are also critical to helping both to enhance their own presence. Two simple self-assessments follow that can help both the supervisor and the supervisee explore how fully present they have been with each other. The first self-assessment appears in Table 8.1, earlier in this chapter; it explores what could be seen and experienced when they are working in a state of presence. The second, in Table 8.2, highlights possible danger signals for when the supervisor and/or the supervisee might be moving away or out of presence. The third, in Table 8.3, provides a format for peer observation on skills practice.

## Feeling and being ready

- Centre: check physical position, movement, body posture and breathing.
- Ask 'What is needed from the session?', 'What will best serve?' and, 'How my/the supervisor's behaviours and interventions might best support?'
- Sensitive use of silence, space and pacing allowing both supervisor and supervisee to listen to their inner voices and inner wisdom.
- Being at ease.

## Finding connection

- Making good contact with the supervisee.
- Touching with full presence.
- Listening with respect and full attention.
- Creating trust, space and safety.
- Honouring the supervisee's work.

## Enabling the learning conversation

- Follows curiosity; providing a clear thread of inquiry through the work.
- Hears what is being said, separating the subjective and the objective for supervisee and for self.
- Supports and challenges appropriately.
- Selects interventions, tools and processes as appropriate.
- Works in the moment and uses also what is being noticed.
- Holds the conversation and the work.

**TABLE 8.2** Working in a state of presence

| Experience of ... | Score 0 – 10 |
|---|---|
| **1** Ego and mind dominated | |
| **2** Retreating, contracting and closing down | |
| **3** Fear, resistance and scarcity | |
| **4** Low trust and honesty | |
| **5** Low safety | |
| **6** Low energy | |
| **7** Shifting away from adult:adult interactions | |
| **8** Voice of criticism | |
| **9** Voice of judgement | |
| **10** Voice of comparison | |
| **11** Limiting beliefs | |
| **12** Collusion | |
| **13** Unnamed psychological games or blind spots | |
| **14** A lack of genuine connection | |
| **15** Lack of authenticity | |
| **16** Power issues and control at play | |
| **17** Search for right and wrong; absolutes or blame | |
| **18** Linear thinking and the language of 'shoulds', 'musts' and 'have tos' | |
| **19** The supervisor is having to work too hard | |

- Uses direct, open and honest dialogue: checks in, reflects back, and uses feedback to facilitate flow.
- Works as appropriate with:
  - psychological mindedness;
  - system awareness;
  - principles of adult learning and change.

**TABLE 8.3** Alerts and danger zones

| Experience of ... | Score 0 – 10 |
|---|---|
| 1 Generosity | |
| 2 Compassion | |
| 3 Abundance | |
| 4 Courage | |
| 5 Respect | |
| 6 Curiosity | |
| 7 Tolerance | |
| 8 Permission | |
| 9 Authencity | |
| 10 Honesty and openness | |
| 11 Trust in self, in others and in the process | |
| 12 Quality of attention and intention | |
| 13 Safety | |
| 14 Space and spaciousness | |
| 15 Possibility and potential | |
| 16 Creating connections and connectedness | |
| 17 Supervisor using only what is useful in the moment and what best serves | |
| 18 Spontaneity | |
| 19 A lightness, playfulness, humour and fun where appropriate | |
| 20 An equal learning partnership | |

● Uses safe and appropriate closure; ending contact and withdrawing.

There are a variety of corrective steps that the supervisor and supervisee can then take when they sense that they might be losing connection; these can include:

- pausing;
- breathing;
- ensuring the interactions are adult to adult;
- checking back in with the supervisee about what best serves;
- naming the confusion;
- following gut instinct and intuition;
- saying sorry;
- using metaphors or images to help reframe;
- scanning the toolkit for interventions that could be offered.

## How does 'presence' link to other supervision models?

Presence offers a quality of being fully present that arguably complements whatever model of supervision the supervisor has chosen to work with. This is because the quality of the state of presence works like an underground stream bringing alive the relationship and the work.

In this book you will have read about a variety of models, and just as coaching practices have grown so have different models of coaching supervision. Key influences have been The Hawkins and Smith Seven-eyed Process Model (2006), Murdoch and Orriss's The Coaching Supervision Academy Full Spectrum Model (2010), Carroll's Five-stage Model (2005), Carroll's Generic Integrative Model of Counselling (2001), Inskipp and Proctor's Working Alliance (1993), Stoltenberg *et al's* Stages of Counsellor Development (1987) and Wosket and Page's Cyclical Model of Supervision as A Container for Creativity and Chaos (2001).

## Caring for ourselves as coaching supervisors

Working with presence requires supervisors to pay attention to their own self-care. Burn out and superficiality can occur if we are not properly caring for ourselves by paying attention to our own safety, personal and professional development and own rest and restoration in a virtuous circle. The deeper we work the more important this becomes.

Here is a quick self-assessment 'health' check to help supervisors test how well they are taking care of themselves.

## Self-assessment 'health' check

Rate 0 – 10

### Quality and safety

- Am I working within the boundaries of my competence?

- Am I working with professionalism and integrity at all times?

- Am I working to my professional ethics and values at all times?

- Am I in regular supervision myself?

- Am I ever feeling compromised in some way with a client, in my relationships or in my work?

### Personal and professional development

- Am I attending to what makes me happy?

- Am I feeling burnt out in some way?

- Am I feeling bored, closed or frustrated?

- Am I getting anxious or fearful?

- Is my ego or mind talking too much?

- Am I at ease and at peace with myself?

- Am I working or trying too hard?

- Am I taking on too much responsibility and falling into 'fix-it' mode?

- Am I investing sufficiently in my own personal development?

- Am I investing sufficiently in my own professional development?

### Rest and restoration

- How are my energy levels?

- Am I creating enough space for myself?

- Are there any particular family or work pressures that might be impacting on my work?

- How good am I at saying 'No thank you'?

- Am I getting cross, impatient or angry too readily?

- Am I eating well? Sleeping well? Am I getting enough exercise?

- Am I paying enough attention to my own friends and family?

- When did I last take a holiday, retreat or total break?

# Conclusion

Working with and in presence is not easy but it is worth the struggle. Presence is a state of being that can offer us the potential to enrich all aspects of our work, lives and relationships. Without it we are denying ourselves and our clients access to a rich tapestry of creativity, inspiration, compassion, possibility and potential that has the power to shift mindsets and perspectives.

## *Acknowledgements*

My thanks to Edna Murdock at the Coaching Supervision Academy for her inspiration and support.

## *References*

Beisser, A (1970) The Paradoxical Theory of Change, p 1, **www.gestalt.org/ arnie.htm**, first published in, (eds) J Fagan and Shepherd, I, *Gesalt Therapy Now. Theory techniques and applications,* Gestalt Journal Press, Gouldsboro, ME

Carroll, M (1996) *Counselling Supervision: Theory, skills and practice,* Continuum International Publishing, London

Carroll, M (2001) *Counselling Supervision: Theory, skills and practice,* Sage, London

Csikszentmihalyi, M (2002) *Flow: The classic work on how to achieve happiness,* Rider, London

de Haan, E (2008) *Relational Coaching: Journeys towards mastering one-to-one learning,* Wiley, Chichester

Gilbert, M (2005) *On Being a Supervisee: Creating learning partnerships,* Vukani Publishing, London

Hawkins, P and Smith, N (2006) *Coaching, Mentoring and Organisational Consultancy Supervision and Development,* Open University Press, Maidenhead

His Holiness The Dala Lama and Cutler, H C (1998) *The Art of Happiness: A handbook for the living,* Riverhead Books, New York

Inskipp, F and Proctor, B (1993) *Making the Most of Supervision and Being a Supervisee,* Cascade, East Sussex

International Coach Federation (ICF) (2010) Coaching Core Competencies, **www.coachfederation.org/research-education/icf-credentials/ core-competencies**

Lucas, B (2003) *Power up your Mind: Learn faster, work smarter,* Nicholas Brealey Publishing, London

Marianetti, O and Passmore, J (2009) Mindfulness at work: paying attention to enhance well-being and performance, in (ed) A Lindley, *Oxford Handbook of Positive Psychology and Work,* Oxford University Press, Oxford

McCongagill, G (2000) The coach as reflective practitioner notes from a journey without end, ch 3, in (eds) C Fitzgerald and J G Berger, *Executive Coaching: Practice and perspectives,* Davis Black Publishing, Palo Alto, CA

Murdock, E (2010) Who you are is how you coach, *Personnel Zone Integration Training Journal,* also published on the coaching supervision website thought leadership page: **www.csa.com**

Murdock, E and Orriss, M (2010) *The Coaching Supervision Academy's Full Spectrum Model:* **www.csa.com**

Page, S *et al* (1994) *Supervising the Counsellor – A cyclical model,* Routledge, London

Parsloe, E and Leedham, M (2009) *Coaching and Mentoring: Practical conversations to improve learning,* Kogan Page, London

Passmore, J and Marianetti, O (2007) The role of mindfulness in coaching, *The Coaching Psychologist,* 3 (3), 131–8

Scharmer, O (2007) Theory U; Leading from the future as it emerges. The social technology of presencing, *Society of Organizational Learning,* 8

Silsbee, D (2010) *Presence-based Coaching; Cultivating self-generative leaders through mind, body and heart,* p 8, Jossey Bass, San Francisco, CA

Stoltenberg, C D, Mcneill, B and Delworth, U (1987) *Supervising Counselors and Therapists: A developmental approach,* Jossey-Bass, San Francisco, CA

Tolle, E (2005) *The Power of Now: A guide to spiritual enlightenment,* Hodder and Stoughton, London

Wosket, V and Page, S ( 2001) The cyclical model of supervision: a container for creativity and chaos, ch 1, in (eds) M Caroll and M Tholstrup, *Integrative Approaches to Supervision,* Jessica Kingsley, London

# PART 2
# Coaching ethics and the law

# Ethical frameworks in coaching

## 09

**CLAIRE TOWNSEND**

## Introduction

**F**or coaching to develop as a profession it is important for coaches to work within an ethical framework that underpins their interactions with their coachees and other stakeholders such as the organization that the coaching client is employed by. De Jong (2006) has argued that sound ethics are the essence and underpinning of good coaching. It is clear that supervision can play a key role in the development and use of ethics in coaching through the 'continuing development of the coach and effectiveness of his/her coaching practice through interactive reflection, interpretative evaluation and the sharing of expertise' (Bachkirova *et al*, 2005). Supervision as a way of helping to develop ethics in coaching is also considered key by Nicklen: 'Ethical issues are becoming more complex, but it is about self-management and coaches need help. Supervision, either on a one to one basis or as part of a coaching circle, is central to this' (Sparrow, 2007).

Work by the Coaching & Mentoring Supervision Project in 2008 highlighted that one of the purposes of supervision was to provide a place to recognize, discuss and address ethical issues or dilemmas. It is important therefore for the supervisor to have knowledge of current ethical frameworks and how to utilize them within the supervision process with coaches.

This chapter will set out to review what ethics is and why it is important in coaching. It will review the ethical frameworks that have been developed by the Association for Coaching, the European Mentoring & Coaching

Council, the International Coaching Federation and the British Psychological Society Special Group in Coaching Psychology.

As coaching is currently an unregulated industry there is no necessity to belong to any of these associations or to abide by any codes of ethics. However, with the growth of coaching there are many advocates for the professionalization of the industry in order to safeguard the quality, effectiveness and ethical integrity of coaching services (Rostron, 2009) and a number of the coaching bodies are working together to develop overarching ethical codes. The UK Coaching Round Table has produced a set of fundamental principles that it expects members of the contributing organizations to operate by, including the statement that 'every coach needs to abide by a code of governing ethics and apply acknowledged standards to the performance of their coaching work'. Coaching supervisors can play an important role in raising coaches' awareness of ethics and their coaching bodies' ethical codes as, although the codes are clearly stated in the bodies' documentation, it cannot always be assumed that the members are actively using them. In addition to this it is likely that many coaching clients and sponsors are unaware of ethical codes (Passmore, 2009) and may not therefore know what to do if they are dissatisfied with the coaching that they are receiving.

## What is ethics?

At its most basic, ethics is a system of moral principles that affect the way in which people make decisions and lead their lives. The word appears to have mixed roots, deriving both from the Greek word *ethikos,* which means habitual or customary conduct, and from the Latin word *ethice,* meaning moral philosophy or the science of right and wrong. Ethics is an established area within philosophy that has many different branches including applied ethics, which attempts to apply ethical theory to real-life situations such as medical, business, professional or environmental ethics. Professional ethics is a sub-section of applied ethics that focuses on conduct and moral decisions within the context of particular relationships in the workplace (Weiner, 2006). It is considered that a professional carries additional responsibilities over and above those of the general population because of the specialist knowledge to which professionals have access and clients do not, which can give the professional power and could be used to deliberately or inadvertently put a client in a vulnerable position.

When looking at the origins of coaching ethical codes they can be seen to have their roots in the ethics of both the therapeutic professions such as counselling and psychotherapy and business, where there are additional issues such as multiple stakeholders and power (Law, 2005).

# Ethical frameworks

To provide effective supervision, knowledge of the ethical frameworks in use by the key coaching associations will be of benefit as the coaches being supervised may belong to one or several of the coaching bodies. The bodies discussed below all have published ethical frameworks that they expect their members to adhere to, and this section will review each framework individually as well as identifying common themes across the frameworks.

In addition to the frameworks that have been developed by the coaching bodies, there has been a number of groups recently who have come together to collaborate on developing shared guidelines for practice including reviews of existing codes of ethics and working together on future developments in this area. These groups have included the Global Convention on Coaching (GCC) and the International Coaching Research Forum (ICRF). In the UK, the UK Coaching Round Table, a group consisting of the Association for Coaching (AC), the Association of Professional Executive Coaching and Supervision (APECS), the European Mentoring & Council UK (EMCC UK) and the UK International Coaching Federation (UK ICF), produced in February 2008 a statement of shared professional values with the meta principle 'to continually enhance the competence and reputation of the coaching profession'. Within this document is the aim that 'every coach needs to abide by a code of governing ethics and apply acknowledged standards to the performance of their coaching work'.

This recognition of the fundamental importance of ethics to good coaching practice highlights the significance of coaches and supervisors understanding available ethical codes and how to apply the contents to their everyday practice. This helps to build coaching competence, which will in turn enhance the coaches' ability to apply ethical standards effectively. This can be complex as there may be circumstances when different principles within a code could be seen to be in conflict and the coach may be faced with an ethical dilemma to resolve. It is considered to be part of the nature of ethics that these issues may be challenging to resolve in some circumstances and this is where supervision can be of great value in helping the coach to resolve more complex dilemmas or to come up with the course of action that leads to the best consequences in that particular situation.

Therefore, for the supervisor to be able to support the coach in resolving ethical dilemmas, it is important that the supervisor is not only aware of the different ethical codes of the coaching bodies but is also aware of his or her own ethical perspective, which can be broadly broken down into the following areas (taken from Rowson, 2001):

- Consequentialist or teleological view. Ethics is concerned with bringing about the best consequences. Ethical obligation is to do whatever will bring the greatest benefits to everyone. Actions are ethically neutral – whether they are right or wrong depends on whether they lead to the best consequences.
- Dutiful or deontological view. Certain actions are intrinsically good and others intrinsically bad. Ethical actions consist in carrying out good actions and avoiding bad actions. Intrinsically good actions include telling the truth, keeping promises and being just.
- Pluralist view. Ethical decision making requires us to be aware of the demands of both perspectives. For example, if keeping a promise would harm others, the pluralist would weigh up the ethical importance of keeping the promise against the importance of not harming others.

The individual's views on these different approaches to ethics can affect the fundamental assumptions that we make about ethics and therefore it is important for supervisors to clarify their ethical perspective prior to working with a coach where they will be in a position to influence the coach's thinking and approach.

## The ethical codes of UK coaching bodies

This section reviews the ethical codes of the following UK coaching bodies:

Association for Coaching;

European Mentoring & Coaching Council;

International Coach Federation; and

British Psychological Society/Special Group in Coaching Psychology.

## Association for Coaching

The Association for Coaching (AC) was launched in July 2002. The importance of ethics within the AC is clear from its dominance in the strap line that appears throughout its website – 'Promoting excellence and ethics in coaching' – and its use in the mission statement:

> We aim to run and operate an ethical and responsible association for our members, based on a framework that incorporates seven core values: High standards – Integrity – Open – Responsive – Client focused – Educational – Progressive.

The Code of Ethics and Good Practice was launched in 2003 and sets out the 'essential elements of sound ethical practice' that it is expected its members will adhere to. There are 13 points within the code that provide a mix of specific requirements and more subjective areas where it could be seen that a consequentialist or pluralist view of ethics may be needed to define the correct course of action in specific circumstances. For example, confidentiality is stated in point 2 as being a key part of the coaching contract. A coach may need to subsequently decide whether some information gained from the client needs to be kept confidential regardless of its content or may need to be discussed with someone else because of what may be considered a more important issue such as concern for the client's health and wellbeing. Many points within this code cannot therefore be seen as a rigid set of rules for how to conduct coaching practice but as a set of guidelines the coach can use to help conduct his or her practice in an ethical way. It could be seen that point 13, 'Coaches must act in a manner that does not bring the profession into disrepute', is an overarching commitment for which many of the other points provide more specific guidance.

Within the Code, however, there are specific requirements that are unambiguous and should help the coach as well as the coaching client to understand the standards of practice that are expected of the coach. These include the requirement for coaches to have professional liability insurance (point 11), 30 hours of continuing professional development on an annual basis (point 9) and to maintain appropriate client records (point 6). It also specifies that the coach ensures that clients are fully informed of the coaching contract and terms and conditions by the time that the coaching begins and that claims made by the coach are honest and accurate (point 2). Acting in an ethical manner is seen therefore to start before the coaching begins and should set the tone for the coaching relationship.

Supervision is specified in point 8 of the Code: 'Coaches are expected to have regular consultative support for their work', and supervision can be valuable in helping coaches to develop their coaching practice in relation to other aspects of the code such as point 1: 'Coaches are required to recognize both personal and professional limitations' and point 7: 'Coaches are required to monitor the quality of their work and seek feedback wherever possible from Clients and other professionals as appropriate.'

The AC code is similar in content to the other codes being reviewed but differs in the specific guidelines that it provides on areas such as the quantity of CPD that coaches are expected to undertake in a year and the necessity of having professional insurance. These specific guidelines may be of particular use to new coaches in helping them to understand what will be needed to continue to build their capability as well as laying out some broad guidelines that can be used as part of a review of practice or of issues arising.

## The Association for Coaching Code of Ethics

1  Coaches are required to recognize both personal and professional limitations:

    *Personal* – with respect to maintaining their own good health and fitness to practice. Should this not be the case, Coaches are required to withdraw from their practice until such time as they are in good health and fit to resume. Clients should be offered appropriate, alternative support during any such period.

    *Professional* – with respect to whether their experience is appropriate to meet the Client's requirements. When this is not the case, clients should be referred to other appropriate services, eg more experienced coaches, counsellors, psychotherapists or other specialist services. In particular, Coaches are required to be sensitive to the possibility that some clients will require more psychological support than is normally available within the coaching remit. In these cases, referral should be made to an appropriate source of care, eg the client's GP, a counsellor or psychotherapist, psychological support services and/or agencies.

2  Coaches are responsible for ensuring that Clients are fully informed of the coaching contract, terms and conditions, prior to or at the initial session. These matters include confidentiality, sessional costs, and frequency of sessions. All claims made by the Coach should be honest, accurate and consistent with maintaining the Coaching profession's good standing.

3   Coaches are required to be frank and willing to respond to their Client's requests for information about the methods, techniques and ways in which the coaching process will be conducted. This should be done both prior to contract agreement and during the full term of the contract.

4   Coaches must be sensitive to issues of culture, religion, gender and race.

5   Coaches must respect the Client's right to terminate coaching at any point during the coaching process.

6   Coaches are required to maintain appropriate records of their work with Clients, ensuring that any such records are accurate and that reasonable security precautions are taken to protect against third party disclosure. Attention must be given to the coachee's rights under any current legislation, eg Data Protection Act.

7   Coaches are required to monitor the quality of their work and to seek feedback wherever possible from Clients and other professionals as appropriate.

8   Coaches are expected to have regular consultative support for their work.

9   A Coach should aim to undertake a minimum of 30 hours of continuing professional development in the theory and practice of coaching on an annual basis.

10  Coaches are required to keep themselves informed of any statutory or legal requirements that may affect their work.

11  Coaches are required to have current professional liability insurance.

12  Coaches are required to consider the impact of any dual relationships they may hold with regards to their Clients and/or any sponsoring organizations.

13  Coaches must act in a manner that does not bring the profession of coaching into disrepute.

## European Mentoring & Coaching Council

The European Mentoring & Coaching Council (EMCC) is a pan-European organization with a local division in 18 countries. The UK EMCC has a mission of defining, creating and promoting best practice for all in mentoring and coaching in the UK. It has four special interest groups of which one is UK Ethics and Research. The current EMCC Code of Ethics, which was updated in 2008, is in use across all member countries and its stated purpose is to 'set out what the clients and sponsors can expect from the coach/mentor in either a coach/ mentoring, training or supervisory relationship and should form the starting point for any contract agreed'. It also states that 'All EMCC Members will make the sponsoring organization and the individual client aware, at the contracting stage, of the existence of the Code of

Ethics'. This emphasis on using and highlighting the Code of Ethics prior to the start of the coaching is an interesting one and could be very helpful in establishing greater clarity and understanding of the coach's responsibilities at the beginning of the coaching relationship. However, it has been noted by the EMCC committee chair on ethics that 'my suspicion is that some members have never even been aware of the code' (Sparrow, 2007).

The Code states the following principles:

- The coach/mentor will acknowledge the dignity of all humanity. They will conduct themselves in a way which respects diversity and promotes equal opportunities.
- It is the primary responsibility of the coach/mentor to provide the best possible service to the client and to act in such a way as to cause no harm to any client or sponsor.
- The coach/mentor is committed to functioning from a position of dignity, autonomy and personal responsibility.

The EMCC Code of Ethics covers the following five areas:

1 Competence: within this area it is specified that coaches will maintain a relationship with a supervisor who will assess their competence and support their development. Supervision could therefore be seen to be at the core of the Competence section as it can help to support coaches in their development of their 'level of experience and knowledge' and 'ensure that their capability is sufficient to enable them to operate according to this Code of Ethics'. It is recognized in the EMCC Guidelines on Supervision that the form that supervision will take will depend on the nature of the coaching being undertaken, so the frequency or duration of supervision is not specified in the Code.

2 Context: referring to the Code at the beginning of the coaching relationship will help to understand and manage the expectations of the client and sponsor and to ensure that the relationship reflects the context in which the coaching takes place.

3 Boundary management: operating within the limits of one's own competence, referring the client on where needed and maintaining awareness of potential conflicts of interest.

4 Integrity: maintaining confidentiality and acting within applicable law.

5 Professionalism: maintaining professional responsibilities including not exploiting the client during and after the termination of the coaching relationship and representing oneself accurately.

Within all of the above areas there is scope for judgement to play a part in the application of ethics and it is in areas such as conflicts of interest within 'boundary management' or maintaining agreed levels of confidentiality within 'integrity' where coaches may need support in deciding on the right course of action. Some aspects of the Code will be more straightforward and less likely to throw up ethical dilemmas, including sub-sections of 'professionalism' such as 'Provision of any follow-up which has been agreed to' and 'Safe and secure maintenance of all related records and data'. These are important areas for the maintenance of professional working relationships and the coach's reputation but are less likely to cause ethical dilemmas.

In addition to the Code, there is a clearly set out Complaints and Disciplinary Procedure that is designed to allow people to make complaints of professional misconduct by EMCC Members and for such complaints to be properly investigated by the EMCC.

This code is clearly laid out and has a strong emphasis on it being used as an integral part of the coaching contract and relationship with the client and not just something to be referred to when there are issues to resolve. It also clearly states the importance of supervision to assess competence and support the development of the coach. The EMCC also appears to be proactive in encouraging clients or sponsors to report breaches of the code by including information within the Code of Ethics document on how to address what may be breaches of the code informally with the coach and how to make a formal complaint if needed.

## 3. International Coach Federation

The ICF was formed in 1995 and is the largest coach membership body with a global membership. Its core purpose is: 'Advancing the art, science and practice of professional coaching'. The ICF has established the ICF Code of Ethics for ICF Members and ICF Credentialed coaches, and the Ethical Conduct Review Process for those who have ethical complaints against an ICF member or Credentialed coach. As a condition of membership, members pledge to uphold the Code of Ethics. The purpose of the code is stated as 'to promote professional and ethical coaching practices, and to raise the awareness of people outside the coaching profession about the integrity, commitment and ethical conduct of ICF members and ICF Credentialed coaches'.

In addition to the Code of Ethics document, the ICF has produced a frequently asked questions document to supplement the code that gives examples of how to use each section of the code in practice. It can be used to clarify any areas that are unclear.

The current Code of Ethics, which was agreed in 2008, is split into three parts. Part One defines coaching, a professional coaching relationship and the specific responsibilities of an ICF professional coach: 'An ICF Professional Coach also agrees to practice the ICF Professional Core Competencies and pledges accountability to the ICF Code of Ethics.'

Part Two sets out the ICF standards of ethical conduct. It states: 'ICF Professional Coaches aspire to conduct themselves in a manner that reflects positively upon the coaching profession; are respectful of different approaches to coaching; and recognize that they are also bound by applicable laws and regulations.'

There are four sections within Part Two. Section 1, Professional Conduct at Large, is concerned with the way in which coaches represent themselves and the profession in terms of ability, qualifications, expertise and research conducted. It specifies that coaches will act in accordance with the Code of Ethics, recognize changes in their own coaching competence and address them appropriately, and maintain client records and contact information in a confidential manner.

Here is an example of an FAQ for this section:

2) I will accurately identify my coaching qualifications, expertise, experience, certifications and ICF Credentials.

Q: I have coached two executives, is it ok to say I'm an experienced executive coach?

A: This could be misleading. Perhaps saying 'I have coached executives' would be appropriate. However, someone who has coached two executives for a length of time through a lot of issues might be experienced. It seems to be a personal judgement call.

Section 2, Conflicts of Interest, focuses on potential conflicts of interest in areas such as remuneration for referrals, any form of reward that may impair the coaching relationships, or any form of benefit from that coach-client relationship that has not been agreed.

An example of an FAQ for this section is:

9) I will seek to avoid conflicts of interest and potential conflicts of interest and openly disclose any such conflicts. I will offer to remove myself when such a conflict arises.

Q: May I accept a contract for a corporate mid-level manager when I am already coaching his boss?

A: You may accept this contract if you think that you can maintain an objective stance and confidentiality with both clients. You can discuss in general terms with the first client how he would feel about coaching someone else in the company. Be aware it could present a conflict of interest while coaching, however, in hiring and firing decisions, etc.

Section 3, Professional Conduct with Clients, aims to provide guidelines about the nature of an appropriate relationship with the client in terms of claims about the coach's own expertise, advice given and agreements made that should be clear and specific in terms of confidentiality, the nature of the coaching and financial arrangements. It also specifies the need for boundaries in terms of physical and sexual contact and the client's right to terminate the relationship if desired. The boundaries of the coach's own capability are also highlighted in the points about knowing when to refer clients on.

Here is an example of an FAQ for this section:

19) I will respect the client's right to terminate the coaching relationship at any point during the process, subject to the provisions of the agreement or contract. I will be alert to indications that the client is no longer benefiting from our coaching relationship.

Q: My client paid in full and we agreed to 10 coaching meetings. After six meetings, my client wants to stop. She says she wants her money back because she has not received the value she expected. Must I give it back?

A: If you did not clarify what might happen under these circumstances then you must discuss this with your client. You may attempt to negotiate with the client to be paid for services rendered to date. It would be advisable to return either the amount beyond services rendered to date, the entire amount minus an administrative fee, or the entire amount. Use your best judgement and remember that how you handle this situation will craft your reputation.

Section 4, Confidentiality/Privacy, refers to confidentiality in relation to the coaching client and the sponsor as well as if training student coaches or working with associate coaches.

An example of an FAQ for this section is:

23) I will have a clear agreement upon how coaching information will be exchanged among coach, client and sponsor.

Q: The supervisor of my new client has a coaching outcome that he does not want the client to know about. I am being paid out of the supervisor's budget. May I keep this information from my client?

A: This sets up an ethical conflict. How can you coach someone without having clarity and an agreement about what is being coached? Whatever you put in your agreement that all three sign is what is acceptable.

Part Three is the ICF Pledge of Ethics, which states:

As an ICF Professional Coach, I acknowledge and agree to honour my ethical and legal obligations to my coaching clients and sponsors, colleagues, and to the public at large. I pledge to comply with the ICF Code of Ethics, and to practise these standards with those whom I coach.

If I breach this Pledge of Ethics or any part of the ICF Code of Ethics, I agree that the ICF in its sole discretion may hold me accountable for so doing. I further agree that my accountability to the ICF for any breach may include sanctions, such as loss of my ICF membership and/or my ICF Credentials.

The ICF ethical code contains the main areas that a coach would expect to see within an ethical framework and includes much of the same ground as that covered by the other coaching bodies' codes. The Pledge of Ethics does not feature specifically in other codes and could be seen as being indicative of the ICF's US roots but does provide a useful summary of what a coach is signing up to when becoming a member of the ICF. The FAQ document offers useful additional guidance on each area of the code and could be used by a coach and supervisor to help clarify any areas of ambiguity. In addition, the ICF provides clear guidelines on its Ethical Conduct Review Process, which is intended to provide a 'model of excellence' for the review of complaints against ICF members and Credentialed coaches.

## The British Psychological Society and the BPS Special Group in Coaching Psychology

The British Psychological Society (BPS) Code of Ethics and Conduct differs from those produced by the coaching associations in that it applies to all members of the BPS regardless of which area of psychology they operate within. These generic standards do therefore apply to coaching psychologists and are also embedded within the Standards Framework for Coaching Psychology that has been produced by the Special Group in Coaching Psychology (SGCP).

The BPS Code of Ethics and Conduct (2009) sets out the broad areas that it is concerned with in the Introduction by outlining the following:

> The British Psychological Society recognizes its obligation to set and uphold the highest standards of professionalism, and to promote ethical behaviour, attitudes and judgements on the part of psychologists by:
>
> - being mindful of the need for protection of the public;
> - expressing clear ethical principles, values and standards;
> - promoting such standards by education and consultation;
> - developing and implementing methods to help psychologists monitor their professional behaviour and attitudes;
> - assisting psychologists with ethical decision making; and
> - providing opportunities for discourse on these issues.

The Code also states that although the aim of the code is that it should apply to all psychologists and provide ethical standards that apply to all, psychologists will also need to familiarize themselves with the legal framework, regulatory commitments and other guidance relevant to the particular context in which they work.

For coaching psychologists this will be the Standards Framework published by the SGCP, which details the standards required to demonstrate competence to practise as a coaching psychologist. In addition, there are further resources available such as the regular ethics column in *The Coaching Psychologist* and 'What Would You Do?' scenarios that are published on the SGCP website and within the ethics column. The BPS has also set up an advisory panel for guidance on ethical dilemmas with access to advisers in the coaching psychology field if needed.

Supervision is considered integral by the SGCP to the work of coaching psychologists and coaches using psychology in their work. It states that there is no one prescriptive model for supervision, but the process is seen as key to the development of skilled, ethical, reflexive and responsible practice. Ensuring high standards of ethics in the coaching process is one of the main aims of supervision as defined by the SGCP.

Within the SGCP Supervision Guidelines document there are a number of examples of ethical situations that could emerge during coaching and need discussing with more experienced people. For example:

Coaching contracts generally imply that a practitioner whether a psychologist or a psychological coach does not work directly with underlying issues and dysfunctions. When the coach or psychologist identifies that a client's 'blocks' to development would be better served by psychological intervention then it can be necessary to refrain from working on the deeper issues. This could be a difficult decision to make without a reflection process facilitated by a supervisor who understands the process of diagnosis and on-referral to appropriate sources of psychological support.

## Management of boundaries

The management of personal as well as professional boundaries is important within the coaching process and supervisors must be competent to ensure that any underlying personal issues that could affect the coaching process are managed effectively and appropriately.

## Management of values conflicts and confidentiality issues

Coaching services are frequently applied within a complex system such as a family, social network or work organization. These environments are unpredictable and complex. Successful management of values conflicts and confidentiality issues are highly dependent on effective and sensitive contracting.

The examples discussed above are all areas that form part of the ethical codes of the coaching associations and highlight the commonality of thinking across coaching psychology and coaching that is undertaken by non psychologists. In addition to these guidelines, the SGCP Standards Framework document makes a number of references to ethics, particularly in the section on 'Knowledge, understanding and skills that underpin the education and training of coaching psychologists', where Ethics has a specific sub-section. There are also additional direct and indirect references throughout the document in areas such as Professional issues, Coachee and client work, Professional relationships, Personal and professional skills and The coaching psychologist as a practitioner, where it is stated that the coaching psychologist should be able to 'adhere to the BPS Code of Conduct, Ethical Principles and Guidelines and the SGCP's Professional Practice Guidelines'.

## Summary of review of ethical codes

The ethical codes discussed above have many areas in common while having distinctive differences in the specific way in which they are presented and in the provision of additional points or further clarification. The use of any of these codes would prove beneficial for coaches and supervisors as a guide to resolving ethical issues.

The main themes emerging from the codes reviewed are:

- professionalism;
- competence;
- confidentiality;
- relationships;
- integrity;
- client-focused;
- boundaries.

These map well onto the common ethical principles that are used in well established fields such as medical and counselling ethics and form the basis of their specific ethical frameworks. Beauchamp and Childress's Four Principles (2001) is one of the most widely used frameworks and offers a broad review of the key areas that are the basis of medical ethics:

1 Respect for autonomy: respecting the decision-making capacities of autonomous persons; enabling individuals to make reasoned informed choices.

2 Beneficence/utility: this considers the balancing of benefits of treatment against the risks and costs; the healthcare professional should act in a way that benefits the patient.

3 Non malfeasance: avoiding the causation of harm; the healthcare professional should not harm the patient. All treatment involves some harm, even if minimal, but the harm should not be disproportionate to the benefits of treatment.

4 Justice: distributing benefits, risks and costs fairly; the notion that patients in similar positions should be treated in a similar manner.

There are many similarities in these principles and those stated in the ethical codes of the coaching bodies reviewed, particularly the focus on being client-centred. It also, however, highlights that coaching brings specific requirements that are different from professionals working in medical and therapeutic fields, particularly areas such as the potential for conflicts of interest between the sponsor and coaching client and the boundaries of confidentiality of information between coach, client and sponsor.

A further way of summarizing the key ethical principles that are shared by the coaching bodies is to review the Statement of Shared Professional Values that has been collated by the UK Coaching Round Table and was signed and agreed in April 2009. This provides a useful meta-view of the ethical principles that all the coaching bodies listed in this chapter view as important as it was collated by the AC, UK ICF, EMCC UK and the Association for Professional Executive Coaching Supervision (APECS), which has not been reviewed here. The statement affirms the following principles:

In the emerging profession of coaching, we believe that:

- Every coach, whether charging fees for coaching provided to individuals or organizations or both, is best served by being a member of a professional body suiting his/her needs.
- Every coach needs to abide by a code of governing ethics and apply acknowledged standards to the performance of their coaching work.
- Every coach needs to invest in their ongoing continuing professional development to ensure the quality of their service and their level of skill is enhanced.
- Every coach has a duty of care to ensure the good reputation of our emerging profession.

*Meta Principle:* To continually enhance the competence and reputation of the coaching profession.

*Principle One – Reputation.* Every coach will act positively and in a manner that increases the public's understanding and acceptance of coaching.

*Principle Two – Continuous Competence Enhancement.* Every coach accepts the need to enhance their experience, knowledge, capability and competence on a continuous basis.

*Principle Three – Client-centred.* Every client is creative, resourceful and whole and the coach's role is to keep the development of that client central to his/her work, ensuring all services provided are appropriate to the client's needs.

*Principle Four – Confidentiality and Standards.* Every coach has a professional responsibility (beyond the terms of the contract with the client) to apply high standards in their service provision and behaviour. He/she needs to be open and frank about methods and techniques used in the coaching process, maintain only appropriate records and to respect the confidentiality a) of the work with their clients and b) of their representative body's members information.

*Principle Five – Law and Diversity.* Every coach will act within the laws of the jurisdictions within which they practice and will also acknowledge and promote diversity at all times.

*Principle Six – Boundary Management.* Every coach will recognize their own limitations of competence and the need to exercise boundary management. The client's right to terminate the coaching process will be respected at all times, as will the need to acknowledge different approaches to coaching which may be more effective for the client than their own. Every endeavour will be taken to ensure the avoidance of conflicts of interest.

*Principle Seven – Personal Pledge.* Every coach will undertake to abide by the above principles that will complement the principles, codes of ethics and conduct set out by their own representative body to which they adhere and by the breach of which they would be required to undergo due process.

This Statement of Shared Professional Values provides a useful summary of the key aspects of a coaching ethical code and if used in conjunction with the specific code of the coaches' own representative body, should provide support coaches in the development of their ethical practice. Other writers (Duff and Passmore, 2010) have offered additional routes for coaches through a heuristic model to guide the coaches' decision making.

## Summary

As coaching is still a developing profession, it is understandable that there are a number of organizations representing coaches. While the field is unregulated it is not necessary for coaches to belong to any of the coaching associations but the benefits in using the information and guidelines they provide are clear. Coaches, if they wish to continue to develop their competence, benefit greatly from being aware of the ethical issues that can arise in everyday practice and in using supervision as a way to continue to develop their competence and ethical practice. Supervision can help with building the competence and awareness needed to recognize that issues may be present that need addressing such as when the coaching client may need referring on to another practitioner or where confidentiality agreements may need reviewing because of potential risks to the client. Inexperienced coaches or those moving into new areas may need to be particularly aware of these types of issues but it can also be of value for experienced coaches to step back and review their practice to ensure that they continue to act in an appropriate way.

One of the clear values in supervision helping coaches with ethical issues or dilemmas is that for many ethical issues there may be more than one option or one right answer that could be chosen. The supervisor can play a valuable role in helping the coach to clarify the issue and review the possible options so that the coach can choose which one he or she thinks is best in the particular circumstances. This can mean choosing between one of several 'right' answers or the least worst option that balances what is right for the coaching client with what is right for the coach. Additional complexity in the coaching arena can also arise where the organizational context can throw up issues such as, 'Who are the clients?', 'Whose benefit has priority?' and, 'What is the responsibility of the coach to manage different values and interests between all the stakeholders?' Coaches therefore need to be aware of the context in which they are working, particularly those providing coaching services within organizations.

This highlights that ethical codes are not there to provide easy answers that can be applied in all situations but are there to guide ethical decision making as well as the way in which the coach approaches the whole of his or her coaching practice. Supervision can play a significant role in supporting the coach's continuing ethical development and in helping him or her to see ethics as an integral part of coaching, not just something to draw on in specific situations.

## References

Association for Coaching, Code of Ethics and Good Practice, **http://www.associationforcoaching.com/about/about02.htm**, accessed 10 August 2010

Bachkirova, T, Stevens, P and Willis, P (2005) *Coaching Supervision*, Coaching and Mentoring Society, Oxford Brookes, Oxford

Beauchamp, T and Childress, J (2001) *Principles of Biomedical Ethics*, 5th edn, Oxford University Press, Oxford

British Psychological Society (2009) Code of Ethics and Conduct, **http://www.bps.org.uk/document-download-area/document-download$. cfm?file_uuid=E6917759-9799-434A-F313-9C35698E1864&ext=pdf**, accessed 10 August 2010

Coaching & Mentoring 'Supervision' Project (2008) Final Document – Part ONE, SSG collation of main themes from Stakeholder Group feedback, **http://www.associationforcoaching.com/memb/PartOneCM SupervisionProject241208.pdf**, accessed 11 August 2010

de Jong, A (2006) Coaching ethics: Integrity in the moment of choice, in (ed) J Passmore, *Excellence in Coaching,* Kogan Page, London

Duff, M and Passmore, J (2010) Coaching ethics: a decision making model, *International Coaching Psychology Review,* 5 (2) 140–51

EMCC Code of Ethics, **http://www.emcouncil.org/fileadmin/documents/ countries/eu/EMCC Code of Ethics.pdf**, accessed 10 August 2010

International Coach Federation (ICF) ICF Code of Ethics, **http://www.coachfederation.org/ethics**, accessed 10 August 2010

Law, H (2005) The role of ethical principles in coaching psychology, *The Coaching Psychologist,* 1, 1, July

Passmore, J (2009) Coaching ethics: Making ethical decisions – novices and experts, *The Coaching Psychologist,* 5 (1)

Rostron, S S (2009) The global initiatives in the coaching field, *Coaching: An International Journal of Theory, Research and Practice,* 2 (1), March, 76–85

Rowson, R (2001) Ethical principles, in (eds) F Palmer Barnes and L Murdin, *Values and Ethics in the Practice of Psychotherapy and Counselling,* Open University Press, Buckingham

Sparrow, S (2007) The ethics boys, *Training and Coaching Today,* April, 26

Special Group in Coaching Psychology (2008) Standards Framework for Coaching Psychology, **http://www.sgcp.org.uk/sgcp/in-practice/useful-documents.cfm**, accessed 4 October 2010

UK Coaching Round Table (2008) Statement of shared professional values, **http://www.associationforcoaching.com/about/UKCRTshared0208.pdf**, accessed 11 August 2010

Weiner, K C (2006) Foundations of professional ethics, in (eds) P Williams and S K Anderson, *Law & Ethics in Coaching,* John Wiley, Chichester

# Coaching ethics – developing a model to enhance coaching practice

10

## JULIE ALLAN, JONATHAN PASSMORE AND LANCE MORTIMER

## Introduction

**C**oaching ethics remains an area of practice frequently discussed by professional associations, but frequently neglected by practitioners. Over the past couple of years one of us has presented several conferences papers on the topic, while at the same event running workshops on other topics including mindfulness and coaching skills. While the ethics event struggled to draw a dozen participants, the session on mindfulness was so popular it was difficult for the presenter to get in the room. Yet despite this lack of interest, ethics remains an important part of coaching practice.

In this chapter we will explore the concept of ethics as it applies to coaching. We will consider why ethics is important in coaching for clients and coaches. We will explore how coaches make ethical decisions and offer a model for enhancing ethical decision making in coaching.

# What is ethics?

Put as plainly as we can manage, 'ethics' is a term used to denote a way of going about things that is consistent with underlying principles concerning what's right. Or what's wrong, for that matter.

Of course, we may differ in our views of what is right and wrong, of what brings about good or brings about harm. And what if the information on which we are making our judgements is incomplete (as it invariably will be) or if we can readily appreciate (as we usually can) that the situation isn't all dark or all light.

Imagine, a coachee in a session tells you that his CV is inaccurate in ways that would have led to him not getting the job he is currently doing. He realized this would be the case so invented experience he didn't have, based on working alongside somebody else who did have that experience and believing that he could easily have managed to stand in that person's shoes. It turns out, by the way, that he was correct in this assessment and the outcome is that a great number of people are fundamentally benefiting from your coachee's current activities.

You could consider that what he has done is probably illegal and certainly against the terms of his employment contract. He has broken rules in that regard. You could consider the evidence you have that many people are gaining from how things are at the moment and this could be jeopardized if your coachee were to be found out. You might find yourself sharply facing your own values base, which holds trust as an important personal value.

Were you to go with a moral stance based on rules and regulations, your view and actions may differ from a stance based on trying to do right by the majority, which may differ from a stance based on your principles – such as trust or compassion or fairness. In the first case the decision would probably seem more clear-cut, in the second a little less so, and in the third you may even experience conflict between your different principles.

There is no shortage of literature defining and exploring ethics, or the development of different moral philosophies, ancient and modern. The three different stances outlined above equate approximately to deontology, utilitarianism and virtue – but there are different perspectives on each, and many a conversation to be had in the move from 'abstracted ethics' to 'applied ethics'.

For those of us working in coaching, the 'What' of ethics might be closely accompanied by the question of 'Why' ethics is so important. In the following section we are going to argue that ethics is not limited to being a matter of law, of religion or even, necessarily, some 'agreed' majority viewpoint – the last of which poses some engaging questions for the developers of ethical codes.

Disciplines including psychology, sociology, politics and anthropology all have something to tell us about the issues of navigating choices in our lives in an ethical way. Many of us have experienced or heard about situations in modern times that raise large and continuing questions about ethics – financial irregularities, political conduct, international relations and trade to name a few. However, where do ethics overlap with the coaching?

Ethical guidance and standards are an output of seeking that which 'works' for us in terms of the behaviours that are acceptable or otherwise. Ethics-in-action is a process of continuing personal enquiry into how we individually behave and what behaviour we will accept or challenge in others and, in considering these questions, understanding more about ourselves and the values we hold.

## Why is ethics important in coaching?

Coaches work with people leading lives in today's society. Coaching has extended from the world of sport, through business and is reaching into aspects of family life through parent coaching, into health through smoking cessation and stress coaching, into education through exams coaching and into learning to drive. In all of these areas ethics is an important consideration to protect both the public and the reputation of individual coaches and the coaching industry.

With no ethical framework, you might, for example, engage in the following:

- Telling your friends and family interesting details about clients.
- Using the names of 'impressive' clients to drum up more business.
- Claiming to have experience you don't have.
- Reading a book on suicide because you have no idea what to say in the next session to a coachee who said she wanted to kill herself.
- Coaching somebody to perform better in an activity he or she hates and believes is morally wrong.

Part of ethical navigation is the self-enquiry into the circumstances in which coaches might find themselves not behaving ethically. What happens if you are tired, or afraid, or feel foolish? What happens if you are in debt? What happens if your loyalty to somebody in an organization who commissions your work comes into conflict with your view on the contract he or she wants to have with you for a particular coachee (eg 'We just need you to deliver three sessions here because we can say we tried, but they are getting the push anyway')? Or you suspect this is the case and don't like the way the individual is being spoken about but you can't be sure what's going on ('Thanks for taking this coachee on, we don't hold out a great deal of hope for them improving').

Ethics is also important in coaching because of the often intimate and personal nature of coaching and the trust which the coachee needs to place in the coach for deep and meaningful conversations to take place.

Sally came to supervision (more on the role of supervision later). She was coaching a successful executive, and was finding the role challenging because while he said he was committed to improving his performance in various ways, he had proved so far unable to identify anything specific that he was less than brilliant at, in his view. Sally had agreed to conduct some 360-degree-type interviews. In doing so somebody had spoken about an affair he was having which they said had impacted on his performance. She didn't pursue any enquiries about it. However, Sally was currently in the middle of a very unfortunate divorce precipitated by her own husband's affair and her state, as reflected in supervision, was of alternate rage and grief. Imagine being Sally. What would you need to do to be able to continue with your coachee?

We could have used a different type of scenario but this does serve to illustrate the interactive and non-simple nature of the task of being a contracted helper to fellow human beings. In this case it was a corporate setting but coaches work in a range of contexts and specialist areas these days, examples being 'youth/teens', 'retirement', 'social enterprise', 'parenting', 'public speaking' … each can bring its own challenges. As a coach, who or what purpose(s) are we serving?

There are other aspects to 'fitness' or suitability. Coaches have a range of skill sets, some drawing heavily on a business background, others on psychological training and experience, others on specific life experience – and with different qualifications or membership specific to coaching. What is the combination of circumstances that would help you decide whether any individual coaching relationship was being conducted ethically?

In most ethical codes related to professions in which people are helping other people, competence is important. For example, the British Psychological Society code, adopted in 1985 and most recently revised in 2009, sets out the BPS position.

---

**BPS Special Group in Coaching Psychology – Code**

**Ethical Principle: Competence**

Statement of values – Psychologists value the continuing development and maintenance of high standards of competence in their professional work, and the importance of preserving their ability to function optimally within the recognized limits of their knowledge, skill, training, education, and experience.

(The British Psychological Society Code of Ethics and Conduct, August 2009, p15)

---

In the Association for Coaching Code of Ethics and Good Practice (2010) coaches are required to recognize both personal and professional limitations.

# The emergence of ethics in coaching

Coaching is by no means a unitary discipline. The emergence of ethical codes has travelled alongside the continuing emergence of a view that coaching is a discrete profession. There are therefore a number of strands of influence. For example, coaching has long existed in sports. Here, the endeavour concerns the means by which teams and individuals can maximize their performance as amateurs or as professionals, in schools and parks or in the Olympics. Then there is something that we might characterize as business mentoring, with the endeavour being to run an effective business by gaining assistance from somebody with appropriate experience and a good way of working to support somebody else. Another substantial strand is drawn from the helping professions including counselling and a variety of therapies, where the restoration (or creation of) 'healthful/well functioning' is the aim. This area has been wide ranging in that it encompasses those who may have been in receipt of a medical diagnosis, and those who have not and are seeking to develop themselves to what they would regard as their full potential.

These and other related professions or activities have developed and required practitioners to work to ethical codes devised for that activity, and what is now being encompassed by the term 'coaching' has drawn on this history. As coaching continues to be defined and applied as a distinct profession, those advocating it have, of necessity, started to articulate what constitutes appropriate skill sets and appropriate conduct. Some of the similarities and differences of approach and content are explored by Claire Townsend in Chapter 9.

What is clear from a review of ethical codes is the diversity, which reflects the history of development of different coaching bodies and those who sit on their boards. With diverse codes there is potential for confusion by clients (Passmore and Mortimer, 2011). There has been some movement to try and create a unified code, but the nature of professional bodies and vested interests has shown in other domains how difficult this can be to achieve.

The capacity to reflect before, during and after coaching sessions, and to act on that reflection, maintaining a high degree of self-awareness, is fairly universal in the available codes and guidelines. However, codes can have their weaknesses. Some are lists of rules. They rarely offer a way to navigate through the process to make an ethical decision.

Carroll (2009) has written about ethical maturity in coaching, with 'ethical maturity' defined as 'having the reflective, rational and emotional capacity to decide what is right and/or wrong, having the courage to do it and being accountable ethically for the decision' (see also Hawkins, Chapter 16). As might be expected as the field develops, there are different expectations of how coaches resolve ethical dilemmas (eg, Brennan and Wildflower, 2010; Moyes, 2009). In relation to ethical development for coaching practitioners there has been emerging recognition of the need for multiple and deliberate opportunities for this, to include course components, scenario-based explorations and reflective practice (Allan, 2010; Allan and Law, 2009; Passmore, 2009a). Research too has made similar points:

> It is imperative that professional bodies provide or accredit opportunities for their members to undertake continuing professional training in ethical issues. There are many ways this can be done including providing specific courses and other materials on ethical dilemmas and the consequences of ethical incompetence. It could be connected to formal requirements for CPD. (Friedman, 2007: 80)

The publications in this area have grown over the past decade, but most remain at the level of commentary on the importance of ethics in coaching or the state of ethics in coaching. Book chapters on ethics include Peltier (2001) and De Jong (2006). There have also been a small number of texts from the United States that have focused on ethical issues such as Williams and Anderson (2006) and Weiner (2007). Some journals have attempted to increase interest in this area, including *The Coaching Psychologist,* which carries an ethics column and fairly frequent ethics-related articles.

We hold the view that coaching needs to move to build models to guide practitioners. In the area of coaching this means complementing codes of practice with an ethical decision-making model. Such a model would offer a structured way to reflect on coaching practice and identify issues and future learning for the practitioner.

# Why is a separate model needed for coaching?

Medicine, law and psychology are seen as professions where individuals are in positions of responsibility in relation to the wellbeing of others. As a result ethics has often taken a higher priority here than in other professions. However, other areas of practice have seen calls for greater ethical practice. The Davos debates in 2009 included a call for business leaders to have an ethical code because of their centrality in the wellbeing of others as mediated through the economy.

Of course, even though professionals may have a code of practice, some still behave badly and to the detriment of others. However, a code goes some useful way to highlighting what is expected and enabling accountability.

The joint endeavour nature of coaching as a relationship between a coach and coachee(s) necessitates the adoption of an approach in which capabilities and values are brought to bear in the service of a developmental outcome. The practitioner needs to be able to adopt a reflexive approach, with attention to what is emerging as the coaching progresses and what will assist the endeavour. It perhaps should go without saying that, for example, deceit, mistrust, incompetence and belittling are incompatible with appropriate coaching but it perhaps too often goes without saying that, no matter what the situation, coaches need to understand their own ethical viewpoint, appreciate any competing interests, have the courage to act on what they believe is right, articulate the reasons for their actions and be accountable.

In 2007, the Professional Associations Research Network published its third title on professional ethics, *Ethical Competence and Professional Associations* (Friedman, 2007). A five-stage model is suggested, shown in Table 10.1, working from Stage 1 to Stage 5.

**TABLE 10.1** Five-stage model

| What is added | Stage |
| --- | --- |
| Experience with ethical dilemmas, recognizing an ethical situation, knowing what is right, ethical reflective practice | 5: Ethical competence |
| Experience with several competencies, tacit knowing what works, technical reflective practice (ie on techniques/approaches) | 4: Technical competence |
| Apply specific knowledge and techniques in practice as defined by profession, employer, could include ethical competency | 3: Competencies |
| Theoretical and technical basis of the profession | 2: Knowledge acquisition |
| Learning and moral judgement capabilities, disposition and motivation to succeed at chosen profession | 1: Personal capability, disposition and motivation |

Achieving Stage 5 in a coaching context would involve as a minimum:

- Having learnt, at Stage 3, the 'do and don't' list (as per a published code) and enacting it.
- Being sensitized to what constitutes a situation with an ethical dimension in the coaching context generally.

- Being sensitized to, and therefore able to recognize, a specific emerging ethical dimension in coaching sessions.
- Being able to notice one's own reactions and responses as a coach and therefore ascertain one's own ethical stance (in a particular circumstance).
- Being able to act on that awareness in an appropriate way, even if difficult.

It is easy to appreciate that ethical competence as a coach is both essential and multi-dimensional.

# A coaching ethics model

Given the issues with ethical codes of practice and a desire to offer coaches a framework that would guide their reflection and learning, one of us undertook research into how experienced coaches make ethical decisions (Duff and Passmore, 2010). The outcome of this process was the development of an ethical decision-making model for coaching practitioners: the ACTION model.

The model consists of six stages to ethical decision making and, in contrast to previous models, which have been largely linear, it aims to offer both iteration and flexibility for coaches to incorporate their own values and beliefs as part of the decision process. The six stages of the ACTION model (Passmore, 2009b) are set out in Figure 10.1.

The stages can be briefly summarized as follows.

## Stage 1: Awareness

This involves being aware of one's own coaching position and the ethical code of the professional body that one is affiliated to. It also involves awareness of one's own personal values and beliefs.

## Stage 2: Classify

This stage involves the identification of the issue as it emerges in practice and the ability to classify the issue as a 'dilemma'.

**FIGURE 10.1** The action model for ethical decision making in coaching

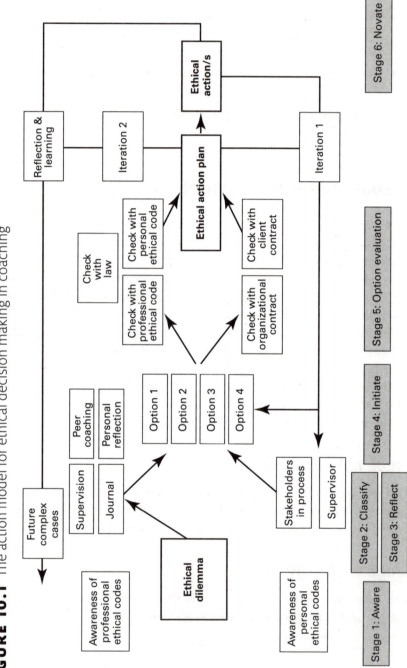

## Stage 3: Time for reflection, support, and advice

Different coaches will use different approaches to suit their own personal styles and needs. One difference that might be expected is between experienced coaches and novices or coaches in training. The experienced coach is likely to have a wide network of support in addition to his or her supervision arrangement. He or she may have a co-coaching relationship in place, or be a member of a peer network. For the novice coach and those in training, the role of the supervisor may be the main avenue and the coach is likely to discuss the issue with a supervisor as part of training. In both routes the key issue is to create some space and time to reflect and consider the issue from various perspectives.

## Stage 4: Initiate

As the reflection occurs the coach may be able to start building a number of solution options to the ethical dilemma. It is advisable to take a period of time to fully explore all of the options available, both self-generated and generated by the coach's support network, including through discussions with peers or a supervisor. In this way the model recognizes the value and real-life iterative nature of solving or resolving dilemmas. Such issues often play on our minds and we resolve them through turning them over, discussing them, turning them over again in our minds, and taking further soundings from others before settling on a course of action.

## Stage 5: Option evaluation

Through this stage, the coach must give time and space to each of the options generated in the initiate stage (4). This will include checking with ethical codes and reflecting on how the decision fits with their own values (revisiting stage 1). It is also likely to involve checking for any multiple relationship issues that may arise when being hired by an organization to coach its staff, and finally reflecting on whether the decision is consistent with the contract established at the start of the relationship with the organizational client and the coachee.

## Stage 6: Novate

Once the decision has been made, the coach must incorporate this scenario into his or her ethical journal or experiences. It may also be prudent to share such a scenario (in a confidential manner), with those within one's own network or coaching body so that colleagues can benefit from the situation. We hold the view that one of the main benefits of developing a process to resolve dilemmas is the value of future learning for the practitioner that can emerge.

# Conclusions

In this chapter we have tried to set out the developing nature of ethics in coaching. We have considered the nature of ethics, its role in coaching and offered a framework for how coaches may complement ethical codes with a structured decision-making model to resolve ethical dilemmas. For us the true value of such a framework lies in the potential it has in helping new as well as experienced coaches, making their tacit decision making more explicit and thus offering opportunities for further learning and personal development.

## References

Allan, J (2010) The ethics column, *The Coaching Psychologist*, 5 (2) 132–34

Allan, J and Law, H (2009) Ethical navigation in coaching psychology – a Socratic workshop, *The Coaching Psychologist*, 5 (2) 110–14

Brennan, D, and Wildflower, L (2010) Ethics in coaching, in (eds) E Cox, T Bachkirova and D Clutterbuck, (pp 369–80), *The Complete Handbook of Coaching*, Sage, London

Carroll, M (2009) Ethical Maturity. Presentation to CSTD and Bath Consultancy Graduate Group, Bath, UK

De Jong, A (2006) Coaching ethics: Integrity in the moment of choice, in (ed) J Passmore, (pp 191–202) *Excellence in Coaching: The industry guide*, Kogan Page, London

Duff, M and Passmore, J (2010) Coaching ethics: a decision-making model, *International Coaching Psychology Review*, 5 (2) 140–51

Friedman, A (2007) *Ethical Competence and Professional Associations*, Professional Associations Research Network, Bristol

Hawkins, P (2011) Building emotional, ethical and cognitive capacity in coaches – a developmental model of supervision, in (ed) J Passmore, *Supervision in Coaching*, Kogan Page, London

Moyes, B (2009) Literature review of coaching supervision, *International Coaching Psychology Review*, 4 (2) 160–71

Passmore, J (2009a) Coaching ethics: Making ethical decisions: experts and novices, *The Coaching Psychologist*, 5 (1) 6–10

Passmore, J (2009b) West Midlands Local Government Annual Coaching Conference, Paper: Looking after yourself as a coach, Coventry, 15 October

Passmore, J and Mortimer, L (2011) Ethics: A balancing act, in (eds) L Boyce and G Hernez-Broome, *Advancing Executive Coaching: Setting the course for successful leadership coaching*, Jossey-Bass, San Francisco, CA

Peltier, B (2001) *The Psychology of Executive Coaching: Theory and application*, Routledge, New York

Weiner, K (2007) *The Little Book of Ethics for Coaches: Ethics, risk management and professional issues*, Authorhouse, USA

Williams, P and Anderson, S (2006) *Law and Ethics in Coaching*, Wiley, New York

# Legal considerations in coaching

**KEVIN M ROGERS**

## Introduction

The relationship a coach has with his or her client is often fruitful and productive. In the vast majority of situations the time spent is helpful and edifying, although in a small number of cases difficulties will arise. This may result in an ending of the arrangement, possible damage to the reputation of the coach, and in some circumstances the commencement of legal proceedings against the coach may follow. The importance of complying with legal requirements cannot be overstated and will assist in ensuring that if an agreement comes to a conclusion the coach can be assured that he or she has complied with his or her legal duties. Furthermore, it is essential that the coach safeguards the information that the client provides in the course of their relationship. The Data Protection Act 1998 outlines a range of obligations that need to be adhered to, while the more traditional common law evolution of confidentiality needs to be factored into a coach's practice.

As coaching is a relatively recent addition to the professions, there is currently little written on the law in relation to coaching – one of the rare examples is the US publication by Williams and Anderson (2005). Although the Association for Coaching states that 'Coaches are required to keep themselves informed of any legal or statutory requirements that may affect their work' a considerable amount of research is still needed in this area (Association for Coaching, 2006). This chapter seeks to contribute to this discussion by highlighting a number of key legal issues that a coach needs to consider when engaging in a new coaching arrangement and how to maintain legal compliance throughout the relationship. An established legal principle is that ignorance is no defence, so coaches need to begin to grapple with some of these important issues, including the establishment and marketing of their services, entering into a contract of engagement with a client and issues relating to data protection and confidentiality. The focus will be on the law relating to England and Wales, although on occasions this may extend to European law.

# Establishment

Before coaches start to contemplate offering their services, they need to decide how they will set themselves up. It may be that a coach will be working alone as a sole trader, or may be working with other individuals in a partnership. A coach may want to consider setting up a private limited company through which he or she will offer his or her services. The main legislation in the UK in the area of company law is the Companies Act 2006, which is the largest statute ever to have gone through Parliament. Incorporation as a private company is a relatively easy process and section 7 of the Companies Act 2006 says that one or more persons can incorporate, provided it is for a lawful purpose. To incorporate, an individual must send the following documents to Companies House:

- the company's Memorandum of Association;
- the Company's Articles of Association signed by the subscriber(s);
- a statement naming the company's first director and company secretary (Form IN01);
- the necessary fee (in 2010 the minimum fee is £20[1]).

Companies House is an executive agency within the remit of the Department of Business, Innovation and Skills, which is responsible for the incorporation and dissolution of companies, collecting and storing required company documentation and ensuring that this is all available to the public.

A company, being an artificial person, can only be identified by its name. It is this which fixes the company's identity. There are certain requirements when it comes to naming a company, including that companies may not register themselves *inter alia* using the name of another existing company (this is the responsibility of the registering company to check), using offensive language or giving the impression that they are connected to the government. Within 12 months of registration the Secretary of State can order a company to change its name if it is too similar to another company.

If a company is a public limited company, as defined in section 4, it must have the words 'Public Limited Company' (or 'Plc') at the end of its name. If the company is a private company, it must have the word 'Limited' (or 'Ltd') at the end of its name. The company name must appear – conspicuously – on the front of the building and all its official paperwork and e-mails that are sent. Upon correct sending of all the necessary forms to Companies House, the registrar will send a certificate of incorporation. This will include the company's name and will also provide a company number. The document will also be dated, and a private limited company can officially commence business as a registered company from the date of the certificate.[2]

A partnership is more informal than incorporation as a company and, provided partners do nothing illegal, the law places very few requirements on a partnership. Perhaps the key difference between a partnership and a company is that of liability. In a partnership, the partners could be held liable for acts of the firm, whereas the liability of a member of a company is limited by shares, or the amount of money that has been invested into the company. A hybrid model is the option of a Limited Liability Partnership, which is similar to a standard partnership, although offers reduced liability for business debts.[3]

It is important to note that different requirements on taxation and employment status exist for these different business models. HM Revenue & Customs provides excellent information to ensure that businesses are not caught out.[4]

# Advertising and marketing

To attract clients, coaches will need to advertise their services. It may be that a particular coach has established a firm relationship with a company or a group of people, although before getting to this stage the coach needs to market his or her services. Word of mouth is an invaluable advertising tool, but a coach may also wish to advertise his or her services in the local press, visual marketing or through employer or employee associations. The internet offers vast potential for advertising, although it is important to note that a website will be available internationally and not just in the coach's domestic jurisdiction. This will mean that the coach needs to exercise a greater degree of caution to ensure that he or she does not upset the sensitivities or the particular rules of any country. For example, the glorification of Nazism is an offence in France, but this is not the case in the United States where this would be protected by the First Amendment Right of Free Speech.

There are a range of strict legislative and statutory controls that regulate both traditional advertising within the United Kingdom and also more dynamic direct advertising carried out over the internet. There are a number of self-regulatory bodies and systems that seek to ensure that advertisements are appropriate for the audience and are not in any way misleading. One such example is the Advertising Standards Agency, which is the independent watchdog responsible for maintaining high standards of advertising within the United Kingdom.[5] Part of its role is to adjudicate on situations where marketers appear to be acting in contravention of the relevant laws and industry codes. The main industry code is the British Codes of Advertising, Sales Promotion and Direct Marketing, which are more commonly known as the CAP Code. This is a comprehensive set of rules that provide a number of basic principles for those engaged in advertising. The principles are that advertisements must be legal, decent, honest and truthful; they should be prepared with a sense of responsibility to consumers and to society and should also be in line with the principles of fair competition generally accepted in business. On 16 March 2010, the Advertising Standards Agency announced that after a substantial two-year consultation exercise (that received over 30,000 responses) a new set of codes would be introduced and these came into effect on 1 September 2010.[6]

The intention behind the new codes was to make the rules more accessible and easier to understand by using a clearer format and greater consistency throughout the document. Introduced for the first time were rules on corporate and social responsibility and advertising to children, guidance on consumer protection; sector-specific rules were also amended.[7] It is therefore important that coaches who seek to advertise their services do so with a sense of responsibility, ensuring that the advertisement is honest and truthful. There are also a number of broader responsibilities in the creation of an advertisement. For instance, it is important that a coach does not infringe another's trademark or copyright. An example of this is creating a website and using images that have been freely copied from another website. Simply because the picture is freely available online does not mean that it is not subject to copyright. In designing a website, it is much safer to either use personal photographs or pay an established agency to use a particular photograph or image.

Finally, it is important to exercise caution in providing advice on a website. In circumstances where advice is provided online, the existence of a simple disclaimer will normally allow the coach to avoid liability in situations where a client takes a course of action based on that advice, which subsequently has unfortunate consequences. In Gary Patchett v Swimming Pool and Allied Trades Association Limited (SPATA)[8] Mr and Mrs Patchett viewed the website of the trade body SPATA to locate a firm that could build a swimming pool for them. The website stated that full checks (including financial) were made on members and, based on the information on the website, the Patchetts instructed a contractor to build a swimming pool at a cost of just over £55,000. During construction the contractor became insolvent and the work was not completed, meaning that the Patchetts had to employ other contractors to finish the job, costing them an extra £44,000. The Patchetts brought proceedings against SPATA for negligent misstatement and sought to recover their losses. The Court of Appeal (by a majority) rejected their argument and held that a duty of care is owed by a website to its visitors, but the existence of a disclaimer may reduce or exclude liability. In this circumstance, the website encouraged people to make further enquiries prior to contracting with a contractor. These further enquiries included obtaining an Information Pack from SPATA, which the Patchetts did not do. Following this case, it appears that a simple disclaimer that appears on a website is sufficient to mitigate against any future potential liability.[9]

# Contract of engagement

Contracts play an important part in everyday life, from the simple purchase of a chocolate bar in a shop, to the mobile phone contract that an assistant asks you to read and sign prior to taking the telephone out of the shop, to the large purchases, such as a property conveyance. As with any legal relationship it is important that all parties are aware of and contract into the terms and conditions of engagements. From the point of view of both the coach and the client (and perhaps any third party, such as the client's employer, who may hold an interest in the arrangement) it is essential that the terms of engagement are clearly set out and agreed to. A contract does not have to be in writing, although it is suggested that in this type of relationship it is appropriate that the parameters of the relationship are written down. This ensures that all parties have a definitive document detailing all of their rights and responsibilities, while also providing assistance in the unlikely event of a legal dispute.

The type of information that needs to be agreed between the coach and a client includes the number of, and length of, sessions, the fee for each session, what will happen in the event of a cancelled session, and termination. It is also important to note the responsibilities of each party (for instance on the part of the coach not to divulge details of discussions) up to and including the notice period that either party must give to bring the relationship to an end.

Once the contractual terms and conditions have been agreed in principle, it is important that both parties sign a document assenting to the agreement. The effect of signing a contract is very clear in common law, which states that an individual is bound by the contents of a document he or she signs even if he or she did not read the document or understand its contents. This principle was seen in the case of L'Estrange v Graucob, which held that when a document containing terms and conditions is signed, the person who signed the document is bound to it and it is wholly immaterial whether that person read the document or not.[10] This signature does not need to be in person as this type of contract can be formed by e-mail as long as each person has typed his or her name at the bottom of the e-mail containing terms and conditions.[11] There are other methods of ensuring that terms and conditions are incorporated, such as through notice and, perhaps more relevantly, course of dealing. If a coach has an established relationship with a client and he or she has taken to working in a particular way, the court is likely to follow this particular method of working and base its judgement on this. In Photolibrary Group Limited (t/a Garden Picture Library) v Burda Senator Verlag GmbH[12] the court held that even though a delivery note (containing details of the photographic transparencies and penalty clauses if the transparencies were lost) was not signed, there was an established course of dealing between the parties to show that these terms (including the penalty clauses) had been adopted.[13] It is important to note, however, that a court may move away from this principle if a clause that a party is trying to enforce is unduly onerous or unusual (Macdonald, 1988).

# Confidentiality

The duty of confidentiality is an established common law principle and is a legal duty that is placed on all coaches. This principle does not simply apply to medical confidences, and the view of the courts is that there is a public interest in protecting the confidences received under a notice of confidentiality or where there is a reasonable expectation of confidentiality, as exists in a coach/client relationship. Traditionally, a breach of confidentiality can be shown through a three-stage test. First, the information divulged by the client to the coach has a quality of confidence about it; second, that information must have been imparted in circumstances where there was an obligation of confidence; and finally, there needs to be an unauthorized use of that information by the coach. There is no requirement to show that the client has suffered any damage.

There are some exceptions to this duty, such as when the client consents to the disclosure,[14] or where the disclosure is in the interests of the client.[15] Additionally, limits of confidentiality could extend to situations where the client may pose a risk of harm to him- or herself or another or where there has been serious illegality. An example of the latter is contained within the Terrorism Act 2000, which places an obligation on all persons to disclose to the police information connected to acts of terrorism. In the majority of cases there is no legal obligation for a coach to report the illegal behaviour of a client, unless statute determines that they must. The nature of confidentiality has been strengthened with the introduction of data protection legislation.

# Data protection

In the UK the Data Protection Act 1998 places requirements on people who process[16] personal data.[17] This extends to schools, universities, businesses, the medical professions, charities, religious institutions and indeed coaches. A coach will invariably hold a large amount of information about the client. This will include personal details (such as name, date of birth, address), payment details, perhaps medical information and certainly notes on their meetings. It is of paramount importance that this information is protected. The UK has witnessed over the past few years a number of very high profile data security breaches, such as the loss by HMRC in November 2007 of two discs containing the personal information of every recipient of child benefit in the UK[18] and the Driving Standards Agency losing the details of around 3 million people who were about to sit their driving theory test.[19] These breaches led to very bad publicity and vast amounts of time and money being spent to secure systems. Although on a much smaller scale, similar breaches could occur to a coach who holds information about his or her clients. Loss could lead to embarrassment for the client and also could damage the goodwill among clients and the profession. It is therefore of paramount importance that a coach complies with the Data Protection Act 1998.

Simply operating a filing system containing details of clients will mean that a coach will need to follow the requirements of the Act. The first requirement is that of notification. As a coach processes personal data he or she will need to notify the Information Commissioner (ICO).[20] Failure to notify the ICO is a criminal offence under section 21 of the Act, leading to a fine. The person (or company) that notifies the ICO is known as the Data Controller. The annual notification requirement is straightforward, and the Data Controller needs to include registrable details (including their name and address, a description of the personal data, the reasons for it being processed, a description of any recipients, and details if the data is to be transferred outside of the European Economic Area). A general description of the security measures that are in place to protect the personal data should also be provided. The annual cost of notification is £35 for the majority of organizations.

Once a Data Controller has notified the ICO they will need to adhere to the eight Data Protection Principles that are found in Schedule 1 of the Act. These principles exist as a 'good practice guide' for Data Controllers who process personal data. The eight principles are:

1 The data shall be processed fairly and lawfully.
2 It is only obtained for one or more specified and lawful purposes.
3 It shall be adequate, relevant and not excessive.
4 It is accurate and up to date.
5 It is not kept for longer than necessary.
6 It is processed in accordance with the data subject's rights.
7 It is kept secure using technical and organizational methods.
8 It is not transferred out of the European Economic Area (EEA) unless there is an adequate level of protection for data subjects.

There are a number of points to address in this list. Principle 1 requires that data must be processed fairly and lawfully. In practice, this means that a Data Controller needs a reason or grounds for processing the data. These conditions for processing are listed in Schedule 2 of the Act:

- the data subject has consented;
- the processing is necessary for contracting;
- it is necessary for legal compliance;
- it is in the vital interests of the data subject;
- the processing is for judicial/governmental purposes;
- the processing is necessary for legitimate purposes.

However, under the terms of the Act there is the concept of 'Sensitive Personal Data'. This is defined by Section 2 of the Act as information relating to an individual regarding his or her:

- racial or ethnic origin;
- religious or political belief;
- trade union membership;
- physical or mental health;
- sex life; or
- criminal record.

If the coach is processing the type of data contained in the list above, then a condition in Schedule 3 of the Act must be met. Specifically:

- The data subject has given his or her explicit consent.
- It is necessary for the purposes of employment obligations on the controller.
- It is in the vital interests of the data subject (if the controller cannot get consent from the data subject).
- It is carried out by a non-profit-making organization.
- It concerns legal compliance.
- It is necessary for the administration of justice.
- It is necessary for medical purposes.
- It is necessary to maintain equal opportunity records.
- It is to be processed following an order from the Secretary of State.

In either case, in the majority of cases a coach is able comply with this element of the law by inserting a clause in the contract of engagement[21] that the client (or 'data subject') is required to sign stating that the client is aware that this arrangement will necessitate the processing of data and consent to this processing.

The second principle relates to processing for specified and lawful purposes. This means that a Data Controller is unable to use the data for any purpose outside that which they have previously notified the ICO. The third principle is a question of fact depending on the purpose of the processing. The fourth and fifth principles are interlinking and relate to accuracy and retention of data. A coach needs to ensure that the personal data held about the client is kept up to date, and once the arrangement has come to an end dispose of the data securely. The length of time that the data may be kept is again a question of fact and could depend on any legislation that may exist relating to the retention of certain data.[22] The recent case of Chief Constable of Humberside v Information Commissioner[23] considered the issue of data retention. In this case, five individuals requested that minor convictions (some of which related to incidents in the 1970s and 1980s during their teenage years) should be deleted from the police record. The difficulty faced by these five individuals was that when they applied for a job requiring a Criminal Records Bureau check, these 'old' offences were being highlighted, even though (in one situation), the police force had said that the conviction would be erased once the individual reached the age of 18. The court held that the chief constables, as Data Controllers, were able to determine the purposes of processing and the length of time the data could be retained. The Court of Appeal was of the view that there is no statutory constraint on any individual or company as to the purposes for which he or it is entitled to retain data. The one exception to this is that the purpose has to be lawful, in order to comply with the first data protection principle.

Principle six states that the data must be processed in accordance with the rights of the data subject. The data subject has a number of rights under the Act, the main one being the right of access to his or her personal data.[24] As a Data Controller, the coach may charge a fee of £10, but must respond within 40 calendar days, which commences once the Data Controller has received sufficient information about the personal data that is requested and the necessary fee. A Data Controller is also able to ask for the data subject to verify his or her identity. The Data Controller must provide the data subject with a description of the personal data held in relation to him or her, a copy of any information held and any information that is needed to make the copy intelligible (for instance a translation for any codes used on the disclosed documents).

The requirement that personal data must be kept secure using technical and organizational methods under principle seven is central to the underlying objective behind the legislation. As mentioned above, a security breach could lead to serious professional damage for the coach because sensitive or even embarrassing information could be released into the public sphere. The European Court of Human Rights recently handed down the judgment in I v Finland.[25] In this case, the applicant was a nurse specializing in eye care who worked in a hospital in Finland. She contracted HIV and needed to be treated at the same hospital. Based on comments that were made to her she formed the impression that her medical records had been accessed by her colleagues. The log kept by the hospital only detailed the last five accesses and only noted the accessing by department, as opposed to the person. This meant the hospital was unable to show who accessed her file. Initially the Finnish court said that as access by unauthorized persons could not be proved there was no case to answer. However, the European Court of Human Rights held that there was a positive duty to secure data – particularly if the data held is sensitive personal data. There is a clear link with Article 8 in the European Convention on Human Rights and confidentiality of health records is fundamental to right to a private life. Therefore, practical and effective protection is needed to safeguard against the misuse of personal data.

A data security breach can happen for a number of reasons. It could be that data (or equipment storing data) is stolen, or is accessed by an unauthorized person and disclosed to a third party, or that computer systems are hacked into. The ICO is keen to ensure that data is kept as secure as possible; evidence for this is seen by the requirements contained within the notification formalities, which requests details of security measures in place. In considering the appropriateness of security measures, the Information Commissioner recommends that regard should be paid to the implementation cost, the technological developments (ie what technology is available to protect data), the nature of the data (sensitive personal data should require greater protection than personal data) and the harm that may result if the data is lost or unlawfully processed. In practice, this means that a coach will need to consider a range of security factors. These could include the physical security of a building. If a coach is storing personal information in an office, he or she needs to ensure that the building is secure and that files are stored in a locked filing cabinet. It may also be that a coach will store personal information on a computer system, in which case it is important that the computer is password protected and that any data stored on a USB disc is encrypted. A coach will also have to consider how he or she disposes of information once the relationship has reached its conclusion. Invariably, this will mean that a coach will need to shred or burn any hardcopy information that he or she still has in his or her possession once the arrangement has ended.

The importance of taking steps to safeguard data has increased since the implementation of the Criminal Justice and Immigration Act 2008, which received Royal Assent on 8 May 2008. Among other things it amends section 55 of the Data Protection Act to make it an offence for a person to knowingly or recklessly (and without the consent of the data controller) obtain or disclose the personal data to another person. This breach needs to be deliberate or reckless and applies in circumstances where the Data Controller knew, or ought to have known, that there was a risk that the contravention would occur and that the contravention would lead to substantial damage or substantial distress and the Data Controller did not take reasonable steps to prevent the contravention. The use of the word 'substantial' in relation to the damage or distress caused may be misleading in suggesting how widely used this provision will be. As an act in contravention of the Data Protection Act can be committed recklessly, this provision has the ability to apply at an early stage. Equally, the ICO is of the view that computer passwords and encryption are standard security measures, so a simple failure in these areas could lead to a monetary penalty (to a maximum of £500,000) being issued against the Data Controller (ICO, 2008a). The monies raised will go into a consolidated fund managed by the Treasury to ensure that there is no incentive for the ICO to pursue individuals under this section. It is possible that this offence will become used regularly by the ICO in situations where a Data Controller has deliberately or recklessly breached any of the eight Data Protection Principles, including by failing to take adequate steps to secure data (ICO, 2008b).

## Conclusion

The legislation implications of coaching practice are still in the developmental stages, although this chapter has sought to highlight and discuss some of the legal issues a coach needs to consider in a coaching relationship. It has considered the initial stages of establishment and advertising services leading to an agreement and contract of engagement. During the coaching relationship there are a number of legal considerations that a coach needs to remember, including confidentiality and data protection. While adhering to the requirements of legislation is good practice to avoid litigation, it also ensures that a coach's practice is fully compliant with the demands of the law to ensure that the reputation of his or her practice and the goodwill of his or her clients will be maintained.

## Notes

1  If a person would like to use the 'Same Day Incorporation' service the 2010 fee was £50.00. The standard turnaround time for Companies House to incorporate a company is eight to 10 working days.

2  For more details on incorporating as a limited company see the guidance provided by Companies House at: **http://www.companieshouse.gov.uk/infoAndGuide/companyRegistration.shtml**.

3  For more on Limited Liability Partnerships see the guidance provided by Companies House at: **http://www.companieshouse.gov.uk/infoAndGuide/llp.shtml**.

4  See: **http://www.hmrc.gov.uk/businesses/index.shtml**.

5  There are other similar industry groups that offer guidance or regulate online direct marketing, such as the Direct Marketing Association, the Interactive Advertising Bureau UK (a trade association for those involved in interactive advertising, electronic commerce and online marketing) and ADMARK, which is an opt-in system for marketers to say that their advertisements are legal, decent, honest and truthful; in return they can display the ADMARK logo on their website. This is similar to the 'Kite Mark' symbol.

6  See Advertising Standards Agency News, New Advertising Codes Launched (16 March 2010). Available at: **http://bcap.org.uk/The-Codes/New-Advertising-Codes.aspx**.

7  For more see: Committee of Advertising Practice New UK Advertising Codes. Available at: **http://bcap.org.uk/The-Codes/New-Advertising-Codes.aspx**.

8  [2009] EWCA Civ 717.

9  For more on this case see: Massey, R Patchett v Swimming Pool and Allied Trades Association Ltd: making a splash – the contextualization of website statements (2010) Computer and Telecommunications Law Review, volume 16, issue 3, pages 78–80 and Farmer, S Patchett v Swimming Pool and Allied Trades Association Ltd (Case Comment) (2009) *E-Commerce Law Reports, 9*, 3, pp 16–17. For an additional Irish perspective: Austin, M Negligent misstatement – where now following Patchett v Swimming Pool and Allied Trades Association? (2010) *Irish Law Times,* 28, 8, pp 122–27.

10   There are some rare exceptions to this. An example is if the signature is obtained by misrepresentation or by fraud, as discussed by the Court of Appeal in Curtis v Chemical Cleaning and Dyeing Company [1951] 1 KB 805, and the person signing the document has to reasonably expect that the document contains contractual terms as in Grogan v Robin Meredith Plant Hire [1996] CLC 1127.

11   J Pereira Fernandes SA v Mehta (2006) 1 WLR 1543.

12   [2008] EWHC 1343 (QB).

13   Another example is found within Hollier v Rambler Motors (AMC) Limited [1972] 2 QB 71, which said that three or four contracts over a period of about five years was probably not sufficient to be a course of dealing for this purpose.

14   Hunter v Mann [1974] QB 767.

15   C v Cairns [2003] Lloyds Rep Med 90.

16   'Processing' has a very wide definition under section 1 of the Act and includes holding, recording, adapting, altering or organizing the data.

17   The key case that defines 'personal data' is Durant v Financial Services Authority [2003] EWCA Civ. 1746. 'Personal data' is data which is biographical in a significant sense and has the data subject as its focus. (The data subject is the person whom the data is about. In the context of a coach/client relationship, the client will be the data subject.) For more on this issue see: Carey, P, *Data Protection: A practical guide to UK and EU law* (2009) Oxford University Press, 3rd edition.

18   For the initial BBC press release on this story see: UK's families put on fraud alert (20 November 2007). Available at: **http://news.bbc.co.uk/1/hi/uk_politics/7103566.stm**.

19   BBC News, Millions of L-Driver details lost (17 December 2007). Available at: **http://news.bbc.co.uk/1/hi/uk_politics/7147715.stm**.

20   The Information Commissioner is responsible for enforcing the Data Protection Act 1998, as well as other legislation such as the Freedom of Information Act 2000 and the Privacy and Electronic Communications (EC Directive) Regulations. It has a very comprehensive and usually helpful website: **http://www.ico.gov.uk**.

21   See above under 'Contract of Engagement'.

22   For instance the Limitation Act 1980 states that an action founded on a simple contract needs to be brought within six years of the accrual of the cause of action (section 5), while an action relating to the recovery of land needs to be brought within 12 years (section 15). These may act an indicators suggesting how long particular personal data should be retained by an organization.

23   [2009] EWCA Civ 1079.

24   Data Protection Act 1998, section 7.

25   (2008) Application 20511/03.

# References

Association for Coaching (2006) Code of Ethics and Good Practice, accessed on 4 June 2010 from: **http://www.associationforcoaching.com/about/about02.htm**

ICO (2008a) Press release: ICO welcomes new powers to fine organisations for data breaches, 9 May. Available at: **http://www.ico.gov.uk/about_us/news_ and_views/press_releases.aspx**

ICO (2008b) Guidance Data Protection Act 1998: Information Commissioner's guidance about the issue of monetary penalties prepared and issued under section 55C (1) of the Data Protection Act 1998. Available at: **http://www.ico.gov. uk/upload/documents/library/data_protection/detailed_specialist_ guides/ico_guidance_monetary_penalties.pdf**

Macdonald, E (1988) The duty to give notice of unusual contract terms, *Journal of Business Law,* September, 375–85

Williams, P and Anderson, S K (2005) *Law and Ethics in Coaching: How to solve and avoid difficult problems in your practice,* John Wiley, Chichester

# PART 3
# Continuous professional development

# Continuous professional development for coaches

## 12

DAVID HAIN, PHILIPPA HAIN AND
LISA MATTHEWMAN

## Introduction

In this chapter we will examine the topic of continuous professional development (CPD). There is a paradox associated with CPD for many coaches. On the one hand, it is clearly a beneficial thing to do, since as coaches we believe in continuing growth. However, making time available can be difficult, and often this is exacerbated by the lack of a compelling rationale to undertake CPD, uncertainty about how to go about it and confusion over how to record development and to generate an appropriate pay-off for the investment made. We will attempt to deconstruct the CPD process and to indicate why it should become a critical element of professional practice and how to make it fundamental to the way coaches go about their business.

## The benefits of CPD

CPD is an integral part of the professional standards of all the coaching bodies. This fact alone demonstrates the weight given to the importance of coaches committing to 'practice what they preach' by undertaking regular and progressive personal learning and development activities. Those who wish to become members of professional bodies must be able to demonstrate their commitment to CPD as part of their registration. Apart from this very practical argument, however, there are good reasons to develop CPD as a critical element of coaching practice.

## 1. Commercial

As the discipline of coaching progressively 'professionalizes' over the next few years, CPD will become a critical feature of demonstrable professional practice. It will become a key focus of whether services offered are taken up by clients. Coaches will need to prove, in a very crowded and competitive field, that they have invested in their own development before being given licence to affect the development of other people.

## 2. Ethical

If coaches want to 'be the change they want to see in the world', it is vital that they regard their own learning and development as a fundamental practice that needs to be reviewed and updated regularly via reflective practice or other methods. Not to find the time and energy to invest in CPD is therefore professional hypocrisy. With no regulation currently, it is easy to avoid undertaking this formally, but it is not helpful to one's development as a coach or of one's professional practice.

## 3. Professional

The professional discipline of coaching is still relatively new and growing hugely. The field of coaching comprises many and varied offerings and the cost of entry to becoming a coach is minimal. It is vital that the field becomes regarded for the highest professional standards and excludes the many people who see becoming a coach as a natural extension of a previous career – and often a good and 'trendy' way to make excellent financial returns for minimal investment in personal skill or depth of knowledge.

## 4. System improvement

As coaching develops both more effective infrastructure and an ever wider and deeper body of professional and technical research and knowledge, CPD is the best guarantee we can have that the most basic element of the system – coaches themselves – is focused on excellence. As in any system, the coaching world changes one coach at a time. Gibb and Megginson (1999) comment that 'people who embrace CPD appear to be more engaged, less stressed, more interested in new opportunities and open to working with new colleagues'.

So the benefits of CPD seem to be many and universally applicable. We aim here to equip coaches with a theoretical overview as well as practical guidance on the many ways of undertaking CPD.

# What is CPD?

Megginson and Whitaker (2004) refer to CPD as 'a process in which individuals can take control of their own learning and development by engaging in an ongoing developmental process of reflection, goal setting and action'. There are a number of reasons why coaches might want to undertake CPD, but the most authentic and compelling ones are based on a desire to develop the skills, knowledge and experience we can accumulate personally, as opposed to doing so simply for job or organizational development initiatives. By undertaking CPD, individuals generally want to facilitate better subject matter knowledge, situational awareness or self-awareness, with the longer term aim of personal, business or career growth.

## *Core concepts*

A key element of CPD is that the learners remain in control of the learning, deciding what to develop and how to do so. Even though they may engage a coach and/or mentor or utilize other learning methods, CPD learners set their own goals and, via reflective practice, regularly calibrate progress and reassess the journey they are making. CPD is most helpfully viewed as having holistic application, covering any or all elements of a learner's life and work, generally ensuring a balance between the two.

CPD is based on the core concepts of action inquiry and reflection. Learners examine and build on their current situation in relation to the future position they desire or aspire to achieve. 'Action inquiry' is an umbrella term for the deliberate use of any kind of a 'plan, act, describe, review' cycle for inquiry into action in a field of practice. Reflective practice, diagnostic practice, action learning, action research and researched action are all terms underpinned by action inquiry. All of them are based on two premises. First, people can accomplish complex tasks more effectively when they also pay attention to personal learning.

Better learners react more quickly, identify issues more effectively, spot trends more reliably and tend to demonstrate more obviously a contagious enthusiasm in their work. Second, what we learn during the course of real work (as opposed to courses, books and other methods) has particular value. Indeed CPD works best when there is support and backing from the employer to legitimate the necessary individual motivation and drive to take it forward.

Another distinguishing feature of effective CPD is that it values and seeks to employ multiple forms of sense-making as the basis for sustainable learning. Activities, as shown in Figure 12.1, can concentrate on diverse goals such as developing further know-how at a very practical level; seeking to further conceptual understanding of a subject or situation; finding new ways of applying imagination, creativity and innovative methods; and attempting to deepen personal experience.

## CPD stakeholders

Figure 12.2 shows how various parties, including the individual learner, can be viewed as having a stake in the process. Employers are increasingly concerned that employees undertake CPD as a way of keeping skills, knowledge and experience up to date. CPD can help with succession planning and staff retention. Clients are increasingly using CPD evidence as distinguishing feature in terms of coaches they employ. Professional bodies encourage CPD because members who manage personal learning and growth more effectively are typically able to deliver the practical application of the professional standards more effectively too. Professional standards are also important to every employer.

## CPD and the coaching professional bodies

CPD is a key requirement of members of nearly all coaching professional organizations and many offer well thought through guidelines on the rationale for and benefits of CPD. Here, space permits us to mention just two.

### Chartered Institute for Personnel Development

The CIPD is a UK-based organization representing trainers and HR professionals. It has set out five key principles for CPD:

1 Professional development is a continuous process that applies throughout a practitioner's working life.

**FIGURE 12.1** CPD framework

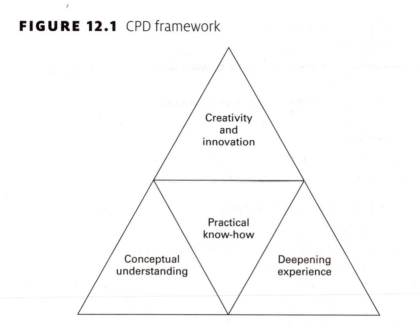

**FIGURE 12.2** CPD stakeholders

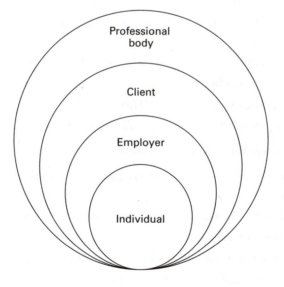

2 Individuals are responsible for controlling and managing their own development.

3 Individuals should decide for themselves their learning needs and how to fulfil them.

4 Learning targets should be clearly articulated and should reflect the needs of employers and clients as well as the practitioner's individual goals.

5 Learning is most effective when it is acknowledged as an integral part of work rather than as additional burden.

## The British Psychological Society

The BPS requires members to maintain CPD records in relation to National Occupational Standards (NOS) for Psychology. NOS are statements of the skills, knowledge and understanding needed in employment and clearly define the outcomes of competent performance. The BPS maintains that NOS can assist the individual psychologists, their employing organization and the Society.

For the individual psychologist:

- helping to ensure that psychologists' skills and knowledge match a job description;
- assisting in providing evidence for an appraisal/staff development review;
- detailing competences, knowledge and skills for use at interview;
- assisting in matching skills and knowledge for a promoted post;
- providing key roles when updating a CV;
- assisting members in meeting CPD requirements.

For the employer/business/organization:

- identifying professionals that are capable, competent and well trained;
- contributing to organizational goals and service provision;
- contributing to clinical governance;
- informing the design and delivery of staff training programmes;
- planning for staff development and retention.

For the Society:

- informing qualifications development;

- informing the design and delivery of professional training programmes;
- informing decision making related to APL;
- informing decision making related to applications for registration.

# Targeting CPD effectively

So, undertaking CPD makes sense for practitioners from nearly every angle – but what kind of CPD should be undertaken?

Our belief is that a sound CPD portfolio would be balanced over time by the need to work on furthering personal knowledge; reviewing and developing attitudinal factors; and consolidating or enlarging personal skill sets. Ideally, all of these areas work together to keep the individual practitioner 'tuned up'. Each of them has a part to play in any coaching intervention, although the balance between them may vary depending on the nature and level of the coaching being undertaken.

## *Knowledge*

The distinguishing skill of the 'super coach', we would contend, is less about the depth of knowledge of any given approach (of which there are many; see Palmer and Whybrow, 2007) to client problems and much more about selecting an appropriate framework from a range of choices to suit client personality and context (see Passmore, 2006). Questions you might ask yourself (or clients) in relation to CPD, therefore, include:

- How wide is your range of interventions?
- From what basis do you select an approach for a given situation?
- Which problems do you struggle (relatively) to help with and which other approaches may assist you?
- Which models and frameworks are of particular interest in developing your range?

## *Attitude*

'Choose your attitude' is an injunction we find ourselves repeating regularly to clients in a range of situations. But are you, as a coach, working on your own attitude? The key to effective coaching, almost regardless of the specific assignment, is the quality of the relationship between coach and coachee. So it is essential to reflect regularly, ideally via feedback, on how we come across as coaches. The components of emotional intelligence, particularly self-awareness, are a lifetime's work, and coaches need to pay close heed to these factors in any balanced CPD programme. Questions in relation to attitude development might include:

- How effective am I at getting regular, evidence-based feedback about my style and impact as a coach?
- How well do I understand my 'hot buttons' and red flags – the triggers to my becoming more judgmental, less good at listening, etc?
- Where am I getting the opportunity to reflect out loud on issues, common elements and incidents that take place during my coaching work – do I understand patterns and trends that may underlie my experience?
- Do I have an effective sounding board with whom I can explore the challenges I face as a coach, identify key areas for development or work through alternative options and approaches?

## Skills

Effective coaches are rightly lauded as highly capable in a range of subtle and difficult to master skills, often, but not exclusively, to do with relationship building, conversation management and influencing. But these skills are notoriously hard to benchmark or to break down into component parts, particularly so when the bulk of a coaching intervention typically consists of a highly dynamic and immediate set of conversational challenges that do not easily lend themselves to immediate insight. In our experience one of the great dilemmas in coaching is how to make sure, as a coach, you get rigorous and detailed feedback without becoming self- (as opposed to client-) centred.

A further skills challenge is closely linked to knowledge. It is one thing to read a book or to watch a video on (say) transpersonal coaching or Gestalt, it is quite another to put the knowledge gained into practice with any degree of mastery. And yet we also know there is a need to move through a number of stages as we progress along skill levels towards unconscious competence. The coach development dilemma, therefore, is about balancing the imperative to become more capable with the even more immediate one of handling each client issue with competence and confidence.

A third skills challenge involves developing bigger-picture thinking. While most coaching interventions are delivered one-to-one and in a very intimate way, nearly all of them take place in a much more complex organizational and social context. Coaches who want to fully develop their effectiveness in a holistic sense, therefore, need to become highly competent in areas such as business understanding, organizational development and systems thinking.

Questions you might ask yourself in relation to CPD include:

- What mechanisms do I employ to benchmark the range and stage of development I have reached in the skills I need?
- Which skills do I most need to practise and how do I do so legitimately without lessening the quality of interventions with clients?
- How well developed are my big-picture skills – for example, how well do I understand the system in which my clients operate?

## CPD dilemmas and paradoxes

In essence, each person's CPD outcomes and challenges will be unique – as are his or her personality, context, experience, aptitude, attitude and skill levels. Effective CPD, therefore, needs to be tailored and fitted to each person pursuing it. Megginson and Whitaker (2004) discuss the many paradoxes and dilemmas that a person might face in relation to CPD. They list seven, which we have presented in Figure 12.3 as a set of continuums.

**FIGURE 12.3** CPD continuum

| | |
|---|---|
| Compulsion _____ | Voluntarism |
| Employer responsibility _____ | Individual responsibility |
| Teaching _____ | Learning |
| Personal development _____ | Organizational learning |
| Life purpose _____ | Life experience |
| Values-driven development _____ | Pragmatic development |
| Journey _____ | Exploration |

We would suggest there is no 'correct' place to be on the scales in Figure 12.3, simply a 'profile' that is most appropriate for individuals. We might invite the coach to reflect on his or her current phase of development and judge where he or she is on each dimension. We might invite the coach to look at the scales again and draw up the profile that he or she would like to have in a year's time. Such simple exercises offer the opportunity for practitioners to reflect on their current attitudes and how they see themselves changing over time.

The first dilemma is based on whether CPD needs to be compulsory or is better as a voluntary activity. The latter choice has a number of potential motivational advantages, including student willingness and more targeted choice-making on topics that really engage learners. On the other hand, sometimes people need a prod to get going, and organizations or professional bodies can provide this. A combination of organizational or professional body CPD requirements in tandem with tailored personal development plans is one way to overcome this dilemma.

To whom should primary responsibility for CPD fall? It is sometimes argued that organizations, particularly ones aspiring to exemplify learning organizations, have a responsibility to ensure that employees complete CPD and that resources should be provided for this purpose. Writers have suggested that CPD should be an element of a modern 'psychological contract' between employee and employer (Herriott, 1995). However, unless ultimate ownership rests with the employee, there is no guarantee that passion and commitment are ignited initially or sustained over time. Some form of joint ownership of the process is probably an ideal outcome, although this depends on the parties concerned.

A further choice relates to whether CPD is seen as extra training or becomes more of a lifelong learning journey. Training courses are obvious and generally easy to access sources of CPD. However, training courses, while readily available and temptingly easy to access, may not on their own be the most useful or appropriate source of CPD experience available. Most courses and skill development activities are not life-changing events. Perhaps longer and more 'blended' programmes including a mix of academic work, personal development and work experience opportunities might be more appropriate, if not so easy to book onto.

It is possible to treat CPD as an isolated and highly focused activity aimed at simply providing personal growth, but undertaking it in conjunction with organizational learning strategies and organizational development often makes the process much more effective. Viewing CPD as an integral mechanism for achieving life goals and consolidating life experience often provides significant enhancement and depth of meaning, but linking this to an organizational context may provide a more immediately practical framework.

CPD activity can often result from personal reflection on core values and can help to ground development activities within key personal principles. However, focusing on contextual issues is often critical to making real progress, since development without context is often unhelpful by way of results. Seeking non-theoretical data such as personal feedback or making meaning of experiences – Chris Argyris's Model II learning (Argyris, 1991) is generally accepted to increase learning effectiveness and therefore may accelerate or deepen personal growth and effectiveness. Considering both personal values and pragmatic opportunities for development is important in a CPD process.

Many metaphors can be used to describe development. It can be viewed as a journey, where there is a destination and the challenge is to find one's way towards it. Alternatively, development can be viewed as exploration of an individual's endless potential. Like a journey, this involves going somewhere but the final destination is probably unknown. Goals for exploration, therefore, can be looser, wider and harder to define. Utilizing both metaphors of development and seeing the CPD process as both a journey and an exploratory activity will more likely permit meaningful and pragmatic goals to be developed, more clearly defined outcomes to be acknowledged and overall success to be evaluated more effectively.

A good starting point in reviewing and strengthening your CPD activity might be to ponder your own responses to the alternatives presented above. Even better, share your insights with someone else such as a supervisor, the benefits of which are explored in the next section.

## Supervision – who coaches the coach?

One of the most effective ways coaches can engage in CPD activity is through entering into a one-to-one arrangement for themselves. For some readers this may entail hiring someone directly as a coach to explore and enhance personal growth and development through being assisted with the identification of issues and development planning. For others, particularly those who already have a portfolio of coachees with whom they have an ongoing relationship, this will entail engaging a supervisor. In using this term, we would distinguish it from simply entering into a coaching arrangement. We mean hiring someone who can help coaches deconstruct their coaching relationships and the challenges and dilemmas they entail, with a view to identifying the strengths the coaches bring to coaching and identifying the development areas that regular practice invariably throws up.

For a very good 'state of the art' discussion about coaching supervision we recommend a paper prepared in 2006 for the UK CIPD Conference, available from the CIPD website. It defines coaching supervisions as 'a structured formal process for coaches, with the help of a coaching supervisor, to attend to improving the quality of their coaching, grow their coaching capacity and support themselves and their practice. Supervision should also be a source of organizational learning' (Hawkins and Schwenk, 2006).

Demand for coaching supervision is on the rise for three reasons. First, at a personal level, coaches increasingly want to improve their effectiveness and results. Organizations hiring coaches increasingly see supervision as a means of maximizing the impact of coaching initiatives, and will, we predict, employ the use of a supervisor as a test for choosing between potential coaches. Research has showed that 88 per cent of organizations believe coaching should be supervised (Hawkins and Schwenk, 2006). Accrediting bodies, while not yet able to insist on supervision, are united in their view that it is an essential mechanism in good professional practice.

A second reason is that supervision is an important element for both relatively new coaches and accomplished veterans, even though the subject matter discussed between coach and supervisor might vary depending on the coach's level of experience. Regardless of capability levels, every coach will benefit from the increased self-awareness, better decision-making options and enhanced autonomy that effective supervision can offer.

Finally, for many coaches, including ourselves, there is an important point about living out personal values. If we are selling ourselves as people who can enhance personal growth and effectiveness in others, we need to take on board the fact that we should be practising what we preach. Since growth is a lifelong journey with no obvious end, there is always something to be developed, and good supervision will bring this out of even the most accomplished individuals. Indeed they are even more likely in our experience to embrace supervision as they understand more deeply how facilitated reflection is more helpful than simply personal review.

One of the main barriers in the past has been the difficulty in finding a qualified coaching supervisor. Today, there are a number of places where coaches can go to find supervisors, and increasingly courses are springing up to teach supervision skills.

However, one-to-one arrangements with a qualified supervisor, while highly effective, are not the only way to achieve guided reflection. Coaches in our experience are increasingly coming together in action learning groups to share their experience and to develop together. These groups may be led by a qualified supervisor, but for people who are used to an action learning format and disciplines, we believe that this is a desirable but not necessary arrangement. Many coaches have developed informal arrangements with 'buddies', often people whom they have met through taking coaching courses – they arrange regular meetings or phone calls to coach each other, with consequent benefits for both. Often these arrangements arise as a result of an in-house coaching programme.

The principle we would suggest is that every coach should accept a personal imperative for guided reflection. While individual arrangements may vary as a result of issues such as supervisor availability, geography or personal comfort levels, we all benefit from facilitated review in the same way that we strive to persuade our clients that they will do likewise.

## *Effective supervision practices*

'Supervision is an opportunity to bring someone back to their own mind, to show them how good they can be' (Kline, 1999). Most of the practices that we use as coaches can be applied to the field of supervision. So whether you are choosing a possible supervisor, setting rules of engagement for peer meetings, or seeking to enhance your own skills to coach other coaches, some of the competencies you may wish to develop include the following. (Several of the other chapters in this book give a fuller description of supervision, as well as offering different approaches to the supervision process.)

## Preparation

Prepare thoughtfully for the session, removing any 'debris' from other activities and getting ready to fully attend to your 'client'. Help colleagues to prepare likewise, particularly if they are in the role of being supervised.

## Contracting

Be clear about your 'rules of engagement', mutual responsibilities and boundaries. Remember the paramount need to build a relationship based on mutual understanding and undertake activities to build this.

## Coaching discussions

Be authentic and true to your own values while genuinely seeking to understand where colleague(s) are coming from. Listen to words and underlying feelings, paying close attention to noticing body language and tone – often the value is in bringing out the unconscious elements of a story. Help to agree and provide a minimal level of structure, and be prepared to review discussions at a process as well as content level.

Try to pitch your own input at the appropriate developmental level of the other party(ies), while offering input that is stretching. Stand ready to share your own insights and experience sparingly but mainly encouraging the other party(ies) to use their own reflections for growth. Encourage story-telling, visualization and other creative mechanisms for encouraging coachee resourcefulness. See the other person(s) as resourceful and creative and show this in your approach to discussions.

Give and receive feedback with empathy and humility, trying to suspend judgement where possible. Aim to understand the 'whole system' of the coachee while also maintaining a systemic perspective of the conversation taking place. Hold a systemic view of the whole process and be able to switch to and from different parts of the system appropriately.

## Review

Routinely review learning, process and contracting issues at regular intervals, at least once per session. Regularly review other learning options – reading material, web resources, contingent ideas and models that may support further development for either (any) party.

# Building knowledge systematically but cheaply

Any time spent in the personal development section of a modern bookshop, far less the Amazon search facility (nearly 11,000 results for 'coaching books') will confirm that the body of information about coaching grows exponentially from year to year. The real skill of the CPD practitioner is to learn how best to extract the required knowledge from all the information available. We are able to use the web, via Google or You Tube, to deliver myriad 'bite size' morsels of knowledge about any or all aspects of coaching. Many of us tap in regularly to coaching blogs or join communities of interest via LinkedIn or other sources. In thinking about building knowledge for CPD, therefore, it seems there is no likelihood of deficiency on the supply side!

They key question for coaches is how much of this knowledge they are tapping into, and to what end. It is all too easy to fall into a habit of 'grazing aimlessly' at the variety of temptations on offer, either as they occur opportunistically or in pursuit of knowledge needed for a particular task, person, situation, etc. We believe the secret of effective CPD knowledge-building is to do so purposefully and in a reasonably systematic manner. This means knowing essentially four things:

1 What is your current level of knowledge, set against some worthwhile framework?

2 What would represent a well rounded body of knowledge of coaching issues at your stage of development?

3 Where can reliable and well validated sources of new knowledge be found?

4 How can you record, or possibly demonstrate, the knowledge you have acquired in a way that facilitates lifelong development of accumulated resources?

More useful, therefore, than another list of recommended coaching books or other sources, which would by definition be partial and idiosyncratic, might be the following four-step process that you can adapt for your own purposes.

## Step 1

Undertake a knowledge audit of your current situation in relation to coaching assignments you are involved with. Use the following categories as a guide to thinking about what criteria are important to your success, and add your own criteria if these are not appropriate. Use the criteria to rate your current capability out of a maximum of 10:

- knowledge of appropriate coaching models (GROW; OSCAR, Learning styles, Cognitive Behavioural Coaching , motivational interviewing, etc);
- knowledge of contextual background (personality issues, sector issues, organization issues, 'political' issues, etc);
- self-knowledge (influencing style, learning style, emotional intelligence quotient, listening skills, bias factors, etc).

## Step 2

Identify the two or three areas of knowledge that would be most likely to materially enhance your ability to deal confidently, knowledgeably and effectively with key assignments.

## Step3

Identify potential sources of information – books, journals, Googling, You Tube, other people, coachees, etc. Work out the knowledge you need from the information available.

## Step 4

Put together a brief development plan to address gaps you have identified. Headings might include:

- What I am going to learn?
- The benefits of doing so.
- The actions I will take.
- Possible barriers.
- Review mechanism and date.

# Accreditation and qualifications

An obvious route to both review existing capabilities and to extend these capabilities in a programmed way is to gain coaching qualifications or accreditation to suitable awarding bodies. Clearly this is, in the main, more expensive than the DIY option explored in the previous section.

However, it has the potential to add significant value to your coaching practice for the following reasons.

The end result will be useful as CPD, but may also have added benefits such as commercial or career ones. Any good accrediting body will have had to set externally validated standards for its programmes, so you can be fairly sure that you are building a portfolio that meets most professional standards or client requirements.

You are going to be able, in most such courses, to learn new knowledge and to practise applying this in informal but observed settings, and the resulting feedback will give you not only a benchmark of the way you apply models, interpersonal skills and so on, but insightful and invaluable feedback about your personal style, attitude, habits and blind spots. As a result it should enable you to build your capabilities in a holistic and comprehensive way.

## What is on offer?

Unlike other professions, such as counselling, psychotherapy and accountancy, coaching is not currently regulated by legislation. This is partly because it is a relatively new profession and some of the infrastructure that surrounds other professions has yet to 'catch up'. It is also true that there is significant diversity of types of coaching (business coaching, life coaching, sports coaching, etc) and in approaches used by coaches. This results in difficulty finding any objective and widely agreed definition of 'best practice', an assertion borne out in a recent research paper on experience in Norway (Svaleng and Grant, 2010). As a result, a bewildering and ever growing number of organizations offer qualifications and accreditation in various aspects of coaching.

So how do you find your way through the maze? The route for a new profession from pioneers through to professionalization is a well trodden one, and it seems that the coaching profession will follow a similar process to the one already experienced by the counselling profession. In the early stages specific training was limited, sporadic and somewhat idiosyncratic, although as the sector has grown a much larger and now quite comprehensive range of short courses has been developed in response to identified needs from the field. Trade bodies have been formed, including the Association for Coaching, the International Coach Federation, the Association of Professional Executive Coaching and Supervision, and the European Mentoring and Coaching Council (UK). There are also more specific discipline-related bodies such as the BPS

Special Group in Coaching Psychology and the Society for Coaching Psychologists. These bodies have started to recognize and recommend private providers. A number of universities are now offering qualifications-based training including coaching at undergraduate, Master's and doctoral level. Such courses are likely to form the main route to qualifications as coaching emerges into a profession, with commissioning managers expecting coaches to have a Master's or equivalent level qualification.

## *Making the right choice*

The qualifications offered by providers vary significantly in duration, learning formats, specialist sectors or coaching approaches, assessment and learning methods and, most important, fees. So it is well worth undertaking the initial analysis offered in the previous section to avoid making a wrong and expensive choice. Questions might include:

- Why is accreditation important, and is it important enough to justify the investment of time and money? The investment of time, effort and money should not be underestimated in gaining a coaching qualification such as an MSc, so it makes sense to have very clear personal goals for doing so.

- What kind of qualifications are needed for the work you are hoping to secure now and in the future? For example, is a postgraduate degree important or are you satisfied with a professional accreditation from one of the various membership bodies such as the Association for Coaching?

- What kind of teaching or learning input do you most value? You will find a range of different delivery mechanisms such as distance learning, webinar, face-to-face (classroom or one-to-one), guided reading or tele-conferencing, often offered in combination. Support mechanisms offered include e-mail-based, telephone support, peer networks and one-to-one supervision.

- How would you prefer to be assessed? You can choose between portfolio accumulated coaching hours, live observation, telephone interviewing, written assignments and 360-degree feedback mechanisms. Again these are often offered in combination.

- How much time and effort are you prepared to invest or is your employer prepared to offer you? Programmes range in duration from around three months to two years, and face-to-face hours vary between 10 and over 100.

## *Taking action*

Finally, having undertaken a personal needs assessment and done your homework on how these needs could best be met, you have to undertake the most difficult bit – getting started. The tips below are included to help you make progress on your CPD without falling into the many traps that can get in the way of doing so.

### 1. Make a resolution

In almost every practical respect, CPD is a discretionary activity. Unless you are specifically studying for a qualification or need to demonstrate evidence of CPD for career, employment or marketing reasons, no one is going to push you to do it. What is more, if you don't plan to take some action your time will inevitably fill up with activities that may or may not be beneficial to your development. So you need to make a decision to push yourself. Activities you can sensibly undertake to give you the impetus you need include the following:

- Make a list of the benefits to you of being able to demonstrate CPD activity. Include personal, organizational and commercial benefits.
- Make a list of learning experiences you have had over the past six months. List the skills you have acquired, the 'aha moments' when an incident has made you really review the way you do things, and the areas of knowledge you have picked up. If the list is substantial, start to classify it and write it down, and you are on your way. If you are struggling to think of anything meaningful in any of these areas, use that as a spur to make CPD a more systematic and planned process in your working life.
- Visualize yourself in three to five years' time. What role are you in? What capabilities are being called on? What could you do now, thoughtfully, to make sure your vision or dreams are realized? What else could you do?

### 2. Make an assessment

As a coach, how effective are you in various areas – personal style and skills, range of approaches to assignments, understanding of key models, commercial or sector acumen, effectiveness feedback from clients? As a quick check on how satisfied you are with your current impact, rate each area on a scale of 1 to 10. If the results are less than eight, you have just started to work out where you could spend some CPD time. If they are higher than eight, congratulations – but how are you going to ensure that you stay at this level?

You may want to become more systematic in how you approach self-assessment as a coach. If so, you could log on to coach improvement organizations like Bullseye Coaching (**www.bullseye-coaching.com**), where you can find systems that enable you to track the ROI you are delivering at a number of levels via reports incorporating direct feedback from clients.

## 3. Make a plan

Hopefully the two previous questions have helped you to identify the specific CPD needs that would be of most benefit currently if you were to address them more systematically. The next step is to identify some learning goals arising from these needs, perhaps using a similar format to the personal development plan described earlier in this chapter. Ask yourself questions such as:

- How much time can I devote to this area?
- What budget considerations do I have to take into account?
- Where can I validate my first thoughts?
- What kind of support would be most valuable – Boss? Peers? External? Academic? Skills-based?
- What kind of input do I need for each goal – reading material, feedback, personal exploration, 'safe' practice time, etc?

The answers to all of these questions will give you a strong initial 'steer' on how you should be targeting your CPD activities.

## 4. Develop some structure

CPD is about reflective learning, based on a distillation of your experience – but remember the two things are different and often separate in time and place. Many people fail to get the most from their experience by omitting to make notes about what happened, their reflections and the lessons they learnt or learning opportunities they identified. While it can be helpful to do this with a third party who can prompt with questions and comments, you can easily get started on your own with a bit of organization.

Start a diary, create a file on your PC or put one together physically; develop a task reminder in your e-mail calendar that prompts you to create some regular reflection time. Basically, do whatever works for

**TABLE 12.1** List of activities

| Development Goal | Options | Ranking by Value to Me | Action |
|---|---|---|---|
| 1 Better use of coaching frameworks | Reading | 4 | Read book on OSCAR model |
| | Coaching/ Supervision | 2 | Explore local supervision options |
| | Web research | 5 | Google GROW model |
| | Peer support | 1 | Start action learning set |
| | Client feedback | 3 | Ask clients |
| | Take course | 6 | |
| | Consider accreditation | 7 | |
| 2. Develop personal influencing style | Coaching/ Supervision | 4 | Explore local supervision options |
| | Peer support | 3 | Undertake 360-degree feedback exercise |
| | Client feedback | 5 | Ask clients |
| | Take course | 1 | Research options |
| | Consider accreditation | 2 | Contact coaching association |

you. The chances are you are already undertaking CPD, but may not be approaching it in a structured enough way to get the benefits.

It is more important to demonstrate what you have done and how it adds to your capabilities than it is to record how many hours you have completed. However, creating a habit is helpful in ensuring regular updating, so try to make a small amount of time to do this regularly (say fortnightly or monthly) rather than leave it for months between reflections. And don't forget to think about opportunistic events such as a meeting that you were really happy with, as well as more planned events such as courses, etc.

The CIPD website, **www.cipd.co.uk**, has a good CPD resource online for members, but also offers some ready-made templates that you can adopt or amend for your own purposes even as a non-member.

### 5. Make a list of activities

Based on the work you have done, list the possible options you could employ to enhance your development. Completing a simple structure such as the one shown in Table 12.1, or your own version, may help you to get started.

As you build the portfolio of options, notice the ones that overlap and consider whether there is any sensible order in which to start.

### 6. Just do it!

Take action. Make reflection time. Start your record keeping. But most important, get going, start to create habits and don't forget to celebrate your successes.

## Summary

It should be apparent from reading this chapter that there are many benefits and relatively few drawbacks to undertaking CPD activities and record keeping. For some readers, the key may be to undertake a benefits analysis. For others, you may simply reflect that you could be better at making regular space to record achievements for the last period and development goals for the next one. Some people may be stimulated to widen their thinking, others to stop thinking about it and just do it.

To summarize the key points we have tried to make. First, CPD is important, personally, professionally and commercially – and only likely to become more so as the coaching profession matures and begins to become regulated, while clients become ever more sophisticated and savvy about engaging coaches. Second, CPD is highly personal, and can be highly eclectic in nature. Practitioners are limited only by their imagination in terms of developing options, mechanisms and plans.

Use some discrimination – do not simply jump at the first workshop opportunity that is e-mailed to you because you can't wait to get started or you are feeling guilty at having missed out. Take some time to make some plans and undertake some analysis, not forgetting to simply write down what you have been 'accidentally' doing in the last few months.

Finally, CPD is a self-development activity, yet one of the paradoxes of self-development is that it is best done with support from other people. That way you are not trapped in your own perception of the world, neither are you limited by only having your own views of a way forward. Ask yourself who else can help you to sharpen your practice – and equally, how you might help colleagues to do likewise.

We recently came across a story about a good lesson on getting started with a course of action. The storyteller had a niece who had just finished college and was looking for her first professional job. When asked what she wanted to do, she said she didn't know. Then she smiled and said she didn't need to know. All she needed to know was what she was going to do *first*. We would urge the same about CPD – make a start!

## References

Argyris, C (1991) Teaching smart people how to learn, *Harvard Business Review*, 69, 3, May–June, 99–108

Gibb, S and Megginson, D (1999) Employee development in Commercial and General Union, (eds) T Redman and A Wilkinson, *Contemporary Human Resource Management*, pp 161–63, Pearson, Harlow

Hawkins, P and Schwenk, G (2006) *Change Agenda. Coaching supervision – maximising the potential of coaching*, CIPD, London

Herriott, P (1995) The management of careers, in (ed) S Tyson, *Strategic Prospects for Human Resource Management*, pp 184–205, CIPD, London

Kline, N (1999) *Time to Think: Listening to ignite the human mind,* Cassell Illustrated, London

Megginson, D and Whitaker, V (2004) *Continuing Professional Development,* CIPD, London

Palmer, S and Whybrow, A (2007) *The Handbook of Coaching Psychology,* Routledge, Hove

Passmore, J (2006) *Excellence in Coaching*, Kogan Page, London

Svaleng, I and Grant, A M (2010) Lessons from the Norwegian coaching industry's attempt to develop joint coaching standards: an ACCESS pathway to a mature coaching industry, *The Coaching Psychologist*, 6, 1, June

# Creative approaches to continuous development

## 13

**ANNE DAVIDSON AND DALE SCHWARZ**

## Introduction

Developing ourselves as coaches is a complex process. It goes to the very core of who we are and the values and talents that led us to enter this profession. And the more accepted and credible we become for the valuable work we do with individuals and organizations, the more is demanded of us. Most of us are challenged to continually expand our repertoire of skills and techniques so that we may go deeper with ourselves and then further with our clients. We believe that a key part of every coach's expanding skill set is to learn to work with creative processes that engage multiple modalities and incorporate the latest learning and research.

In this chapter we explain our rationale for using creative processes to help you do your own inner work. We believe each of us must start with his- or herself; only then can we consistently model the very transformative processes we ask of our clients; only then can we be completely present with coachees as authentic, trustworthy and wise guides. We illustrate some of the primary processes we use by providing two exercises to address an issue that frequently arises when coaching: the voice of the inner critic. The same approaches we advocate to help you do your own inner work are easily adaptable for working with other coaches and, in many cases, your clients. We encourage you to try the exercises yourself and then creatively adapt them for your own purposes using the guidelines for designing interventions at the end of the chapter.

# The value of using creative approaches

We believe that fully meeting the needs of our clients means developing our whole selves: mind, body and spirit. We must engage in and mirror the same creative process that is at the heart of innovation, personal change and organizational development. As we train coaches from around the globe in our facilitative coach methodology, we find that most of us can deepen our own development and the effectiveness of our work with coachees by engaging a wider range of learning modalities, or 'multiple ways of knowing'. These are often referred to as 'creative approaches' because they frequently go beyond logical, rational analysis and dialogue. Many draw from the expressive arts of visualization, writing, body movement, music and the practice of ritual and celebration, but applied in a very purposeful, results-oriented manner. They are used to help us get to the heart of issues and obstacles that can be difficult to access and verbalize. They produce a real, in-the-moment experience that can rapidly shift a mindset and open expanded possibilities. Here we highlight two important aspects of using creative processes: accessing the adaptive unconscious and working with preferred and less-preferred learning styles.

## 1. Accessing the adaptive unconscious

Most of us have followed a cognitive, rational model of learning. Modern society and our educational system generally emphasize logical, analytical, conscious thought. In the process of this education and through our early psychological responses to life's situations, we tend to under-develop or cut off a large part of our brain's capacity. Neuroscientists tell us, in fact, that cognitive, rational processing uses only a small portion of our brain (Szegedy-Maszak, 2005). Underneath this rational brain we have layers of unconscious awareness that process our feelings and sensations. What psychologists refer to as the 'adaptive unconscious' drives many of our internal processes, including feelings, emotions, how we deal with real or imagined danger, initiate actions and set goals. It is also the source of the intuitive intelligence that allows us to recognize seemingly unrelated patterns, develop creative solutions, work with metaphors and images, and to 'know without knowing why'.

If you have ever found yourself overreacting to a situation, losing your temper, or getting emotionally grabbed (and who among us has not?), you are experiencing some of the power of the adaptive unconscious. Wilson (2002) shows from his research on the adaptive unconscious that we develop unconscious traits and tendencies that are like habits, ingrained because we practise them over and over. Wilson argues that trying to introspectively, rationally determine the unconscious motives and 'stories' that drive much of our behaviour is not productive. He found that much of what people say about their feelings and attitudes is misleading because they focus on reasons that come to mind but that might not reflect the truth behind their feelings. They filter the intuitive, adaptive unconscious through the rational mind and, in the process, distort what is actually going on.

Many coaching breakthroughs are achieved by using exercises and techniques that bypass the rational mind. Visual expression, body awareness and reflective writing are some of these. Other breakthroughs come from working directly with the rational mind by exploring our deeply held values and beliefs through inquiry, cognitive reflection and dialogue. Much of our coaching focus is tapping into wisdom that resides outside of most people's daily awareness. We know that in both rational and intuitive thinking our deeply held values, beliefs, assumptions and fears frequently function like invisible operating systems that drive our behaviour.

No one way is right. Research in human intelligence clearly points to weaknesses in both intuitive and rational decision making (Myers, 2007). More often than not, work done in several modalities, when combined, achieves more effective results. To be comfortable integrating multiple approaches with clients, we see it as essential that coaches work with themselves and each other, using multi-sensory exercises like the ones included in this chapter. More detail is offered in our earlier work, *Facilitative Coaching: A toolkit for expanding your repertoire and achieving lasting results* (Schwarz and Davidson, 2009) and *The Skilled Facilitator Fieldbook* (Schwarz *et al*, 2005). We suggest you choose one exercise or modality, test it with a colleague, integrate it into practice with a few clients, capture your learning, and then move to another.

## 2. Working with learning styles

In our experience, the most productive way to work with the values and beliefs that hold the seeds of unfulfilled possibilities or that create problematic obstacles is to change modalities or ways of knowing. There are many models of human intelligence or information processing. These include, for example, research on left- and right-brain processing and The Myers-Briggs Type Indicator, which present models of distinct ways of taking in and processing information (Myers and McCaulley, 1985). Gardner (1999) suggests that we have at least seven different forms of intelligence: linguistic, logical-mathematical, spatial, bodily-kinaesthetic, musical, interpersonal and intrapersonal. More recently, Medina's work (2008) on 'brain rules' highlights practical learning applications of some of the current neuroscience research. He emphasizes the importance of stimulating multiple senses, engaging the emotions and visualizing concepts. His view from his research is that 'vision trumps all other senses'.

Obviously, psychologists and researchers do not agree about how to describe human intelligence. The human brain is still one of the greatest frontiers known – or unknown – to mankind. Yet we all know from our own school experiences and from watching the growth and development of children, colleagues and friends that we have different ways of understanding and interacting with the world. Most of us seem to have a small set of preferred modalities or preferences that we gravitate to when we seek to learn something new or change our behaviour. These become habits of the mind that serve us well and help us use our natural gifts. At the same time, our preferences can blind us to valuable information that is more easily accessed in other ways.

Our experience is that coaches can use multiple ways of knowing to work with learning styles in two significant ways. First, in early work with yourself or a client, it is helpful to make at least an informal assessment of preferred learning style(s) and to use that information in initially exploring issues. You can get at this by simply asking, 'When I learn something new, how do I prefer to learn it? Do I like to read about it? To watch someone else do it? To have a list of steps or to explore freely? Does it help me to hear the information first or read it first?' Answers might guide you to start with visualizing, diagramming or mind-mapping an issue or exercise before trying to work step-by-step or talking it through.

Second, many substantive breakthroughs come from intentionally using modalities that engage less-preferred learning styles. Many times we find thinking-dominant individuals have incredible breakthroughs by visualizing an issue and creating a simple stick-figure drawing or symbol to represent what came up. We might have got to the same issue through dialogue, but often it would take much longer. This is true in part because the less preferred modalities frequently unearth 'buried treasure' from the adaptive unconscious.

We encourage you, in your coaching role, to master a variety of techniques that access multiple ways of knowing and being. We think that the more fluid you are in moving among ways of making sense of your own human experience, the more you will grow and the more you can help your clients move into the purposeful, creative action that is best for them. At a minimum, you will develop awareness of your own potential biases toward using your preferred modalities rather than working through your clients' learning preferences. Exploring this territory is also a way to build your own creativity. As practitioners we continue to develop our professional expertise by discovering new ways to use a wide variety of exercises and approaches. Carl's story (below) illustrates how this worked when Anne was training a new coach.

## CASE STUDY 1  Carl

Anne worked with Carl to train him to coach leaders in his organization. Carl had a tendency to jump to problem-solving prematurely with and for coachees. Anne discussed this issue with Carl and modelled options for him to handle issues in a more curious and exploratory way. She also helped him follow up with clients after sessions to track the results and consequences of his coaching. In several situations it became clear that Carl had encouraged the coachee to move to solutions before an issue was clearly defined or to work on a symptom rather than uncover root causes of obstacles. Still Carl's pattern of jumping to solutions did not change.

Carl is a very linear, rational thinker, and Anne had worked with him using similar modalities. Finally, she suggested to Carl that there might be some unidentified barrier or obstacle making it difficult for him to hold back on solving problems for coachees. She asked if he would be willing to explore that possibility using some of his less preferred ways of knowing, like guided imagery, drawing and reflective writing. 'That seems too touchy-feely,' was Carl's first response. Anne offered that this would just be an experiment to see if using a less-preferred modality would uncover something new. She shared experiences of other coaches who had found the approach useful, even though it was not their preference. 'If this works,' said Anne, 'that will be helpful. If not, we will both learn what did not work, and we can explore other options.'

Carl agreed to try an experiment. Anne led him through a guided imagery that helped him get in touch with how he coached and collaborated with others when he felt most successful. She asked him to recreate one experience in detail, to notice his body (how centred he was, where he was holding tension, energy movement), to notice feelings and visual images that arose. Then she asked Carl to sketch a symbol or image that represented visually what arose. Carl drew a big yellow sun illuminating the centre of a complex set of lines. Next Anne led Carl through a guided imagery that recreated one of the times when he jumped to problem-solving and when the client later told him this was not effective. Carl noted that in recreating this experience, he felt his chest collapse and his stomach tense. He drew a dark cloud. He spent a few minutes in reflective writing about the contrast between his two symbols: when he was effective, he was helping to shed light on complex issues and problems. When he was ineffective, Carl felt this dark cloud of pressure on his head – pressure to succeed, pressure to be right. He was turned in on himself, not present with the client, and just wanted to solve the problem and move on.

In subsequent discussion about Carl's drawing and writing, he recognized a lifelong pattern of putting pressure on himself to 'have all the answers'. He connected it to early experiences of trying to meet high demands from parents and teachers and frequently feeling he fell short. In a new learning situation, all the tension of trying to 'get it right' and produce results created a mindset for Carl that caused him to work with clients in a way that produced just the opposite.

Using guided imagery, body awareness, visual expression and reflective writing allowed Anne and Carl to uncover this pattern and discuss it in less than an hour. Carl's awareness of this pattern (and of the physical tension that indicated he was falling into it) almost immediately shifted his coaching style. Something we had spent hours trying to shift through dialogue and observational feedback changed in just one session through using interventions that could bypass his defences and rationalizations to work with rich data held in the adaptive unconscious.

# Creative approaches for working with our inner critic

We'd like to more completely illustrate how creative processes that engage multiple ways of knowing can aid your development by addressing a specific issue that frequently arises: dealing with our 'inner critic' – that negative voice that harshly judges our actions and effectiveness. It takes us away from being fully present with our clients and distracts us from addressing challenging issues that would help us and/or our clients resolve obstacles. Below is a brief explanation, followed by two exercises you can use for self-coaching and for coaching others.

## Our inner critic began as a coping strategy

Our critical voice results from early shaming or humiliating and from fear-based experiences instilled by authority figures (parents, teachers, religious leaders) or by older children and/or peers. For example, shame or humiliation can result from being reprimanded or laughed at in a classroom for responding with an incorrect answer to a teacher's question. We internalize these negative messages about ourselves and replay them in our minds. The inner critic evolves as a creative coping strategy in response to these early experiences. We criticize ourselves as a pre-emptive measure to avoid public criticism and humiliation. We also develop the critic as a way of acclimatizing ourselves to the prevailing culture. Early on, our critic enables us to cope with and survive difficult situations.

Basically the underlying message of the inner critic is, 'You are not acceptable or worthy as you are.' The outcome is generally distress and suffering. Our critical, fearful inner voice is the basis for much of our ineffective behaviour. It is often the trigger that sends us into a downward spiral of unilateral control, fear-based choices and inappropriate rescuing or persecuting of others. (For models of the specific ways we behave when we get triggered by our inner critic, see Schwarz and Davidson, 2009.)

## From inner critic to compassion

When our inner critic rears its head, our experience is painful and distracting. The good news is that by addressing our inner critic, we can develop our compassion for ourselves and for others. Compassion is the antidote to the inner critic. By compassion we mean developing the ability to suspend judgement of ourselves and others, appreciating that each of us makes choices based on the information and skills we have at any given time. Compassion is about appreciating that our own struggles and those of others are a natural part of the human condition while at the same time holding ourselves and others accountable for our choices. Effective coaches are not harsh critics of themselves or stern judges of others. At the same time, we refrain from using past choices as excuses for behaving ineffectively in the present. Often it is easier to act compassionately towards others. It can be more challenging to be genuinely compassionate towards ourselves. Yet only when we become truly compassionate towards ourselves can we fully extend compassion to others.

**FIGURE 13.1** A client depicts the aspects of her inner critic

Though it may seem counter-intuitive, the critical part of us is actually our ally in this process. The critical voice is a reminder that we can shift from judgement to compassion. We can notice how and why we criticize ourselves so that we reframe how we approach certain issues. It is possible that a hidden talent resides behind the 'I am no good at this' or 'I can't do this' messages. Many people discover previously unknown aspects of creative ability once they learn to address the inner critic appropriately.

When the inner critic arises, we can listen and make a choice about how much power and attention we will give that part of ourselves. We can also identify any useful, valid information our inner critic may have for us. Gradually, by paying attention to our inner critic in this way, its strength diminishes. Each time we hear the inner critic's voice we can acknowledge it and make a choice for compassion. Getting to know and making peace with your inner critic is a continuous, often uncomfortable process. Yet in this way we develop the ability to further empower ourselves and embrace compassion. We begin to move more quickly through the cycle of acknowledging, choosing, and then releasing that part of ourselves. Figure 13.1 illustrates how one of our clients began using visual expression to understand and make peace with her critic.

**CASE STUDY 2**   Dale

Dale was visited by her inner critic while preparing to lead an important event. To release herself from the grip of her inner critic she made a series of three drawings (Figures 13.2 to 13.4). Here is her story.

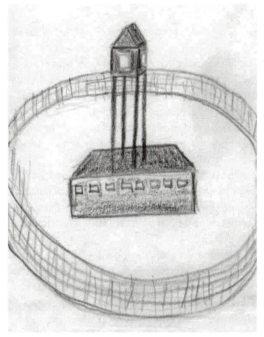

Figure 13.2
Dale's critic as prison guard tower

Figure 13.3
*Critic as ally sweeps away the crumbs*

Figure 13.4
*Dale's critic transformed: Bermuda Lighthouse*

I began walking myself through the same exercises that I frequently use with clients. I focused my attention on my bodily awareness and feelings. Then I summoned a visual image that resonated with these sensations, feelings and my inner critic. Instantly, I saw a picture of a prison guard tower and drew it in my sketchbook. The words, 'judge as prison guard tower' popped into my head. The drawing and words described precisely how I felt: 'I'm judging and imprisoning myself – blocking my creativity, productivity and excitement about this event.'

I asked myself, 'What can help me address the judge/inner critic?' An image formed in my mind's eye and I drew it, even though I didn't know how it connected to my question. Reflecting on the drawing, I wrote, 'The judge (my ally) arises, preparing me for the event. I am sweeping the hametz out from the corners. The hametz symbolizes that which ferments and doesn't serve my purpose.'

Sweeping bread crumbs, hametz, from the corners of the room is a Jewish ritual done in preparation for Passover. (As it happens, it was Passover. Though I've never done this practice, it was part of my adaptive unconscious.) Taking a moment for reflection, I felt the tension leave my body and self-compassion return. By befriending my inner critic, I'm on track, doing the necessary work of readying myself and clearing out what doesn't serve me.

Next, I invoked an image to anchor my shift in consciousness. I drew the Bermuda Lighthouse. I wrote, 'The prison guard tower transforms into the Bermuda Lighthouse.' This final picture was a celebration. I became the beaming lighthouse ready to shine.

# Befriending your inner critic

It is important to recognize that there is a distinction between the uncompassionate, judgmental inner critic and the analytical, evaluative function of the mind often referred to as the 'discerning mind'. The discerning mind is the thought process that enables us to distinguish and determine what we value, what we believe and what we deem important. The discerning mind provides us with useful judgements and thinking that help us make astute and clear decisions congruent with our purpose. It is the part of our mind that allows us to make a clear choice for compassion over unilateral judgement.

Talking directly with your inner critic helps you further investigate and learn about this aspect of yourself. By doing so, you take responsibility for your critical self. This can be advantageous when you (or your client) feel stuck or when you do not see progress towards a stated goal. After the inner critic is identified, conversations can take place between the discerning mind and the inner critic.

This dialogue can be expressed verbally or through writing, through visual expression or movement and through combinations of these and other modalities. The outcome of the exercises is to surface any valid information the critic may have; to gain some perspective, compassion and objectivity towards oneself; and to use the discerning mind to untangle and learn about any underlying beliefs that are obstacles to moving forward.

Rich rewards accrue when you can shift your inner critic into your ally and sit side by side with ease. We think addressing the critic is an important part of any coach's professional development so that we do not become triggered or distracted by a client challenging or questioning us or presenting an issue we are uncertain how to address. Below we provide two exercises proven in our practice to effectively address inner critic issues using the multiple ways of knowing and creative practices we described at the beginning of this chapter. We encourage you to test and adapt them to your own purposes and learning needs. The exercises include guided imageries that you can record in your own voice and play back to guide yourself.

# Inner critic exercises

## Exercise 1.
## Forming and conversing with your inner critic

*Purpose:* This exercise develops a concrete, objective form for the inner critic and generates learning about its qualities.

*When to use:*

- to identify the presence and qualities of the inner critic;

- to appreciate the ways the inner critic may interfere with effective coaching;

- to understand the impact of the inner critic on creative, purposeful action;

- to learn to treat the inner critic compassionately and as an ally in the development process.

*Time frame:* 10–12 minutes
*Materials:* Crayon, marker, blank paper, and/or plasticene modelling clay, blank paper and pen.

*Instructions*
Step 1: A brief guided imagery can help you visualize the inner critic's form. Here is a sample dialogue to guide yourself through this process, which includes body awareness and visualization. Remember to pause between each statement to allow time for observation and imaging:

> Get comfortable in your seat. Allow your eyes to close or cast them down. Notice your breath … Notice the rise and fall of your breath ….

> Notice where you sense the inner critic in your body. Bring your attention to your upper body, your head, … face, … neck … and shoulders. Now your arms and hands. Notice where the inner critic may be present. Now bring your attention to your torso, to your lungs, … your chest, … your belly. Notice if your inner critic lives in these places.

> And now scan your pelvis, … your upper legs, lower legs and feet. Notice where in your body you feel the presence of your inner critic. It is often the places of tension or stress.

Now let yourself begin picturing the inner critic's size. How much space does it take up? What is its' shape? What colour or colours is it? Notice its texture. If it moves, how does it move?

Now let an image, symbol, or picture come that reflects the inner critic. The image may or may not make sense to you. Capture its qualities and characteristics in any way that has meaning to you. It can be realistic or abstract. There is no right or wrong way to do this. Just let the inner critic emerge and come to life.

When you are ready open your eyes.

Step 2: Bring the inner critic to form by drawing your image of the critic or sculpting it with clay.

Step 3: Learn more about the inner critic with reflective writing. Ask the inner critic to write responses to the following questions:

- What do your form, colours, shape, texture say?

- What are your characteristics?

- Where did you come from?

- What do you want from me?

- How do you keep me stuck?

- How can you help me?

- What can you teach me?

Step 4: Conclude the exercise by asking yourself questions such as:

- What key insights did I gain from my responses to the questions?

- Were there other feelings or thoughts that came up for me as I brought form to my critic?

- How might my insights help me move forward?

## Exercise 2.
## Forming and conversing with your compassionate self

*Purpose:* This exercise develops a concrete, objective form for the compassionate self. It helps facilitate a shift away from the critical self by providing a clear contrast between the inner critic and the compassionate self. This is useful in developing self-caring, confidence and self-worth.

*When to use:*

- to identify the presence and qualities of the compassionate self;

- to appreciate and develop access to your compassion;

- to further develop a practice for shifting from inner critic to compassionate self;

- to develop appreciation for the usefulness of the compassionate self for creative, purposeful action.

*Time frame:* 10–12 minutes
*Materials:* Crayon, marker, blank paper, and/or plasticene modelling clay

*Instructions*
Step 1: Use a guided imagery like the one below to help you visualize a form for your compassionate self:

> Let yourself get comfortable in your seat. Allow your eyes to close or cast them down. Shake out your hands and wrists or make another movement to release tension. Notice your breath. Notice the rise and fall of your breath.

> Recall a time when you felt compassion towards someone or something. This could be a person, a creature, or situation in the world. Notice the sense of caring, respect and regard you feel. Notice where in your body you feel the presence of your compassion. It is often around the heart area, though you may experience it elsewhere. Place your hands where you feel this bodily connection with your compassionate self. Allow yourself to breathe deeply into this place and fully experience your compassion.

> As the strength and power of your compassion grow, allow yourself to turn this feeling and sensation towards yourself. Reflect towards yourself the compassion you offer others. Open your heart and offer your compassion to yourself and your own struggles, whatever they might be.

> Now let an image, symbol, or picture come to mind that reflects or resonates with this sense of compassion. Notice the shape, colour and texture of this image. The image may or may not make sense to you. Capture its qualities and character in any way that has meaning to you. It can be realistic or abstract. There is no right or wrong way to do this. Just let your compassion emerge and come to form.

Step 2: Bring your compassionate self into form by drawing it or sculpting it with clay.

Step 3: Ask yourself reflective questions like the ones below to learn more about the compassionate self. Respond verbally by sharing with someone or with reflective writing. Ask the image of your compassionate self to respond in first the person. (I ...). Ask:

- What do your form, colour(s), shape and texture say?

- What are your attributes?

- How can you help me?

- What can you teach me?

- How can I deepen my experience of you?

Step 4: Develop a practice to regularly reconnect with your compassion by placing your hands where you felt the bodily connection with your compassionate self. Then recall your compassion image. With a deep inhale and exhale of breath, acknowledge and celebrate that you reconnected with your compassionate self.

## Results from creatively engaging multiple modalities

Here are some of the results we achieve from using multiple ways of knowing to help ourselves and the coaches we train develop our abilities:

- *Deeper learning.* The more modalities we engage, the more likely we are to create a powerful, memorable experience that increases commitment to follow through on insights.

- *Improving communication and decision making.* More relevant information becomes available by clearly defining ideas and feelings, by contrasting them through visual metaphors, and by writing about and experimenting with issues.

- *Fostering innovative thinking.* By enabling ourselves and others to view a situation from a fresh perspective, we make new connections and generate creative ideas. By surfacing, reframing, or letting go of old stories and defensive routines, we free mental and emotional energy to work toward new possibilities.

- *Strengthening personal awareness and compassion.* The results of experiential and multi-sensory coaching interventions give us a deeper reflection of ourselves at a given moment in time. They exist outside of ourselves. Individuals can gain perspective, objectivity and acceptance about themselves through these approaches. Compassion towards self expands and leads to increased compassion towards others, particularly those we coach.

- *Increasing risk taking.* Creative techniques are an invitation to experiment and take manageable risks. When people take risks, the unexpected often emerges. Practice venturing into unknown territory and gaining new insights builds capacity for greater risk taking in other arenas, including taking risks in the service of an important dream or goal.

- *Moving towards, through, and beyond difficult and undiscussable issues*. We find that identifying difficult issues and working through them is more productive than avoiding them. But frequently issues that are not brought out into the open are poorly defined. Attached to such issues are unidentified feelings, unrecognized personal hot buttons and irrational fears growing out of previous experiences. They unconsciously lead us into ineffective thinking and behaviour. Interventions that access and more clearly identify the territory around difficult and undiscussable issues helps address them.

- *Building trust*. When we more truly know ourselves as coaches, we can show up with a level of authenticity that helps establish trust with our clients. Particularly when we have our own experiences of working with our adaptive unconscious and working in less preferred modalities, we can advocate credibly for doing this work while giving our coachees clear choices. We can speak about the validity and efficiency of using a particular modality without it coming across as flaky, vague or un-purposeful.

- *Developing professional competencies*. As coaching certifications become more common and specific coach competencies are clearly identified, it is evident that they emphasize many skills that are specifically developed by using an expanded repertoire of creative processes. For example, in the United States, the International Coach Federation specifically lists three competencies that our process develops efficiently: coaching presence, creating awareness and designing actions (including engaging the client to explore alternative ideas and solutions, promoting active experimentation and self-discovery and celebrating client successes).

## Designing your own interventions

Designing your own interventions is not only a way to customize your coaching of yourself and others, but it also keeps you in touch with your own creative process. The more you use your creative muscle, the stronger it will become. We believe that the more you expand your own creativity, the more curious and alive you will be and the more creative you can become with your clients. Here are some guidelines for creating interventions.

## Give yourself permission to create

There is no 'right' way to design interventions. Make them up. Most of your designs will serve their purpose. Sometimes they won't. The consequences are minimal. There will be something for you and your clients to learn from each intervention, and as long as you gain learning, you will progress.

## Mine your life experience

Ideas can come from anywhere. All that is required is to remain present with your life experiences and open to possibilities. If you read a great poem, see an inspiring movie, or observe a bird building a nest, think about how that might be useful.

## Use whatever is available

Many of the interventions we use require few props or materials. Most of the art exercises can be conducted with simple items at hand like pen and paper. The environment around us is rich with possibilities. Nurture your own spontaneity and 'kid spirit'. If you watch young children, they are generally more engaged in playing with whatever they find around them – stones, water, pots, pans, the forks and spoons and their food – than they are in the fancy toys adults buy. Rediscover this part of yourself and use it to enhance your coaching.

## Use your intuition

Intuition plays a huge role in ideas for interventions. Sometimes you just get a 'sixth sense' about an approach that might work. If you are not in the habit of accessing and trusting your intuition, work with some expressive modalities (artistic expression, reflective writing or story-telling, for example) to develop your intuitive abilities.

## Build on contrasts

Much of delineating issues and ideas involves comparison and contrast. Building contrast into experiential exercises helps clarify what is desired or what is working well and what is not. It is important to complete these interventions by focusing on how to shift from what is not desired to what is. Otherwise, actions are built to avoid what is not wanted, rather than to generate genuinely creative responses and options.

### Listen for metaphors, analogies or colourful language

Build on and expand visual or comparative language as the basis for an intervention. If you hear yourself saying something like, 'My life feels like being lost in the forest', draw and write what this feels like and contrast it with your dream or vision. List what would help you get out of the woods and make comparisons with what would help you get your life on track.

### Remain curious and playful

Trying to get things 'right' or make them predictable will quickly shut down your creative energy. The great creators and inventors of our time are known for being curious and playful. So squint at the page. Look at things from a new perspective. It won't hurt you and you may discover a new intervention possibility.

### Co-create with clients and colleagues

We create and test a lot of interventions together. Creating is easier and more fun when you can play off someone else's ideas. And you can make mistakes, laugh about them and then figure out what would work in an actual coaching situation.

## Conclusion

Using multiple ways of knowing to access inner wisdom can be an efficient and highly effective approach to raise and address unseen possibilities and obstacles to development. The inner critic exercises offered here serve as a template for using creative process to address a number of issues that arise with both coaches and their clients. We encourage experimentation through self-coaching and peer practice. Many coaches who cannot envision using creative approaches with their clients find that after they become familiar and comfortable with them through their own inner work, they can advance their practice to work with wider range of clients. By entering into a continuous practice of learning and creating new approaches and interventions, more can be achieved with clients, often in less time. Coaches who can skilfully, credibly use multiple modalities help a wide range of clients achieve powerful insights and significant shifts. These coaches often see new possibilities for maximizing their own personal and professional potential.

## References

Gardner, H (1999) *Intelligence Reframed: Multiple intelligences for the 21st century,* Basic Books, New York

Medina, J (2008) *Brain Rules: 12 principles for surviving and thriving at work, home, and school,* Pear Press, Seattle, WA

Myers, D G (2007) The powers and perils of intuition, *Scientific American Mind,* 18 (3) 24–31

Myers, I B and McCaulley, M H (1985) *A Guide to the Development and Use of the Myers-Briggs Type Indicator,* Consulting Psychologist Press, Palo Alto, CA

Schwarz, D and Davidson, A (2009) *Facilitative Coaching: A toolkit for expanding your repertoire and achieving lasting results,* Pfeiffer, San Francisco, CA

Schwarz, R, Davidson, A, Carlson, P and McKinney, S (2005) *The Skilled Facilitator Fieldbook: Tips, tools, and tested methods for consultants, facilitators, managers, trainers, and coaches,* Jossey-Bass, San Francisco, CA

Szegedy-Maszak, M (2005) Mysteries of the mind, *US News and World Report Online Newsletter,* February. Available at: **http://health.usnews.com/ usnews/health/articles/050228/28think.htm**

Wilson, T D (2002) *A Stranger to Ourselves,* Belknap Press, Cambridge, MA

Note: Portions of this chapter were adapted from Schwarz, D and Davidson, A (2009) *Facilitative Coaching: A toolkit for expanding your repertoire and achieving lasting results*, Pfeiffer, San Francisco, CA. These sections are modified and reprinted with permission of John Wiley & Sons

# Undertaking and reviewing coaching research as CPD

## 14

**MAX BLUMBERG AND DAVID A LANE**

## Introduction

In this chapter we first consider the nature of CPD as a continuous endeavour for practitioners, explaining what CPD is as well as what it is not, and setting out some of the reasons for and benefits of coaching research. We also consider the significance of the term 'scientist practitioner'. Outlining the centrality to CPD of developing frameworks for sharing the impact of coaching on clients, we consider the importance of scientific evidence to coaching and of how this component differentiates coaching psychology from other coaching modalities.

We then introduce the idea of coaching practitioner research along with a general framework for how to go about the research process. Focusing on the importance for practitioners of identifying a purpose and focus for their CPD activities, we discuss how to generate topics as well as setting out and identifying options in research paradigms, methodologies, theories and modes of research.

We look at both quantitative and qualitative methodologies, considering research design, credibility, rigour and reporting. We also identify the different strategies and assumptions of both quantitative and qualitative methodology, and outline some of the issues around them. After also identifying and underscoring the importance of research ethics to practitioner research, we conclude by highlighting the chapter's key points, reflecting on the perceived validity of practitioner research, and on providing examples of organizational-level outcomes that may be influenced by coaching and CPD.

## What is CPD?

The time has long passed when practitioners could qualify and expect to offer a service to clients without a continued emphasis on staying up to date and developing professionally. Additionally, the scientific credentials of professionals in coaching psychology are highly prized. For many it is a matter of professional integrity that their work with clients is informed by research and that they are able to interpret that research for the benefit of clients. In many service settings, evaluation of practice forms a key part of the quality system to ensure increasing value to clients and commissioners. So, as practitioners we engage with research as consumers, as participants in it, and also as researchers ourselves. In one way or another, then, understanding or undertaking research forms a central part of our continuing professional development (Lane and Corrie, 2006).

## What is practitioner coaching research?

Coaching research, of which there is an increasing amount, provides a framework for understanding and sharing the impact of coaching on client outcomes (Fillery-Travis and Lane, 2007). In attempting to achieve this there are two areas that as consumers or researchers add particular value to our work with clients. The first of these involves seeking to minimize hidden assumptions when using exploratory models by attempting to rely on evidence that is transparent (whatever methodology is used). Sometimes this is about using agreed, replicable, consistent methodologies. But even where we are using – or commenting on – interpretive frames, we make clear the limits of these and the basis for the judgements. The second area involves the rigorous and systematic generation and/or testing of hypotheses when relying on experimental frames.

## What is not practitioner coaching research?

Traditionally, research operated in what was called Mode 1 (Gibbons, *et al*, 1994), epitomized by the single-discipline researcher whose research did not necessarily have to relate to practice. There is now, however, a near universal requirement to show a return on investment. Therefore, issue-led research sits neatly as a Mode 2 type of activity (Fillery-Travis and Lane, 2008), and Mode 1 activity is not considered to be practitioner coaching research. (For clarification and examples of Mode 1 and Mode 2 research topic types and generators, see Table 14.2 on page 242.)

As Mode 2, practitioner coaching research is controlled by the practitioner and can be co-constructed with clients. Also, the practitioner is explicit about the purpose of the research activity, which is very much embedded in practice rather than being caught in what Lane and Corrie (2006) have referred to as a straitjacket based on scientific philosophies sitting outside of the concerns of practitioners.

## Why practitioner coaching research?

Psychology differs from related professions because it uses interventions based on scientific evidence (Lane and Corrie, 2006: 66). While not limiting itself to an empirical 'scientist practitioner' mode, there is an opportunity for coaching psychology to differentiate from other coaching types by applying evidence-informed interventions – provided there is agreement as to what constitutes evidence (whether quantitative, qualitative, or expert-based). There are three main benefits to this stance. First, coaches can optimize delivery of their own practice by enhancing the skills required to evaluate research and practice (Stoltenberg *et al*, 2002, cited in Corrie and Lane, 2010). Second, it facilitates experimentation – which is particularly important in a young discipline. Third, as Miller and Frederickson (2006) remind us, it underscores that research does not exist for its own sake but to help us examine and reflect upon our professional practice. This is why practitioner research is so central to fully developed and effective CPD.

**FIGURE 14.1** A general process for coaching practitioner CPD research

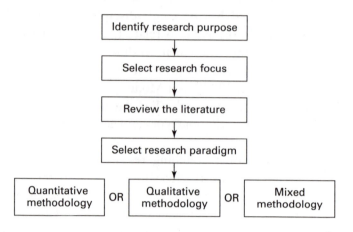

## Introduction to a research process

The research process outlined in Figure 14.1 and described in this chapter seeks to meet the following criteria (Anderson *et al*, 2001; Robson, 2002):

- It is designed for practising coaches wishing to use research as a contribution to their continuing professional development.
- It is both academically rigorous and relevant in practice.
- It can be used as a framework for practitioners to evaluate existing research.

### *Identifying the research purpose*

Corrie and Lane (2006: 30) insist that when 'undertaking any psychological enquiry, it is vital to be clear about its fundamental purpose'. In the context of CPD-based coaching research, this is particularly important. This is because a clearly defined research purpose not only influences the nature of the primary research question but also encourages an orientation to the future that encourages practitioner-researchers to consider the personal and professional ramifications of their work (Fillery-Travis and Lane, 2008). Table 14.1 presents examples of coaching research purposes.

**TABLE 14.1** Examples of coaching practitioner research purposes

| Personal and professional development | Development of the coaching psychology discipline | Commissioned research |
| --- | --- | --- |
| Meeting CPD requirements | Contributing to the coaching psychology body of knowledge | Fulfilling requests for commissioned research |
| Deepening professional knowledge | Publication in a peer-reviewed journal | **Client benefits** |
| Preparing for a new coaching role | | Demonstrating the benefits of a coaching intervention |
| Practice personalization | **Commercial benefit** | Improving existing interventions |
| Aligning interventions with evidence-based coaching practice | Acquiring and retaining more clients | Planning new intervention strategies |
| | Proving the value of your practice | |
| **Client project** | | |
| The research may form part of a larger client project | | |

**SOURCES:** Corrie and Lane, 2010; Crane and Haffen, 2002; Kampa-Kokesch and Anderson, 2001, Lane and Corrie, 2006

## Selecting a research topic

As an emerging discipline, a variety of coaching psychology topics are suitable for CPD research. Some of those ripe for research include the predictors of coaching effectiveness, the nature and timing of coaching interventions, the development of effective coaching performance measures, and the incremental performance value added by coaching. Other topics include the nature of client–coach relationships of various types (external, internal, mentor, HR, etc), coaching industry profiling (eg training, professionalism and practice), and more wide-reaching research topics such as the theoretical underpinnings of human performance (Grant and Cavanagh, 2007; Rostron, 2008; Spence, 2007). There are a number of useful sources for topic generation. These include traditional sources (Mode 1), but for practitioners also include issues arising in and from practice (Mode 2); see Table 14.2.

**TABLE 14.2** Two modes for research

| Mode 1 | Mode 2 |
| --- | --- |
| • The coaching psychology literature<br>• Extensions to or replications of existing research<br>• The 'future directions' and 'research limitations' sections published in many peer-reviewed articles or books<br>• Academic researchers working in the coaching arena are often willing to share topics with a view to extending their own research | • Brainstorming discussions with coaching supervisors, academic researchers or colleagues<br>• Themes arising within a practitioner's own practice<br>• Themes raised by clients<br>• Coaching conference networking<br>• Policy makers from regulatory coaching bodies |

Issues to be considered when selecting a research topic include the feasibility of the research in terms of time, resources and data availability, whether an appropriate research design is available, and whether the necessary data collection and analytical skills for the proposed investigation are available. Also important is whether the primary research purpose is to meet CPD requirements; if so, topic approval should be obtained from a supervisor. It is also worth considering that to maintain motivation throughout the study, researchers may find it helpful to select a topic in which they have a personal interest (Creswell, 1994; Hussey and Hussey, 1997; Neuman, 1994; Robson, 2002).

## Reviewing the literature

The literature review is 'a systematic, explicit, and reproducible method for identifying, evaluating, and synthesizing the existing body of completed and recorded work produced by researchers, scholars, and practitioners' (Fink, 2005: 3). In essence, its objectives are to:

- Identify background theories that have been used to inform existing research, and those that have the potential to inform existing research, but have not yet been applied.

- Identify research questions that have been asked and adequately addressed, as well as those that have been asked but not adequately addressed, and those that have not yet been asked.
- Identify the strengths and weaknesses of existing research methodologies, participant samples, analytical methods and conclusions.

The following ideas may be helpful when undertaking a literature review:

- Include both topic literature and research methods literature in the review, but as a practitioner also include the journals that address practice concerns.
- Undergraduate and graduate textbooks are a useful resource and frequently provide information about topical theories, debates and key studies undertaken, as well as useful keywords for literature searches.
- Reference sections of scholarly articles can be used to identify further useful literature (a process referred to as 'snowballing' – Hussey and Hussey, 1997).
- PhD theses on related topics usually offer a scholarly treatise and further literature references. They can be located, for example, via the British Library and Dissertation Express published by UMI.
- Google Scholar is an effective research tool that meta-searches traditional academic sources including Science Direct, Informa, Ingenta and Psychinfo. It often provides free links to articles that must otherwise be purchased from the publisher or accessed via a university or professional body affiliation.
- As part of the literature review, a note should be made of each source's research question, hypotheses, background theories applied, research sample demographics, data collection techniques and instruments, dependent and independent variables, analytical techniques used, and hypothesis testing outcomes, as well as any directions for future research.

Many tools are available for capturing the above information, ranging from spreadsheets to specialist reference management software such as Bookends, Citation or Bibus (the latter being open-source and free at the time of writing). Always have in mind our earlier point that it is about understanding and making transparent underlying assumptions, as well as considering the extent to which the studies you read and review address the questions raised and the rigour or the process they employ.

## Selecting a research paradigm

Research methodologies are generally underpinned by a knowledge paradigm that governs the research design and the collection, analysis and interpretation of empirical data (Guba, 1990; Kuhn, 1962). Modern psychological research methodologies are usually based on what are termed positivist, relativist or interpretative paradigms, or some combination of these (Creswell, 2002).

Positivist methodologies – such as the scientific method – are usually referred to as quantitative methodologies and are based upon a deductive process that uses *a priori* theory (that is, inferring/deducing from a general principle) to generate research hypotheses that are then tested using empirical data (Black, 1993). They are useful when:

- The purpose of the research is to measure how and how far coaching interventions lead to particular coaching outcomes.
- The research protocol (for example, the number of constructs, research methodology and data collection methods) can be pre-specified and are unlikely to require change upon commencement of the investigation (Robson, 2002).
- Experimental conditions and extraneous variables can be rigorously controlled (Kerlinger, 1986).

In contrast, qualitative methodologies – often based on relativist and interpretative paradigms – employ an inductive approach where hypotheses are developed *a posteriori* based on observed empirical data (Creswell, 2004). Qualitative approaches are usually most appropriate where:

- The purpose of the investigation is to understand the meaning and subjective experience of phenomena (such as clients' experiences of coaching interventions).
- Existing research on the topic is limited.
- The research focus embraces a large number of constructs.

Table 14.3 presents a selection of assumptions underpinning quantitative and qualitative methodologies.

**TABLE 14.3** Comparison of quantitative and qualitative methodology assumptions

|  | Quantitative methods | Qualitative methods |
| --- | --- | --- |
| Epistemological position | Objectivist | Constructivist |
| Relationship between researcher and subject | Distant/outsider | Close/insider |
| Research focus | 'Facts' | Meanings |
| Relationship between theory/ concepts and research | Deduction/ confirmation | Induction/emergent |
| Scope of findings | Nomothetic | Ideographic |
| The nature of data | Data based on numbers | Data based on text |

**ADAPTED FROM:** Gray, 2004: 200

# Quantitative research strategies

Figure 14.2 outlines a quantitative research process suitable for practitioner research and described in the sections below.

## 1. Theory selection

Theories with potential relevance to coaching psychology include:

- Practice-based theories: for example cognitive behavioural therapy, existential, psychodynamic, positive psychology, or the medical model. These usually reflect practitioner training.
- Outcome-based theories: theories and models relevant to the client domain. For example, industry-based performance models, sales and marketing theory, work–life balance, relationship intimacy, or organizational development models. They do not typically include coaching psychology constructs.

**FIGURE 14.2**  A quantitative research process

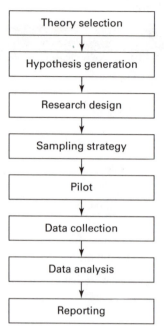

- Organizational theories: for example complexity, systemic and networking theories.
- Mixed theories: these include models that link coaching psychology antecedents to client domain outcomes.

## Developing a research question

Quantitative research questions ask about the impact of independent variables on a dependent variable. Grant *et al* (2010) recommend that in coaching research, dependent variables should reflect the efficacy of coaching. Table 14.4 lists examples, and Table 14.5 provides examples of antecedent constructs used in existing research to date.

Some extraneous or confounding variables that may affect the coaching psychology research outcomes include market context, team input, senior management, products/services, and the economic climate in which the research is carried out, including any relevant mergers/acquisitions or organizational strategy.

**TABLE 14.4** Examples of client-level coaching efficacy constructs

| | |
|---|---|
| Stress | Self-efficacy |
| Work–life balance | Interpersonal skills |
| Coaching return on investment | Strategic thinking |
| Resilience | Time management |
| Decision making | Conflict management |
| Goal-attainment | Delegation |
| Mental health: eg stress, anxiety, | Staffing issues |
| depression, etc | Workplace absence |
| Wellbeing | Learning agility |
| Leadership and management | Goal self-concordance and |
| styles | attainment |
| Body mass index | Engagement |
| Self-reflection and insight | |

**SOURCE:** Grant *et al* (2010); Kampa-Kokesch and Anderson (2001)

## Types of quantitative research questions

De Vaus (2001) identifies three types of quantitative research and associated research questions.

### a. Explanatory research

Explanatory research aims to establish a causal relationship between one or more independent variables and a dependent variable. Associated research questions are usually of the form: what effect does X have on Y? To what extent does M mediate/moderate the relationship between X and Y?

### b. Descriptive research

Whereas explanatory research tests causal relationships, descriptive research focuses on the characteristics of individual variables; for example central tendency, dispersion and frequency distribution of a variable, or comparing these factors across two or more variables. Data is usually collected via survey or interview and examples of research questions might include: what is the mean and standard deviation of X? Is X normally distributed? How has X changed over the past five years? What is the incidence of X compared to Y?

**TABLE 14.5** Examples of independent variables used in coaching research

**Performance improvement modality**
Life coaching, executive coaching, health coaching, training, mentoring, managing, process consulting, psychotherapy, etc

**Coaching model**
CBT, GROW, positive psychology, psychodynamic, existential, solution-focused, mindfulness, metacognition, etc

**Coach-client relationship**
HR, external, manager, mentor, etc.

**Coach role**
Facilitator, expert, psychotherapist

**Coaching delivery**
Group versus individual, in situ, telephone, internet, etc

**Coaching process**
Number and timing of coaching sessions

**Client factors**
Education, personality, attitudes, self-regulation, neurophysiological factors, interaction style, readiness to change, job role, etc

**Coach factors**
Education, competencies, confidence, personality, attitudes, motivation, insight, experience, listening skills, etc.

**Coach-client dyad**
Interactions between coach and client factors

**Organizational context**
Objectives for coaching, required organizational competencies, organizational culture, etc

**Coaching supervision**

**SOURCE:** Grant *et al* (2010); Kampa-Kokesch and Anderson (2001)

### c. Exploratory research

Exploratory research establishes the feasibility of proposed investigations where topic knowledge is limited. It seeks to establish, for example, the feasibility of a proposed research methodology; the resources required to conduct the research; participant and data availability; appropriateness of the proposed measures for the proposed sample; and/or possible effect sizes, extraneous and nuisance variables.

## 2. Generating hypotheses

Scientific research hypotheses operationalize research questions by transforming them into null and alternative hypotheses. These are testable propositions expressed as follows: null hypothesis (H0) – any observed change in the dependent variable was caused by factors other than corresponding changes in the independent variable(s), or alternative hypothesis (H1) – any observed change in the dependent variable was caused by corresponding changes in the independent variable(s).

If the probability of an obtained experimental outcome is below the level where such an outcome might be expected simply by chance alone (the significance level of the experiment), the null hypothesis is rejected and the alternative hypothesis accepted. Incorrectly rejecting the null hypothesis and accepting the alternative hypothesis is referred to as committing a Type I error and the probability of its occurrence is the significance of the experiment.

Conversely, incorrectly accepting the null hypothesis and rejecting the alternative hypothesis is a Type II error and the probability of its occurrence can be reduced by increasing the significance level of the experiment. This, however, reduces the power of the study to detect small changes in the dependent variable resulting from manipulation of the independent variable.

## 3. Quantitative research designs

### Credibility, rigour and precision in quantitative research

The extent to which experiments establish causal outcome relationships depends largely on the effectiveness of research designs. Robust research designs enhance research outcomes by maximizing the effect of independent variables, minimizing error variance, and controlling the effects of extraneous variables (the MaxMinCon principle; Kerlinger, 1986). These in turn depend on the internal and external validity of the study (Campbell and Stanley, 1963; de Vaus, 2001; Robson, 2002).

Internal validity is the confidence with which changes in the dependent variable can be attributed to changes in the independent variable rather than to other causes. External validity (or generalizability) is the extent to which experimental sample findings can be applied to the population from which the sample was drawn.

## Types of quantitative research designs

Quantitative research designs can be classified as experimental or non-experimental, where the key difference is that experimental designs manipulate the independent variables whereas the latter do not.

## Experimental designs

Experimental designs can be classified as true experimental and quasi-experimental designs. In experimental designs, participants are experimental groups to optimize validity whereas this does not occur in quasi-experimental designs.

### True experimental designs

True experimental research designs exhibit the following characteristics (de Vaus, 2001; Robson, 2002): the selection of sample participants from pre-defined populations; the random allocation of participants to different experimental conditions; planned independent variable manipulation (treatment, intervention); measurement of the variables and control of extraneous variables; and statistically-based hypothesis testing. Variations on true experimental designs include:

- Randomized controlled trials (RCT): referred to as the 'gold standard' of experimental designs (Grant *et al*, 2010: 19), RCT includes a control group that receives no treatment, thereby increasing the likelihood that groups differ only in respect of the independent variable rather than on extraneous or selection-based factors.
- Factorial designs: designs that test the impact of multiple independent variables.
- Matched participant designs: matching of participants across experimental groups on a factor known to correlate with the dependent variable. This design increases the variance explained by the independent variable by accounting for the variance of the matching variable.
- Between-subjects designs: each experimental group receives a different treatment and group differences in the effects of treatments are assessed.
- Within-subjects designs: each participant receives multiple treatments and the effects of treatments on each individual are assessed. Repeated measure designs should only be used where order and practice effects are unlikely.

- Pre-intervention and post-intervention testing: pre-testing accounts for possible differences in the initial levels of the dependent variable between experimental groups. The dependent variable under these circumstances then becomes the difference between the pre- and post-test scores (change scores) and has the effect of increasing internal validity. Pre-tests should only be used where they are unlikely to sensitize participants or influence the treatment outcome.

### Quasi-experimental designs

A design is considered to be quasi-experimental if the independent variables are manipulated, but participants are not randomly allocated to comparison groups (Campbell and Stanley, 1963). Quasi-experimental designs therefore reduce internal validity because they do not manage the threats of history or maturation. Non-random participant allocation is a common reality in organizational research where groups (for example, work teams) must remain intact and should be noted as a research limitation (Phillips and Phillips, 2003; Stober, 2005).

## Non-experimental research designs

Because non-experimental designs do not manipulate independent variables, typical features include:

- selection of samples from pre-defined populations;
- allocation of samples to various experimental conditions;
- measurement of variables;
- control of extraneous variables;
- may or may not include hypothesis testing.

Non-experimental design can be categorized as correlational, comparative and longitudinal:

### Correlational designs

Correlational designs investigate relationships (correlations) between variables. Examples include cross-sectional designs and prediction designs.

Cross-sectional designs provide a snapshot of a number of variables within a single group at a moment in time; for example, the relationship between attitude towards coaching and coaching outcome. Because non-experimental designs cannot establish causality, the terms 'independent' and 'dependent' variables are replaced by 'explanatory' and 'outcomes' variables, respectively. Prediction designs establish the extent to which one set of variables predicts another; for example, the extent to which attitude towards coaching predicts coaching outcomes. The investigation must therefore extend over time and independent variables are termed 'predictor' and 'criterion' variables.

### Comparative designs

Like correlational designs, comparative designs analyse relations between explanatory and outcome variables. They differ, however, in that comparisons are made between two or more groups: for example, comparing the relationship between senior and middle management attitudes towards coaching and coaching outcomes.

### Longitudinal designs

Longitudinal designs use repeated measures to establish how variables change over time. They are useful, for example, in establishing the sustainability of coaching outcomes. They can be used with both correlational and comparative designs, and with panels and cohorts. They are, though, resource-intensive and tend to suffer from sample attrition and practice effects.

## 4. Sampling strategies

A population is the total potential number of cases or entities that share characteristics that are relevant to the research focus. Because it is usually impractical to assess an entire population, a representative sample is drawn using a sampling frame. Sample representativeness is maximized when sample participants are randomly selected.

The entities constituting the sample are referred to as the experimental unit of analysis, typically the client in coaching outcome research. Other possible units of analysis include educational establishments, organizations or coaches themselves.

The size of the sample influences the power of the study and the confidence with which sample findings can be generalized to the population of interest. Required sample sizes vary according to research design and the statistical technique used to test hypotheses (Borg and Gall, 1989; Cohen, 1992).

# 5. Piloting the study

Prior to commencing data collection, researchers are encouraged to conduct a pilot study with a few randomly selected participants to assess the adequacy of the design, sampling frame and data collection instruments; the feasibility of addressing the research question; any logistical issues; construct variability; the suitability of the intended analytical techniques; and the financial and human resources likely to be required (van Teijlingen and Hundley, 2001). Pilot studies are also useful for the development of research plans and in obtaining funding for research.

## Creating a research proposal

Research proposals are useful for planning the investigation, for obtaining expert assistance regarding feasibility and design improvement, and as a basis for CPD review. They can be structured as follows (Gray, 2004; Punch, 2000; Robson, 2002):

*Title:* This should encapsulate the central research question and also mention the constructs if possible.

*Abstract:* This should provide a concise outline of the background theory and gaps, the research question, the hypotheses, the research design, and sample used.

*Objectives:* These articulate the measurable outcomes desired from the study.

*Literature review:* This provides an overview of the topic, its history and any knowledge gaps. This heading is optional for practitioners not intending to publish their research.

Research questions.

*Methodology:* This is an explanation of the research design and process, sampling method, and measurement instruments.

*Limitations:* Known limitations, for example, issues with internal consistency or limited power.

*Work schedule:* Optional timetable of activities.

*References:* Works cited in the proposal.

# 6. Data collection

Once a research design has been defined and participants selected, measurement instruments are used to assess participant attributes of interest, and to convert them into numerical values for statistical analysis to follow (for example, hypothesis testing, group comparison and predicting outcomes).

Psychometric tests measuring personality, ability, interest, motivation and attitude are frequently used in psychology, with data gathered using self-reports, observation, peer-ratings and interviews (Furnham, 2008; Sapsford, 2006). In addition to psychometric instruments, executive coaching researchers are encouraged to seek domain-specific measures for measuring, for example, financial or sales and marketing outcomes.

## Selecting data collection instruments

Practitioner-researchers can use published measures or create their own (Punch, 2000). That said, Grant and Cavanagh (2007: 247) caution against using practitioner-developed 'idiosyncratic self-report measures' because they frequently lack validity and reliability, and inhibit cross-study comparisons and meta-analyses thereby limiting the research base.

The validity and reliability of measuring instruments are important for establishing scientific credibility. Validity is the extent to which instruments measure what they purport to, while reliability is the consistency with which an instrument measures underlying phenomena (Black, 1993).

While few coaching-specific instruments have been developed to date, psychometric measures are available from bodies such as the British Psychological Society, the Australian Psychological Society and the American Psychological Association. These bodies also accredit the use of these tests as required. Two measurement approaches that may be of particular interest to coaches include Goal Attainment Scaling (Grant *et al*, 2010; Spence, 2007) and positive psychology measures (Positive Psychology Centre at the University of Pennsylvania).

# 7. Quantitative data analysis

Once data have been collected, quantitative analysis can commence using a process similar to the following.

**Dataset preparation**

- Coding non-quantitative items.
- Checking for errors such as out of range or non-allowed values.
- Processing missing data.

**Exploratory analysis**

- Using tables and graphs to highlight the characteristics of all variables such as central tendency, dispersion and frequency distribution.
- Eliminating variables with low variance.

**Confirmatory analysis**

There are three primary classes of confirmatory analysis: comparing group differences, measuring associations between variables, and predicting values from given data. Within each group, the selected technique depends on the frequency distribution of the variables involved:

- Normally distributed variables are analysed using parametric analytical techniques.
- Non-normally distributed variables are analysed using non-parametric analytical techniques.

## 8. Reporting quantitative research

The structure of research reports depends largely on the purpose of the research and its audience. Researchers wishing to publish in peer reviewed journals will generally find guidelines in the publication; these are likely to be similar to the following (Gray, 2004; Punch, 2000; Robson, 2002):

Title: Encapsulates the central research question and should mention the outcome construct if possible.

Abstract: A concise outline of the main research question and hypothesis, the research design, sample, major findings and conclusion.

Introduction: Justification of the research, research questions and hypotheses.

*Literature review:* Background theory, existing research and knowledge gaps.

*Methodology:* Research context (academic, organizational), sampling strategy, research design and the procedure, analytical techniques used.

*Results:* Summary of raw findings without interpretation.

*Discussion:* Discussion of hypotheses comparing results obtained with studies mentioned in the literature review, contribution of new knowledge if any, limitations, and recommendations for future research.

*References:* Works cited in the proposal.

# Qualitative research: the case study

A number of researchers argue that the case study is a useful qualitative design for coaching research (Bachkirova and Kauffman, 2008; Harding, 2009; Lowman, 2001). Case studies are in situ, rigorous and detailed examinations of a single entity or small number of related entities of interest (Yin, 2003).

A case study research strategy might consist of the following components (Creswell, 2004; Gray, 2004; Robson, 2002). First, the research questions and hypotheses are developed, preferably linked to existing theory and research where available. They are provisional and subject to modification as data is collected. Once this is done, one or a small number of cases is selected using purposive sampling based on criteria relevant to the research focus. After deciding on a pertinent case or cases, research measures and instruments as well as research protocols can be developed, using multiple data sources to increase validity and reliability. These might include, for example, interviews, participant and direct observation, and documentation analysis.

Once these steps are covered, data are collected and research instruments and protocols can be altered based on what has been learnt, if required. Once the data are collected, they need to be analysed. Techniques for analysing case study data vary and include pattern matching and explanation building, which compares hypothesized and observed outcomes; time series analysis, which compares actual and hypothesized longitudinal changes; and programme logic models, which combine pattern matching and times series analysis by predicting the evolution of an outcome from an initial event. Finally, analytic generalization can take place, whereby data is analysed with a view to testing support for initial hypotheses.

## *Reporting case studies*

Passmore and Gibbes (2007: 122) recommend the following structure for reporting case study findings. First, there is a clear description of the context of the research, as well as of the coachee's issue and the objectives agreed by the coach and the coachee. Then, there is an explanation of the selection approach chosen by the coach, and a description of what happened during the coaching relationship. Crucially, the outcomes of the coaching relationship and how these were measured/assessed should also be included, as, finally, should reflections on lessons learnt by the coach.

## *Rigour in case study designs*

Qualitative scholars frequently argue that the criteria required for scientific rigour are irrelevant in qualitative research. Given the argument, however, that social policy decisions are frequently based on positivist research with measurable outcomes, the validity and reliability of the case study method are considered here.

# Research ethics

Researchers affiliated to regulatory bodies such as the British Psychological Society should be aware of the ethical guidelines issued by those bodies (eg British Psychological Society, 2009). In general, the guidelines set out in Table 14.6 are recommended for coaching research (Gray, 2004; Robson, 2002).

**TABLE 14.6** Dos and don'ts of research ethics

| Do | Do not |
|---|---|
| • Treat participants fairly and with consideration and respect <br> • Ensure informed consent <br> • Respect privacy of participants | • Involve people without their consent <br> • Coerce participation <br> • Withhold information about the true nature of the research <br> • Deceive participants <br> • Induce participants to commit acts that reduce self-esteem <br> • Violate rights of self-determination <br> • Expose participants to physical or mental stress <br> • Withhold benefits from some participants relative to others <br> • Harm participants |

# Conclusion

This chapter has outlined how to approach practitioner research, what its benefits are, and how and why it can be a useful and integral part of practice and CPD. Outlining how to engage with the research process, and what to consider in selecting a methodological and theoretical approach, we have suggested what considerations might usefully be undertaken in selecting research topics and hypotheses as well as strategies and protocols. Finally, we have suggested how research can be structured, and how it is usually reported.

Coaching psychology is an applied discipline and, as such, its practitioners are potential vehicles for much needed field research. Coaching practitioners should take advantage of their in situ roles to add value to the coaching research base by focusing on designs that determine the extent to which client-level coaching outcomes mediate or moderate the effect of coaching interventions on organizational outcomes (see Table 14.7).

While not all practitioners have the research resources and competencies available to research academics, most can access one rare

**TABLE 14.7** Examples of organizational-level outcomes that may be influenced by coaching

| Output: | Work habits | Quality |
|---|---|---|
| Units produced | Absenteeism | Scrap |
| Items assembled | Tardiness | Rejects |
| Items sold | Visits to the | Error rates |
| Forms processed | dispensary | Rework |
| Loans approved | First aid treatments | Shortages |
| Inventory turnover | Violations of safety | Deviation from |
| Patients visited | rules | standard |
| Applications | Excessive breaks | Product failures |
| processed | | Inventory |
| Productivity | **Work climate** | adjustments |
| Work backlog | Number of | Percentage of |
| Shipments | grievances | properly completed |
| New accounts | Number of | tasks |
| opened | discriminations | Number of expenses |
| | Charges | |
| **Time** | Employee complaints | **Customer Service** |
| Equipment downtime | Job satisfaction | Churn rate |
| Overtime | Employee turnover | Number of satisfied |
| On time shipments | Litigation | customers |
| Time to project | | Customer satisfaction |
| completion | **Costs** | index |
| Processing time | Budget variances | Customer loyalty |
| Cycle time | Unit costs | Customer complaints |
| Meeting schedules | Cost by account | |
| Repair time | Variable costs | **Development/** |
| Efficiency | Fixed costs | **advancement** |
| Work stoppages | Overhead costs | Number of |
| Order response time | Operating costs | promotions |
| Late reporting | Number of cost | Number of pay |
| Lost time days | reductions | increases |
| | Accident costs | Number of training |
| | Sales expense | programmes |
| | | attended |
| | | Requests for transfer |
| | | Performance |
| | | appraisal ratings |
| | | Increases in job |
| | | effectiveness |

**SOURCE:** Phillips and Phillips (2003)

resource: research collaborators, our client base. This strength points to potentially fruitful practitioner-academic collaborations. Further, being effective consumers as well as practitioners of research may be a matter of professional integrity (see Dawes, 1994, Jones, 1998, Lane and Corrie, 2006). This debate is not one that practitioners can ignore: our responsibilities to our clients require us to engage fully with it as part of our continuing professional development and practice.

## References

Anderson, N, Herriot, P and Hodgkinson, G (2001) The practitioner-research divide in industrial, work and organisational (IWO) psychology: where are we now, and where do we go from here?, *Journal of Occupational and Organizational Psychology*, 74, 391–411

Bachkirova, T and Kauffman, C (2008) Many ways of knowing: how to make sense of different research perspectives in studies of coaching, *Coaching: An International Journal of Theory, Research and Practice*, 1 (2) 107–13

Black, T (1993) *Evaluating Social Science Research*, Sage, London

Borg, D and Gall, M (1989) *Educational Research*, Longman, New York

British Psychological Society (2009) *Ethical Guidelines and Support*, The British Psychological Society, Leicester

Campbell, D T and Stanley, J C (1963) *Experimental and Quasi-experimental Designs for Research*, Rand McNally, Chicago, IL

Cohen, J (1992) A power primer, *Psychological Bulletin*, 112 (1) 155–59

Corrie, S and Lane, D (2010) *Constructing Stories, Telling Tales: A guide to formulation in applied psychology*, Karnac Books, London

Crane, D and Haffen, M (2002) Meeting the needs of evidence-based practice in family therapy: developing the scientist-practitioner, *Model Journal of Family Therapy*, 24 (2) 113–24

Creswell, J (1994) *Research Design: Qualitative and quantitative approaches*, Sage, Thousand Oaks, CA

Creswell, J (2002) *Educational Research: Planning, conducting, and evaluating quantitative and qualitative research*, Pearson Education, Upper Saddle Creek, NJ

Creswell, J (2004) *Research Design: Qualitative and quantitative approaches*, Sage, Thousand Oaks, CA

Dawes, R M (1994) *House of Cards: Psychology and psychotherapy built on a myth*, The Free Press, New York

de Vaus, D (2001) *Research Design in Social Research*, Sage, New York

Fillery-Travis, A and Lane, D A (2007) Research: does coaching work?, in (eds) S Palmer and A Whybrow, *Handbook of Coaching Psychology: A guide for practitioners*, Routledge, London

Fillery-Travis, A and Lane, D A (2008) How to develop your research interests, in (eds) S Palmer and R Bor, *The Practitioners Handbook*, Sage, London

Fink, A (2005) *Conducting Research Literature Reviews: From the internet to paper*, Sage, New York

Furnham, A (2008) HR professionals' beliefs about, and knowledge of, assessment techniques and psychometric tests, *International Journal of Selection and Assessment,* 16, 301–06

Gibbons, M, Limoges, C, Nowotny, H, Schwartzmann, S, Scott, P and Trow, M (1994) *The New Production of Knowledge: The dynamics of science and research in contemporary societies,* Sage, London

Grant, A and Cavanagh, M (2007) Evidence-based coaching: flourishing or languishing?, *Australian Psychologist,* 42 (4) 239–54

Grant, A, Passmore, J, Cavanagh, M and Parker, H (2010) The state of play in coaching today: a comprehensive review of the field, *Review of Industrial and Organizational Psychology,* 25, 125–67

Gray, D (2004) *Doing Research in the Real World,* Sage, New York

Guba, E (1990) *The Paradigm Dialogue,* Sage, Newbury Park, CA

Harding, C (2009) Researcher as Goldilocks: searching for a methodology that is 'just right' for a coaching and mentoring study, *International Journal of Evidence Based Coaching and Mentoring,* 3, 11–21

Hussey, J and Hussey, R (1997) *Business Research: A practical guide for undergraduate and postgraduate students,* Macmillan, London

Jones, A (1998) 'What's the bloody point?' More thoughts on fraudulent identity, *Clinical Psychology Forum,* 112, 3–9

Kampa-Kokesch, S and Anderson, M (2001) Executive coaching: a comprehensive review of the literature, *Consulting Psychology Journal: Practice and Research,* 60 (1) 205–28

Kerlinger, F (1986) *Foundations of Behavioral Research,* Holt, Rinehart, and Winston, Fort Worth, TX

Kuhn, T (1962) *The Structure of Scientific Revolutions,* University of Chicago Press, Chicago, IL

Lane, D A and Corrie, S (2006) *The Modern Scientist Practitioner: A guide to practice in psychology,* Routledge, London

Lowman, R (2001) Constructing a literature from case studies: promise and limitations of the method, *Consulting Psychology Journal: Practice and Research,* 53 (2) 119–23

Miller, A and Frederickson, N (2006) Generalisable findings and idiographic problems: Struggles and successes for educational psychologists as scientist-practitioners, in (eds) D A Lane and S Corrie, *The Modern Scientist-Practitioner: A guide to practice in psychology,* Routledge, London

Neuman, W (1994) *Social Research Methods: Qualitative and quantitative approaches,* Allyn and Bacon, Boston, MA

Passmore, J and Gibbes, C (2007) The state of executive coaching research: what does the current literature tell us and what's next for coaching research?, *International Coaching Psychology Review,* 2 (2) 116–28

Phillips, J and Phillips, P (2003) *Return on Investment in Training and Performance Improvement Programs,* Butterworth-Heinemann, Burlington, MA

Punch, K (2000) *Developing Effective Research Proposals,* Sage, New York

Robson, C (2002) *Real World Research,* Blackwell, Oxford

Rostron, S (2008) White paper: Research agenda for development of the field, Global Convention of Coaching, available from **http://www.instituteofcoaching.org/images/pdfs/State-of-Coaching-Research.pdf**

Sapsford, R (2006) *Survey Research,* Sage, London

Spence, G (2007) Further development of evidence-based coaching: lessons from the rise and fall of the human potential movement, *Australian Psychologist,* 42 (4) 255–65

Stober, D (2005) Approaches to research on executive and organisational coaching outcomes, *International Journal of Coaching in Organizations,* 3 (1) 6–13

van Teijlingen, E and Hundley, V (2001) The importance of pilot studies, *Social Research Update* (online), Winter. Available: **http://sru.soc.surrey.ac.uk/ SRU35.pdf** (accessed 20 April 2010)

Yin, R K (2003) *Case Study Research, Design and Methods,* 3rd edn, Sage, New York

# PART 4
# **Personal reflection**

# Coaches' use of reflective journals for learning

**DECLAN WOODS**

## Introduction

**S**uccess in the marketplace increasingly depends on learning, yet most people don't know how to learn (Argyris, 1991). This is worrying because knowledge and skills can quickly become outdated and competence is not a constant, and to adapt to what tomorrow may bring people will need to continue to learn (Lewis, 2003). If this was true before, nowhere is this truer now than in the fast evolving world of coaches and their work with coachees. There are, however, opportunities every day for coaches to learn through their coaching. The trick is for them to find ways of maximizing these learning opportunities. Keeping a journal on their coaching and reflecting on it may help.

A literature review reveals confusion over both the definition and practice of reflection. This is consistent with the findings of a small-scale study with several executive coaches carried out in writing this chapter; their comments and experiences are included here. Despite wide variations in approaches to reflective activity, the research participants all recognized the potential value in reflecting on their practice and sought guidance on how to do this better. This should be of interest to coaches because, as Johns explained (2004), reflection should be a core activity and quality of a professional coach. Yet despite this, Boud and Walker (1998) advise that many learners either resist reflecting, have difficulty understanding how they should go about it, or simply cannot reflect. This chapter therefore aims to demystify reflection and provide guidance to coaches on how to go about it, using case examples. After defining key terms, the chapter is structured around a coach's work with clients and the review, reflection and learning derived from it.

# What is reflection?

To many, reflection is an intangible, woolly concept. Some clarification might help demystify it. Most theorists (eg Raelin, 2001) agree that reflection means 'to bend back, stand apart from, stand outside of'. Carroll and Gilbert (2005) also refer to reflection as gaining a new and perhaps different perspective after having stepped back from one's coaching. Dewey (1933), an early proponent of reflection, believed reflection fell into two parts: questioning (often based on some doubt) and searching (for new material to overcome the doubt). But what makes a coach step back, question and search?

For many, the first step in reflection is a feeling of discomfort arising from an (coaching) experience and the start of recognizing that their normal response to a situation was insufficient (Atkins and Murphy, 1993). One of the coaches surveyed said they wrote: 'Notes to self eg, 'cleaner contracting', 'next time I need to ...'; my reactions or what's working well and [my practice would be] even better if ... ; observations on the client' and commented they typically log gaps in their practice or ideas about practice improvements.

Hinett (2003) and Mackintosh (1998) recognized a trigger for learning was sometimes from recognized error or ineffectiveness in practice. Hackman and Wageman (2007) extended this view, believing errors and failure provide more opportunities for learning than do success and achievement: failure provides data that can be explored for insights into the selected approaches and how these might be improved.

If true, a key challenge for coaches seems to be overcoming a natural defensive reaction and not overly-rationalizing their approach to coaching. Hay (2007) recognized this response in herself when she described her development through tape-recording her work and reviewing this with a supervisor:

> I persevered and gradually learned to accept these insights and improve my competence for the future instead of beating myself up over my perceived inadequacies (p7) ... once you get beyond the natural tendency

to punish yourself for being so unaware at the time, you begin to learn a great deal more about how you function (p 25).

Recognition, time and timing are also important. Adult learning theories (eg Knowles, 1985) suggest that managers learn most when they are ready to learn – that is, when they recognize in themselves that their past experience is no longer proving useful in the current situation. It may take a particular event to trigger this awareness and being conscious of areas for development in their practice. However, while coaches may realize they are ready to learn, they may be less aware that their prior experiences might affect their openness to reflecting and learning. While a shocking or ineffective coaching intervention or outcome might cause coaches to stop and 'reflect', they still need to be open-minded enough to evaluate the situation, take in different viewpoints and consider fresh possibilities. This may prove uncomfortable for many coaches and require courage to do so and a willingness to accept the unknown for a time. Given the above, establishing a safe environment seems an important element to encouraging effective reflective learning.

For those coaches who accept this discomfort, there are strong arguments to the benefits of reflective practice, including:

- increasing ownership of the material and encouraging the learner to have a more active role in the learning process (Jensen, 1987);
- personal development – through the exploration of self and personal meanings to events (eg Christensen, 1981);
- improving thinking skills (Moon, 2005);
- supporting behaviour change – 'offloading of the burden of unpleasant events or experiences', an 'emotional dumping ground' (Moon 2006: 49).

# Gathering material from coaching sessions

This section looks at coaches' initial gathering of material from their coaching on which they can reflect later.

## *Capturing material from coaching sessions*

In my experience, judicious note-taking can help a coach reflect and learn. The use of note-taking in coaching is widely debated, however. While some coaches like to take notes during a coaching session, others prefer not to, believing it can get in the way of being present with a client. Provided the client agrees to the coach taking notes (this needs to be contracted for), it can have advantages including providing a more detailed session record than if a coach relies on memory alone. However, note-taking can lead to a coach failing to spot or hear vital clues provided by the coachee at the time. If no notes are taken, the coach is able to focus on developing an effective working relationship with the coachee. An alternative for the coach is to take notes after a session ends, which can act as a form of 'clearing' of the client and his or her issues and allow a fuller concentration on the work ahead.

Alternatively, a session can be recorded. While it could be video recorded, often an audio recording will provide most of the important information a coach will need. It is common for therapists (and coaches) in training to audio record their work and transcribe it for further analysis, with the support of a supervisor with a view to finding ways of doing it even better. After all, as Hay (2007: 23), said, 'reflection is setting aside time to think about what you've done in the past and what you might do in the future'.

A key advantage of recording over notes is that note-taking is subject to a coach's own biases, preferences and selective attention. This starts during the coaching itself where a coach, if unaware of a particular occurrence, is unlikely to note it and pay attention to it subsequently in his or her review and analysis. Recording can help offset these limitations.

Knapman and Morrison (1998, in Carroll and Gilbert, 2005) refer to the practice of writing up notes as producing a process report: 'Recording in detail either during the interview or immediately afterwards what was said by both parties, recording the non-verbal cues given by both parties and any analysis of what you thought might be happening' (p 33). These notes might be based upon what a coachee says or coach observes in a particular session, thus providing a short-term reaction to this, or when kept chronologically over a number of sessions, may form a coaching diary.

The next section goes beyond the notes a coach takes during a session to how he or she might collate these in different formats, including in logs or diaries.

## Logging material from coaching in journals

### What are reflective journals?

The focus of this chapter is on coaches' use of journals and diaries for learning. Moon (2006) calls learning journals a vehicle for reflection, saying there are many different words used to describe them including diaries, logs or learning logs. She differentiates them by saying a learning journal is likely to include some factual recording (eg the time and place of the coaching) but is not necessarily limited to these details.

The literature tells us journals help people think about their attitudes, beliefs and assumptions in order to promote self-evaluation. This study seems to support this view as the following quotations from the study participants indicate:

- It's about deep self-awareness and knowing myself.
- As I'm an extrovert, I need to write to 'hear myself speak'. Journaling is therefore a way of externalizing an otherwise internal process.
- I ask myself questions: where is my life going? Where am I in relation to my purpose and passion? It tends to be philosophical.
- I've been journal-writing for 20 years. Every six months I look back and identity patterns and themes.
- It's what's going on for me in my world at that time.

Chi *et al* (1994) describe making sense of something through journaling as a place for self-explanations, which aligns with the coaches surveyed:

- It's for me. It's my self-coaching journey.
- It's my learning journal. This is personal to me and my way of learning.

As well as a philosophical benefit, journals also appear to have a practical one, with coaches reporting:

- It's a professional tool.
- Part of (my) toolkit.
- Keep on track and key things.

## What format do reflective journals take?

This study reveals that the structure of coaches' journals varies. They appear in a wide variety of formats and dimensions, including bound diaries, blank loose-leaf pads, scrap books, and audio and visually recorded media. The literature also charts the increase in electronic media in the form of blogs and Wikis.

With one exception of a coach who captured their journal on a laptop, all of the coaches surveyed used paper-based journals. For example:

- I keep a personal journal (for my learning), and a small moleskin book (a reminder of key coaching models and to capture themes and reflections to take to supervision).

- [I have a moleskin book] The feel is very important to me and how it looks, such as the texture/colour especially as it lasts a long time. I want to keep it; it's not disposable.

Journals are typically thought of as written – often handwritten – accounts, and pen and paper are easily transportable and provide low-technology solutions for quick recording and reflective writing. This was the most common means by which the coaches surveyed collected material. What is important is that coaches find a format that works quickly and easily for them and allows them to organize material in a way that they can reflect on it.

## What do coaches write in reflective journals?

The content of coaches' learning journals also varies. Irrespective of the format, the content need not be limited to handwritten or typed notes and could be in the form of, or supplemented by, diagrams, sketches, relationship maps and materials added from other sources, eg, coachee organizational information such as an organogram. Moon (2006: 3) says 'learning journals are close or coincide with the idea of an artist's notebook' and 'words can be mixed with drawing or drawings may predominate'. When asked about the format they used, the coaches surveyed said:

- It is my personal reflections and also includes sketches, diagrams, mind-maps.

- Words (at a deeper level), pictures (eg 'I use light bulbs a lot'), photos, scrapbook. My words take me straight back into it [the coaching session].

A key question in determining the content is the purpose and intended audience of the journal – principally for whom it is being written and who, therefore, will see it. For example, it is common for a journal to be used as part of the assessed work of formal coach training or by a professional coaching body (eg Association for Coaching) as part of its individual coach accreditation. Whether for personal or professional development, if the journal is to be viewed by others (such as fellow trainee coaches or the coach's supervisor) it will need to be recorded in a format that is understandable by others.

Gray (2004: 65) tells us that a 'reflective journal is a document that contains personal anecdotes, stories, or descriptions of work-related problems' and this is consistent with these findings:

- I write about everything – ideas; creative thoughts; feelings; things to do; stories.
- A diary's what I keep dates in and log sessions (timing and process) – this is different from my reflective journal.
- What I write varies. Sometimes short, eg key things remembered/ prompts for next time; sometimes longer, eg positive work goals; key life events.

The literature tell us that a reflective journal can contain a description of critical learning incidents, reflections on personal and professional values and an analysis of the contradictions between what the person wants to do (espoused theories) and what they do in practice (theories-in-use) (Ghaye and Lillyman, 1997). It is not uncommon for coaches to record critical incidents in journals. While Gray (2004: 66) says that descriptions of these incidents tend to be more detailed than ' mere diary entries', they need not be particularly sensational events. They can often be highly personal and the cause of deep (and uncomfortable) introspection, which can become 'developmental turning points' (Skovholt and McCarthy, 1988: 69). The following quotes show the degree of emotional content in some coaches' journals:

- It charts my ups and downs – I use it to control them and me. I use it to help me step back particularly during the downs.
- I keep a diary of my thoughts/emotions to 'get it out there' – I look back on these later and find this 'very therapeutic'.
- If I'm emotional (angry) I'm impulsive. Journaling is a 'safe environment to get some feelings out.'
- It helps me distil [how I feel about my coaching] and make it real rather than talking to someone about it.

Cormier (1988) goes so far as to say these critical incidents could be categorized as 'mistakes' and, while challenging at the time, they can act as useful developmental fulcrums. He reminds us there is a long history in psychological practice of therapists analysing critical incidents to develop self-awareness and professional practice. Coaches could learn much through adopting this practice.

## Organizing reflective journal material

Journals often consist of an 'accumulation of material' (Moon, 2006: 2), implying a lot of material has been generated over time. Here, gathering and organizing this material to make it manageable for the coach to reflect will be important, especially for those verbose in their writing! The following extract from the children's favourite wizard, Harry Potter (Rowling, 2000: 518–19, in Moon, 2006) illustrates this:

> I sometimes find, and I am sure that you know the feeling, that I simply have too many thoughts and memories crammed into my mind ... At these times ... I use the Pensieve [a stone basin]. One simply siphons the excess thoughts from one's mind, pours them into the basin, and examines them at one's leisure. It becomes easier to spot patterns and links, you understand, when they are in this form.

Some writers (eg November, 1993) believe that the best results are achieved when significant guidance on journal-writing is provided. Moon suggests those unfamiliar with journaling 'start with a journal that is relatively structured and move on to a freer format' (2006: 52) believing this approach can help learners obtain greater benefit from the journal-writing process by helping them not 'going around in circles'. Having a pre-determined approach will help a coach manage large amounts of data. A structure for this could include themes for writing, and Knapman and Morrison (1998) suggest items that could be used to organize coaching material:

1 What I said.
2 What the coachee said.
3 What I felt.
4 What I told myself.
5 What I did.
6 What the coachee did.
7 What seemed to be happening at this point.

An example of an extract from a transcript of a tape-recorded session (with a coach's subsequent immediate reflections) is shown in Table 15.1 to illustrate this approach.

**TABLE 15.1** Case study 1

Contextual background

The session tape-recorded and transcribed below is the fourth session out of six contracted for with the client and took place several months after the third session had been held.

What emerged from the first session was a range of inter-connected presenting issues covering:

- Personal issues such as confidence levels, raising his profile, networking
- Resourcing issues around staff shortages, lack of personal and staff capacity
- Working method and work–life balance issues manifesting itself in limited work role effectiveness and a negative impact on his personal life and relationship with his wife.

At sessions 2–3, the client reported good progress on the above and in the 4th session wanted to focus on an internal promotion opportunity that had arisen between sessions.

| Transcript extract from a recorded coaching session | | Coach's post-coaching reflections |
|---|---|---|
| **What the coachee said** | **Coach's in-the-moment thoughts (shown in) and actual responses** | |
| I should have done it by now but I'm finding I can't clear space in my diary to address these higher level things, which unfortunately will affect my future because if I don't do it I'll have to accept what happens. | (Uses silence to encourage the coachee to tell his story) | His issue could be organizational but could equally be a lack of people resource in his team and him being overloaded. He seems to recognize the realities of his situation. |
| There could be talk of a re-organization but that might mean someone of a higher level replacing my boss. I'm not sure if that's what I want, it might be too much. | | I sensed we had hit upon the core issue but the coachee, perhaps projecting his anxiety, feels the need to tell me all the details. I continue listening for further info. |

**TABLE 15.1** continued

| Transcript extract from a recorded coaching session | | Coach's post-coaching reflections |
|---|---|---|
| **What the coachee said** | **Coach's in-the-moment thoughts (shown in) and actual responses** | |
| What I need to think about is getting my boss to let me do it [temporary promotion to Dept Head] | Yes. And what else? | Trying to encourage the recognition. |
| To backtrack a bit, I think I'm not perceived as being a Dept Head and so people probably formed their own opinions no matter what I say, won't actually change anything. | (Decide the relationship isn't strong enough to challenge his self-limiting belief yet and so adopt a more supportive stance): 'That sounds difficult for you.' | Backtracking happens often making it difficult to keep track let alone on track! Trying to suspend my judgement on his promotability and stay neutral! |
| Conversation continues | | |
| I'm starting to babble now. | | Relieved client recognizes this part of the conversation isn't helping him. |
| | [Enquiring tone] My question was 'What's your feeling at this stage?' [about whether you want the Dept Head role.] 'Do you want it and why?' | I try to keep the conversation focused. He seems to prefer a cognitive style & so I try a different approach here – accessing how he feels rather than thinks about it. Try to uncover his motivation for the job. |

**Coach's subsequent reflections on this session**

Having had the opportunity to reflect upon the session, I conclude that there were patterns of behaviour here that had surfaced in previous sessions. With this awareness I actively tried to break these patterns in this session by remaining neutral and thus encouraging the client to make his own decisions. Although I am aware of the power dynamics between coach and client and had tried not to collude with the client in earlier sessions, I think I may have done this unconsciously by directing the coaching process more than may have been necessary. In so doing, I may have fallen into the role of Rescuer (one of my own patterns of behaviour) – something I was keen not to repeat in this session and largely achieved. This change in intervention style from me led to a degree of circling in the session, with the client stating his views several times and an apparent lack of progress in terms of moving the work forward. I experienced this as frustrating at the time and with hindsight could have used my felt-experience by sharing this with the client during the session.

On reflection, I recognize that there were some possible parallels between how the client behaved towards me in the session (defers decisions and acts passively) and how he probably behaves towards others (especially superiors) at work. Although I didn't feel it necessary to share this with the client in the session, I feel this is material that could be used to support the client in challenging others perceptions of him in the Dept Head role. I didn't possess sufficient awareness to see this issue as clearly in the session as afterwards.

This example shows how, through a simple, structured approach using several of Knapman and Morrison's themes, the coach organizes her material and used this to help her reflect later.

# Reviewing and analysing reflective journal material

The next step after having gathered material is to review it and start the process of making sense of it. There are various options open to the coach. As well as reviewing a specific coaching session, much can be learnt by reviewing material from across a range of sessions, whether with the same client or across several different clients. For example, a coach could reflect on the same stage across different coachees and identify patterns and themes, or on the transition between stages with either the same or different coachees. In my experience, reviewing material from across sessions has proven particularly enlightening and developmental in identifying patterns of habitual practices over different coachees.

As noted, taking a focused approach to managing large volumes of notes and journal material seems sensible. Hay (2007) suggests prioritizing areas to target for development to help this. One approach is to review data from across different stages of the coaching process alliance. Alternatively, a coach could review his or her work against a set of coaching competencies, as the example in Table 15.2 shows.

While this example is based on a single session with one coachee, it could equally be reviewed across several clients. In fact, it was the reflection from this session that encouraged the coach to think about her coaching and recognize broader patterns and implications for her coaching practice.

# Learning from reflection and learning how to reflect

### *How does a coach learn through a reflective journal?*

While reflective practice is still loosely defined, many definitions in the literature imply that a person is reflecting on activities and deriving learning from them. Yet despite Carroll and Gilbert (2005: 61) telling us that 'reflection is a crucial element in learning', learning from journals is often assumed to be an outcome in a largely uncritical way. This is particularly telling because although some might argue that reflection is no more than a form of thinking, it is generally agreed that learners have difficulty starting reflective writing and, when they do, it is typically descriptive, superficial, and does not lead to significant learning (Lyons, 1999; Samuals and Betts, 2005).

Moon (2006) strongly asserts that learning should be an outcome of journal-writing and reports that there is no one type of learning arising from them. She discusses several elements to how people learn from journals, saying that learning is deliberate, probably organized and formal in nature. While some of the coaches consulted reported they need to allocate time for reflection, others preferred to do this on a more ad hoc basis: '[I reflect ...] Spontaneously. Often in the early hours of the

**TABLE 15.2** Case study 2

**Contextual background**
The material below is partly recorded from notes taken during a coaching session – the last of four sessions. In reviewing her notes, the coach noticed:

| Competencies frequently demonstrated | Competencies not (frequently) demonstrated |
| --- | --- |
| She frequently demonstrated the following competencies:<br><br>● Establishing the coaching agreement<br>● Active listening<br>● Managing accountability and progress<br>● Powerful questioning | She also noticed the following competencies were less evident in this coaching session:<br><br>● building the relationship; and<br>● developing trust and intimacy. |

**Post-coaching reflections and learning**
On reflection, I recognize my coaching had become stale over recent weeks and I was bored by the typical pattern of my coaching, ie listen; reflect back; work the issue towards achieving goals. I notice these elements are areas where I have received very positive feedback from coachees and peers (acute ability to listen; ability to connect issues/threads and offer insights and use of my cognitive skills to manage accountability towards achieving a practical task). My coaching seemed to lack depth and connection, however, and I felt jaded by the *sameness* of it.

I realize my coaching had hit a plateau and I was searching for ways of moving through this and developing my coaching skills. Through supervision, I found focusing on emotions (my own and the coachees) helpful, which led to bolder interventions on my part and a greater use of self as an instrument of change for the client as part of my expanded everyday practice.

morning or late at night.' However, the same coach also commented: 'recognize the need [for me] to be disciplined. Journaling provides that discipline and structure', suggesting that a degree of organization and formality might be useful for some coaches.

This is interesting because it sits at odds with the way learning at work has evolved in recent years. While people learn everyday both formally and informally, Eraut *et al* (1998) tell us that most of the learning that takes place in organizations is informal, with responsibility for it having moved from the organization to the individual in recent years (Megginson, 2004), and a shift from formal to more informal development with increasing use of self-managed learning (Woodall and Winstanley, 1998). Learning journals seem to fit within this vogue.

Although reflection can take place unconsciously, we focus here on a more conscious approach to evaluating a situation from which learning emerges. Kolb (1984) recognized this, having identified reflection as one stage of learning in his popular learning cycle.

Rather than a traditional teacher-led accumulation approach to learning with knowledge poured in, in reflection on journal-writing the learner guides the learning journey. Learning is therefore not about accumulating knowledge per se but changing one's views. A journal can play a central role in this by helping coaches decide what they already know and expanding their schema of it. Equally, coaches recognizing what they don't know or the limits of their practice could be the trigger for starting to reflect, as the following examples imply:

- I compare my ideal self with my practice and where I'm 'off kilter'.
- [When reflecting, I look for] 'Even better if ...' – what's the client style and what worked well for them from my practice so I can be better prepared next time.

The act of journal-writing allows coaches to revisit their practice and expand this by building on existing learning, examine existing internal experiences, the fit between these internal experiences and new external ones, and the meaning made of these. Cognitive structures can change without any new knowledge being added – we may just change our point of view on an issue. Moon (2004) coined the phrase 'cognitive housekeeping' to describe this re-ordering of internal experience, particularly if there is no new material added.

However, in the same way as earlier experiences of reflection can shape our attitude and approach to it, the knowledge we already possess may affect what we learn. This is partly because prior experiences are likely to have influenced the way in which we receive and process new information and because it is possible that the process of acquiring new knowledge may well cause a conflict with a coach's established and dominant beliefs. Festinger (1957) coined this 'cognitive dissonance' and there are strong reasons for the use of journals to support professional development where this might occur (Moon, 2004; Trelfa, 2005). Several of the coaches surveyed commented on their use of journaling for professional development:

> I see it [journal] as an aid for learning. I intend to use it to support my accreditation as a coach. It's not formal learning. I can share my coaching journey and open up myself to others eg in co-coaching or supervision.
>
> I found journaling on [coach training] courses and supervision courses to be excellent learning.

The act of writing itself seems to provide conditions for learning. For example, we can learn through writing because it:

- forces time ... for reflection (Holly and McLoughlin, 1989);
- forces learners to organize and to clarify their thoughts ... In this way they reflect on and improve their understanding (Moon, 1999);
- helps learners to know whether or not they understand something. If they cannot explain it, they probably cannot understand it (Moon, 2006).

Given that the above seem important in encouraging coaches to reflect, it begs the question: what might get in the way of coaches reflecting?

## What are the barriers to reflective learning?

A range of things can block reflection: tiredness, stress and other preoccupations can all 'get in the way'. In today's fast-paced world, finding 'quality' time is a challenge for many of us. Walker (1985) and Wildman and Niles (1987) recognized that writing takes 'time and intellectual space', which can sometimes be difficult to achieve. Selfe and Arabi (1986) cited a lack of time as a reason for journal-writing failing.

Many coaches will be familiar with Nancy Kline's *Time to Think* (1999) in which she emphasizes the components necessary to maximize a quality thinking environment, including 'ease' – slowing down before asking questions that facilitate reflection. The act of journal-writing may help because it encourages the writer to stop and think, as we saw earlier and is reinforced below:

- My ideal is to finish coaching, sit for 10 minutes to dump down my thoughts when they're fresh. I find it frustrating if I have to go straight onto another activity, I lose the richness and have difficulty recalling the granularity.
- It's easy to go from one thing to the next and disregard and for it [coaching] to feel superficial. In other words, I *need* to do it.

- I do feel I work better if I stop and reflect. It frees me up and calms me down and makes me more resourceful.
- Embedding my learning – otherwise it will float away.

Time does appear to be an important ingredient in effective reflection. Although important, preserving regular time for it may not be realistic or possible for some. With this in mind, Carroll and Gilbert (2005) argue that reflection-in-action (as something happens or occurs) could suit the speed of contemporary life better, with the onus on us needing to learn this way to derive maximum learning from everyday activities.

Another contentious area seems to be the quality of reflection itself. It is argued that if reflective quality is poor then resultant learning will be poor. Ferry and Ross-Gordon (1998) and McAlpine and Weston (2002) provide verification that people do vary in the effectiveness with which they reflect, saying this is not limited to experience. Gray (2004) advises that, while informal learning experiences are an important means through which people can develop critical reflection, it does not come naturally to most. This could be because coaches do not understand the differences between description and critical reflection. Clear definitions and an example (provided below) might help.

So, what is the difference between describing coaching and critically reflecting upon it? Reflection is often thought of as existing at different levels, suggesting an order or hierarchy from a shallower descriptive level through to a deeper level of critical reflection. While some theorists give different levels of reflection names (eg, Van Manen, 1977), this does not imply that they are qualitatively different. There seem to be consistent views that superficial reflection is descriptive (Moon, 2006); Kim (1999) uses the phrase 'non-reflexive' to refer to material that is non-critical or non-reflective. Hatton and Smith's (1995) work has become a well known framework to depict the different levels of reflective activity, and coaches might use this to develop their writing to become more reflective. This framework is shown in Table 15.3 along with an example of the differences in a coach's reflections on three levels.

None of the coaches who formed part of this study commented upon the different levels of reflection, indicating a possible lack of awareness of the deeper levels of reflection, at least in theory. From the sample coach reflective materials disclosed and reviewed in writing this chapter, most fell into the 'descriptive' category, pointing to critical reflection being an area for development, even for experienced coaches.

**TABLE 15.3** Hatton and Smith's (1995) framework of the different levels of reflective activity, adapted by Moon (2006)

1 **Descriptive writing** – writing that is not considered to show evidence of reflection: it is a description with no discussion beyond description.

Example coach reflection:
- The coachee achieved her outcome.
- The coach was content with the session.

2 **Descriptive reflection:** There is description of events. The possibility of alternative viewpoints is accepted but most reflection is from one perspective.

Example coach reflection:
- The coachee achieved her outcome. The coachee appeared happy. I wonder how satisfied the coachee really was. How might I find out? What might the sponsor's perspective be?
- I [coach] was content with the session. I wonder if this matches the client's view.

3 **Dialogic reflection:** The work demonstrates a 'stepping back' from events and actions leading to a different level of contemplation about discourse with self and exploring the discourse of events and actions. There is a recognition that different qualities of judgement and alternative explanations may exist for the same material. The reflection is analytical or integrative, though may reveal inconsistency.

Example coach reflection (on what would make the session even better):
- Could cut out detailed reflecting back to coachee (What I'm hearing is ...') and explain the *essence* of what I've heard – this would help make the session pacier. At what pace is the coachee experiencing the session and is this helpful (from the coachee's perspective)?
- Noticed over-use of question 'Is that it or ...?' to check understanding. Wondered why I need to understand? Who am I understanding for? What if I don't? Wonder if that's polarizing choices for client into only two possible options (one or another) and how I can create consideration of greater possibilities
- Repeated use of the word 'Okay' – is this an acknowledgement or a verbal tick? Need to self-check to make sure I don't over-use.

The sharing of journal material raises ethical and practical issues of confidentiality and readability. Interestingly, 50 per cent of the coaches surveyed said they typically share or would be prepared to share the content of their journal with their coachee. Another coach commented, 'I'm conscious of the ethical position and the DPA [Data Protection Act] – and aware of what could be read by anyone if a case goes to court.' This suggests a degree of caution as to what may be written in a journal.

There is always the danger that knowing a journal will be seen by others may have both a conscious and unconscious influence on what is written by the coach. As one coach surveyed pointedly put it: 'I retain much of my journaling in my head for safety. Don't want top secret documents falling into enemy hands.' Another commented that a barrier to learning would be: 'If others invaded or intruded on my log.'

This research seems to support the view that other people viewing a journal may constrain the flow of reflection and freedom of expression on the part of a coach, highlighting another barrier to learning from journals.

## Conclusions

Learning is vital to develop our practice as professional coaches and journal-writing and reflection can play an important role in this. Yet for many, reflecting on experience does not come easily and few of us do it effectively. For those who already reflect, the benefits are numerous and high despite the trigger for reflecting often inducing real (emotional) discomfort in the coach.

The most common approaches to gathering material for reflecting are in writing or by audio-recording, and to capture this in semi-structured, paper-based journals in words and pictures. Having developmental experiences in the first place is vital and recognizing the need to learn, being ready for it, and setting aside time are all important ingredients in helping promote successful reflective practice. Breaches in confidentiality, distractions and not knowing 'how to' all inhibit reflection.

This chapter has provided examples of how to gather, organize and review raw journal material and presented different possibilities for how to go about reflecting, particularly at a deeper, more critical level from which even more learning can be gained. Hay (2007: 8) tells us 'The point of reflection is to enhance capability, so time spent reflecting on how to behave in future situations allows you to identify more options and to plan for increased flexibility, with specific clients and more generally.' It is hoped that this chapter will, in some small way, encourage wider and improved reflective learning which, in turn, enhances coaches' work with coachees.

# References

Argyris, C (1991) Teaching smart people how to learn, *Harvard Business Review*

Atkins, S and Murphy, K (1993) Reflection: a review of the literature, *Journal of Advanced Nursing*, 18, 1188–92

Carroll, M and Gilbert, M C (2005) *On being a Supervisee – Creating learning partnerships,* Vukani Publishing, London

Chi, M, de Leeuw, N, Chiu, M and La Vancher, C (1994) Eliciting self-explanations improves learning, *Cognitive Science*, 18, 439–77

Christensen, R (1981) 'Dear Diary', a learning tool for adults, *Lifelong Learning in the Adult Years*, October, 158–62

Cormier, L S (1988) Critical incidents in counselor development: themes and patterns, *Journal of Counseling & Development*, 67 (2) 131–32

Dewey, J (1933) *How We Think: A restatement of the relation of reflective thinking to the educative process,* D C Heath, New York

Eraut, M, Alderton, J, Cole, G and Senker, P (1998) Development of knowledge and skills in employment, Final report of a research project funded by the Learning Society Programme of the Economic and Social Research Council, University of Sussex Institute of Education

Ferry, N and Ross-Gordon, J (1998) An inquiry into Schön's epistemology of practice: exploring links between experiencing and workplace practice, *Adult Education Quarterly*, 48, 98–112

Festinger, L (1957) *A Theory of Cognitive Dissonance,* Stanford University Press, Stanford, CA

Ghaye, T and Lillyman, S (1997) *Learning Journals and Critical Incidents: Reflective practice for health care professionals,* Quay Books, Salisbury

Gray, D E (2004) Informal management learning – developing critical reflection through reflective tools, 11th European Mentoring and Coaching Conference, 17–19 November

Hackman, J R and Wageman, R (2007) Asking the right questions about management: discussion and conclusions, *American Psychologist*, 62 (1) 43–47

Hatton, N and Smith, D (1995) Reflection in teacher education – towards definition and implementation, *Teacher and Teacher Education*, 11 (1) 33–49

Hay, J (2007) *Reflective Practice and Supervision for Coaches (Coaching in Practice),* Open University Press, Buckingham

Hinett, K (2003) Improving learning through reflection, Parts 1 and 2, reprinted from the Institute for Learning and Teaching in Higher Education (ILTHE) members' website (no longer available)

Holly, M and McLoughlin, C (1989) *Perspectives on Teacher Professional Development,* Falmer Press, London

Jensen, V (1987) Writing in college physics, in (ed) T Fulwiler, *The Journal Book,* Heinemann, Portsmouth, NH

Johns, C (2004) *Becoming a Reflective Practitioner,* Blackwell Science, Oxford

Kim, H (1999) Critical reflective inquiry for knowledge development in nursing practice, *Journal of Advanced Nursing*, 29 (5) 1205–12

Kline, N (1999) *Time to Think – Listening to ignite the human mind,* Cassell Illustrated, London

Knapman, J and Morrison, T (1998) *Making the Most of Supervision in Health and Social Care,* Pavilion, Brighton

Kolb, D A (1984) *Experiential Learning: Experience as the source of learning and development,* Prentice-Hall, Englewood Cliffs, NJ

Knowles, M (1985) *Androgogy in Action,* Jossey-Bass, San Francisco, CA

Lewis, P (2003) Improving performance. Why is coaching (and its cousin mentoring) so much in the public eye?, *Edge,* 2, 4, Autumn

Lyons, J (1999) Reflective education for professional practice: discovering knowledge from experience, *Nurse Education Today,* 19, 29–34

McAlpine, L and Weston, C (2001) Reflection, improving teaching and students learning, pp 59–77, in (eds) N Hativa and P Goodyear, *Teacher Thinking, Beliefs and Knowledge in Higher Education,* Kluwer, Dordrecht

Mackintosh, C (1998) Reflection: a flawed strategy for the nursing profession, *Nurse Education Today,* 18, 553–57

Megginson, D (2004) Planned and emergent learning: consequences for development, in (eds) C Grey and E Antonacopoulou, *Essential Readings in Management Learning,* Sage, London

Moon, J A (1999) *Learning Journals: A handbook for academics, students and professional development,* 1st edn, RoutledgeFalmer, London

Moon, J A (2004) *A Handbook of Reflective and Experiential Learning,* RoutledgeFalmer, London

Moon, J A (2005) First Person, unpublished short story in Moon, (2006) *Learning Journals: A handbook for academics, students and professional development,* 2nd edn, Routledge, London

Moon, J A (2006) *Learning Journals: A handbook for academics, students and professional development,* 2nd edn, Routledge, London

November, P (1993) Journals for journey into deep learning, *Research and Development in Higher Education,* 16, 299–303

Raelin, J A (2001) Public reflection as the basis of learning, *Management Learning,* 32 (1) 11–30

Samuals, M and Betts, J (2005) Crossing the threshold from description to deconstruction: using self-assessment to deepen reflection on lived scenarios. Paper presented at Institute of Reflective Practice Conference, 'Scenario-Based Learning', Gloucester, June

Selfe, C and Arabi, F (1986) Writing to learn: engineering students journals, in (eds) A Young and T Fulwiler, *Writing Across the Disciplines,* Boynton/Cook, Upper Montclaire, NJ

Skovholt, T M and McCarthy, P R (1988) Critical incidents: catalysts for counselor development, *Journal of Counseling and Development,* 67, October, 69–72

Trelfa, J (2005) Faith in reflective practice, *Reflective Practice,* 6 (2) 205–12

Van Manen, M (1977) Linking ways of knowing and ways of being, *Curriculum Inquiry,* 6, 205–08

Walker, D (1985) Writing and reflection, in (eds) D Boud, R Keogh and D Walker, *Reflection: Turning experience into learning,* Kogan Page, London

Wildman, T and Niles J (1987) Reflective teachers, tensions between abstractions and realities, *Journal of Teacher Education,* 3, 25–31

Woodall, J and Winstanley, D (1998) *Management Development. Strategy and practice,* Blackwell Business, Oxford

# Building emotional, ethical and cognitive capacity in coaches

## a developmental model of supervision

**PETER HAWKINS**

## Introduction

In recent years I have been concerned that the challenges for leaders in all sectors have been growing exponentially and those working in leadership development have not been developing their craft and themselves at the rate these new challenges demand and that the leaders we are there to support deserve. One of the limits of leadership development is the coach's own personal capacity and maturity. In Hawkins and Smith (2006) we showed how quality supervision will increase the necessary capacities of coaches, mentors and consultants so that they become more effective. However, we wrote less about how to work with supervisees when their development comes up against the limits of their current frame of reference (Laske, 2009) or their action-logic (Torbert and Associates, 2004). It is at this juncture that supervisees can either be supported in making a developmental transition, and radically increase their emotional and ethical capacity, or become stuck in trying to meet new challenges with old frames of reference.

In our training of several hundred coaching supervisors we have found that generally they are less skilled at attending to the overall development of the supervisee's capacity than they are at attending to the current client work. So in this chapter I will specifically focus on the developmental aspects of supervision and how supervision can help take supervisees to their learning edge, confront their limiting beliefs and mindsets, and grow their emotional and ethical capacity to more effectively engage with their clients. In this chapter I will propose that:

- An individual coach's frame of reference both enables and limits his or her ability to develop those he or she coaches.
- Coaches' 'frame of reference' or 'action-logic' is like the seat of a three-legged stool, the legs being their relational engagement capacity their ethical capacity, and their cognitive capacity to embrace and work with complexity.
- To enlarge the stool it is necessary to develop all three legs and transform the seat that connects them.
- Supervision can be a suitable place for helping coaches transition to new frames of reference and grow these three key capacities.

## Coaching supervision – its development and definition

In 2006 we defined supervision as:

> The process by which a coach with the help of a supervisor, can attend to understanding better both the client system and themselves as part of the client-coach system, and by so doing transform their work and develop their craft. (Hawkins and Smith, 2006)

To this could be added:

> Supervision does this by also attending to transforming the relationship between the supervisor and coach and to the wider contexts in which the work is happening.

At the core of continuing professional development is continual personal development, where our own development is weaved through every aspect of our practice. When this happens every coachee becomes a teacher, every piece of feedback an opportunity for new learning, producing practices that support the balanced cycle of action, reflection, new understanding and new practice. Elsewhere (Hawkins, 2006; Hawkins and Smith, 2006) we have shown why we believe that having supervision is a fundamental aspect of continuing personal and professional development for coaches, mentors and consultants. Supervision provides a protected and disciplined space in which coaches can reflect on particular client situations and relationships, the reactivity and patterns these evoke in them and, by transforming these live in supervision, can profoundly benefit the coachee, the client organization and their own professional practice and development.

Coaching and mentoring have been areas of enormous growth in the last 10 years (Berglas, 2002; CIPD, 2004; Grant *et al*, 2010). Despite this, coaching supervision was noticeable by its absence in the first 20 years of the growth of this new profession. In the early part of the 21st century very few coaches were receiving supervision (Hawkins and Schwenk, 2006), and those who did so were going to supervisors trained in psychotherapy or counselling. It was not until 2003 that the first specific training was offered for coaching supervisors and 2006 that the first book on coaching supervision was published (Hawkins and Smith, 2006).

Over the last 25 years I and my colleagues have written extensively about supervision and for the last five years about coaching supervision. Throughout that time I have emphasized how supervision has three key elements or functions – the qualitative, the developmental and the resourcing or supportive. Much of this work has focused on the qualitative aspects and the ways supervision can attend to the work with clients, treating the educative or developmental benefits for the supervisee as a natural by-product of this focus on the client work. In Hawkins and Shohet (1989) we created a developmental model of supervision, based on much research and writing in the United States in the field of counselling psychology and in particular the work of Stoltenberg and Delworth (1987). The developmental model we created is helpful in distinguishing some of the core concerns that typically manifest at different stages of professional development and how supervision of students needs to be different from supervision of master practitioners. However, the model says little about how a supervisor can enable a supervisee to move from one stage of development to another, nor does it distinguish clearly between more advanced levels of development.

# What are capacities?

Hawkins and Smith (2006), influenced by Broussine (1998) and others, distinguished between the 'Three Cs': competencies, capability and capacity. These were defined as:

*Competencies:* the ability to utilize a skill or use a tool.

*Capability:* the ability to use the tool or skill, at the right time, in the right way and in the right place.

*Capacity:* a human quality, rather than a skill and more to do with how you are, rather than what you do.

Capabilities, like competencies, can be learnt and developed; the difference between the two is seen in the way the learning is generated. Competencies can be learnt in the classroom but capabilities can only be learnt live and on the job.

Capacities, on the other hand, relate to one's being rather than one's doing. They are human qualities that can be nurtured and refined. Capacities can also be thought of in their root meaning of the space you have within you for engaging with a wide range of individuals and situations and for holding complexity in relationships. We have all met people who seem to have little internal space from which to relate to you – and others who carry a seemingly infinite internal spaciousness, which tells you that they are fully present with whatever you feel you need to share or do.

# From emotional intelligence to relational engagement capacity

Most of the literature on emotional intelligence focuses on emotional competencies and capabilities. For instance, Salovey and Mayer (1990) define emotional intelligence as: 'The ability to perceive emotion, integrate emotion to facilitate thought, understand emotions and to regulate emotions to promote personal growth.' Their ability-based model views emotions as useful sources of information that help one to make sense of and navigate the social environment. Their model proposes that individuals vary in their ability to process information of an emotional nature and in their ability to relate emotional processing to a wider cognition. Their model claims that emotional intelligence includes four types of abilities:

1 Perceiving emotions – the ability to detect and decipher emotions in faces, pictures, voices, etc, including the ability to identify one's own emotions.

2 Using emotions – the ability to harness emotions to facilitate various cognitive activities such as thinking and problem solving. The emotionally intelligent person can adapt his or her changing moods to best fit the task at hand.

3 Understanding emotions – the ability to comprehend emotional language, including the ability to be sensitive to slight variations between emotions, and the ability to recognize how emotions evolve over time.

4 Managing emotions – the ability to regulate emotions in both ourselves and in others.

I believe what is more important in both leaders and coaches is emotional capacity in the midst of relating to others and I have termed this 'relationship engagement capacity'. This too has four elements:

1 Rapport – the capacity to achieve rapport not only with people like ourselves, but across a wide breadth of differences.

2 Sustained presence – the capacity to stay engaged and fully present with another without becoming reactive, when the relationship is full of difficult emotions, eg you may be attacked, or re-stimulated by your clients' distress or anxiety. This capacity closely links with the concept of the good-enough supervisor and the good-enough worker, who can hear the communication of their client without becoming reactive to the client or feeling bad about themselves (Hawkins and Shohet, 2006).

3 Depth of engagement – the capacity to gauge the level of depth of engagement needed and respond at that level, be it content, behaviour, mindsets, feelings, values or higher purpose.

4 Inspiration – the capacity to open new windows and doors for other people, to connect with new worlds and possibilities.

Figure 16.1 provides a map on which individuals can plot their own capacity using a 1 to 10 scale (numbering from the centre to the outside)

**FIGURE 16.1** Relationship engagement capacity

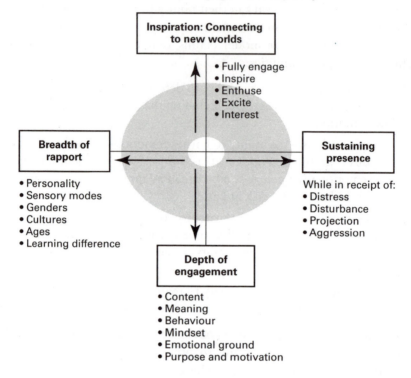

on each dimension. The area covered by joining the four plotted scores provides a self-evaluation of one's own current capacity.

If you shade in the area inside the lines, the shape of the area will also tell you something about your engagement style (see Figure 6.2). Those who have the most shaded area in the top left quadrant tend towards the style of 'charismatic motivator'. Those who have shaded mostly in the bottom left are more the 'facilitator' with the ability to create deep connections between those who are present in the room. Those in the bottom right will be predominantly 'counsellors' and 'supervisors' who can attend well to the inner life of those they lead or coach. Those in the top right are more the 'coach', engaging with the client at the edge of what they do not know. Those whose shape is drawn out along the horizontal dimension tend more towards a supportive and enabling style, while those who have a shape drawn out along the vertical dimension tend more to a challenging and impacting style.

**FIGURE 16.2** Relationship engagement capacity styles

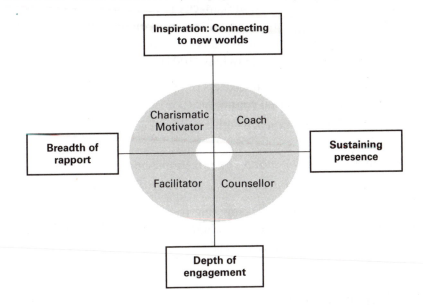

I have found it useful to help coaches in supervision to plot three different facets of their own capacity:

- their capacity when at their worst;
- their capacity when functioning at their best;
- what they believe their potential capacity could be.

This can provide the springboard for other types of inquiry:

- What conditions and stressors in themselves, their personal life, their agency or organization and the profession, push or shrink their capacity to this lower level?
- What conditions and enablers in themselves, their personal life, their agency, the organization and the profession, support their capacity to flourish at this higher level?
- What development in themselves, their personal life, their practice, the organization and the profession would grow their capacity towards their full potential?
- What capacities do they exhibit outside work that they leave at the door inside work?

Relational engagement also involves a fifth capacity that combines all four of the other dimensions: the capacity to be authentic and congruent in a way that creates trust from others. In working with both coaches and leaders, I have discovered that it is useful to distinguish four levels of authenticity or congruence (Hawkins, 2001):

1 Congruence between all aspects of oneself (words and action, verbal and non-verbal communication).

2 Rapport and congruence with another in generative dialogical engagement.

3 Congruence to the group, organizational and cultural setting.

4 Alignment to the purpose of what we are there to serve.

I have also discovered that being able to expand one's own relational engagement capacity requires the ability to be authentic and congruent in all four dimensions simultaneously.

# Ethical capacity

To engage emotionally, non-reactively, at depth, with rapport and presence and in a way that opens new possibilities, is necessary but not sufficient for being a quality coach. Leaders and coaches are both constantly faced with complex moral and ethical dilemmas. Coaches often find they are faced with ethical dilemmas that cannot be resolved within their current frame of thinking and look for help from their supervisors. At this point supervisors can acutely feel the increased pressure to give advice and come down on one side or the other of the dilemma, rather than focus on using the dilemma to help grow the ethical capacity of their supervisee.

Carroll (1996, 2009) defines ethical maturity as: 'Having the reflective, rational and emotional capacity to decide what actions are right and/or wrong, having the courage to do it and being publicly accountable for my decision.' He also articulates how acting ethically is full of complexity and ambiguity. He provides a very useful five-stage process for ethical decision making:

1 Creating ethical sensitivity – involves becoming aware of the implications of behaviour for others and insight into the possibility of ethical demands within interpersonal situations.

2 Formulating a moral course of action – represents how the interplay between the facts of the situation, professional ethical rules and our ethical principles may jell into a moral course of action.

3 Holding ethical conversations – the ability to go public with your course of action and respond appropriately to feedback and reaction.

4 Implementing an ethical decision – refers to the need to follow through and implement the ethical decisions made while coping with the resistances both inside and outside, such as politics, self-interest, protection of a colleague, or fear of making a mistake.

5. Living with the ambiguities of an ethical decision – indicates that coping with doubt and uncertainty is a vital capability for containing a moral dilemma.

A typical ethical dilemma that can occur in supervision is a coach reporting that his client has asked him to reassure her that the coaching is confidential, because she would like coaching on being interviewed for a new job outside the company, which she does not want her company to know about. The current company is paying for the coaching and this work is outside the current agreed focus. How this is approached by the coach can be seen as a reflection of his current frame of reference or action-logic, which I will explore in the next section, before returning to the dilemma.

# The capacity of cognitive complexity

The third leg of the stool is the capacity of cognitive complexity, the capacity to hold in dynamic relationship and integrate differing and conflicting perspectives, ideas and beliefs. Laske (2003, 2006a, 2006b and 2009) describes four stages in the adult development of cognition:

- common sense – based on observation and belief;
- understanding – based on formal logic;
- reason – based on dialogical thought forms; and
- practical wisdom.

Laske has written extensively about the need for coaching to move its focus beyond behaviour change to encompass the development of clients' fundamental 'frames of reference'. He distinguishes between social-emotional development, which he sees as being about 'meaning-making' and cognitive development, which he sees as being about 'sense-making'. Both of these combine to create the person's 'frame of reference' or his or her *weltanschauung* on which he or she bases his or her thinking, feeling or doing. This is the seat of the stool, to which I will now turn.

## Our action-logic or frame of reference

Laske's concept of the individual's 'frame of reference' is similar to Torbert's 'action-logic', which we will explore below, but Torbert is particularly interested in how our meaning-making and sense-making translate into behaviour and action in the midst of challenge and daily pressures. Both Laske and Tobert build on the psychological theories of adult development.

In the 20th century much work was done studying the developmental stages of children (Erickson, 1968; Piaget, 1955, 1977; Stern, 1990), but it was only a few psychologists who recognized that development does not stop after childhood and adolescence, as development is a lifelong process. Erickson extended his developmental stages into adulthood and psychologist and Jungian writers began writing about mid-life development (see Lachman, 2004). The work of Loevinger (1976), Kohlberg (1981) and others extended and clarified the stages of adult development towards maturity. Their particular interest was in the increasing capacity to engage with the complexity of moral and ethical choices. They utilized a number of ethical dilemmas to study how individuals justified the ethical choices they made. They noticed how adults can progress from operating out of self-interest, to conformity with social norms and rules, to a more utilitarian concept of serving the greatest benefit, to finally embracing ethical complexity and differing world views, while being able to reflect on themselves and the choices they were making.

Torbert built on the work of Loevinger and Kohlberg and specifically applied it to leadership. He has spent many years researching, testing and refining his model of levels of leadership development and the shifts they require in the individual (Torbert and Associates, 2004; Rooke and Torbert, 2005). Many developmental psychologists agree that what differentiates leaders is shown by their preferred ways of acting under severe pressure or challenge. This often reveals their perception and interpretation of the situations they find themselves in. Their specific

**TABLE 16.1** Seven stages of leading

| Action Logic | % Sample Profile |
|---|---|
| Opportunist | 5 |
| Diplomat | 12 |
| Expert | 38 |
| Achiever | 30 |
| Individualist | 10 |
| Strategist | 4 |
| Alchemist | 1 |

mode of responding to these pressures constitutes their internal 'action-logic', and this is what discriminates different types of leaders. Torbert emphasizes how important it is for a leader to understand his or her own action-logic and then explore how he or she can change it – through what he calls 'a voyage of personal understanding and development'. Such a journey not only transforms the capacity of the individual but can also transform the capacity of an organization. Torbert's research with thousands of executives shows the positive impact of understanding their own action-logic on their ability to lead. Research conducted over 25 years indicates that levels of corporate and individual performance vary significantly according to the prevailing range of action-logics preferred by these leaders.

Torbert and Associates (2004) suggest seven definable stages of adult development in leaders, shown in Table 16.1. Rooke and Torbert (2005: 68) wrote:

> The research shows that three types of leader (Opportunists, Diplomats and Experts), some 55% of Torbert's sample, associate with below average corporate performance. They were significantly less effective at implementing organizational strategies than the 30% of the sample, who measured as Achievers. Moreover, only the final 15% of managers in the sample (Individualists, Strategists, and Alchemists) showed consistent capacity to innovate and to successfully transform their organizations.

From the many years of working with this model in leadership development in a great variety of organizations, I would suggest that most organizations are severely limited in their change agility and their capacity to respond to the complexities of today's challenges because they do not have enough leaders with high-order action-logics. One of the potential contributions of leadership development and in particular coaching is to enable the transition of leaders to high-order action-logics, and we have written about this in Hawkins and Smith (2006: 48–60). To enable this development, the coach also needs to ensure his or her own development to increasing levels of action-logic and this should be a key aspect of supervision. So here I will look at how coaches at different levels of action-logic can be recognized in supervision

## The opportunist

*Focused upon:* personal wins, and other people as opportunities to be exploited.

*Characterized by:* mistrust of others, egocentric behaviour, manipulation and ruthlessness of action.

Only about 5 per cent of leaders seen in Torbert's research came into this category. They have a strong need to be in control because they have to have what they want. They treat other people as pawns, as objects to be manipulated to get what they want, or as competitors. It is very rare to find coaches who only operate in this mode, but some will regress to this action-logic, wanting to focus in supervision on how they 'get the better of their clients' and how they commercially win out as successful coaches.

## The diplomat

*Focused upon:* belonging, avoiding conflict and gaining control over own behaviour, rather than other people or external events.

*Characterized by:* cooperating with group norms and performing daily roles well.

Around 12 per cent of Torbert's sample population of leaders used a diplomat action-logic. Their wish to be liked and to create harmony means that they naturally try to ignore conflict. As coaches they look for approval from their clients and fear challenging or upsetting them and come to supervision looking for approval and wanting the supervisor to show them how to be effective and successful.

## The expert

*Focused upon:* developing control of the world of thought by perfecting their knowledge both in professional and personal lives.

*Characterized by:* reliance on 'hard data', trying to develop watertight thinking, wanting continuous improvement, driving efficiency, doing what they know to be right.

Torbert's research has shown that experts make up the most common group at all levels of management, including executive leaders, forming almost 40 per cent of the managerial population. Many professional routes to becoming a leader strongly develop an expert mindset, based on specialist technical expertise, be that as an accountant, HR professional, production manager, sales director, etc.

The expert coach arrives at supervision wanting to focus on problems that have arisen and the best way of overcoming them. They are often in love with techniques and models and less able to focus on the relational (mode 3 of the Seven-eyed Model; Hawkins and Smith, 2006: 164–65) and themselves as part of the coaching relationship (mode 4; Hawkins and Smith, 2006: 166–67).

These first three developmental stages have only limited viability as action-logics for leaders of large or complex organizations or for their coaches. Each of these three logics tends to locate change externally as a problem to be sorted out and lack the capacity to:

- question and reflect upon what they are doing;
- be open to personal change in behaviours, and
- be sensitive to the real needs of others.

Each of these previous stages is driven by the needs of the coach, in some shape or form, and the coach will struggle to focus on the combined needs of the individual client, the organization and its stakeholders.

## The achiever

*Focused upon:* deliverables, positive influence, and making it happen.

*Characterized by:* creating a positive work environment, open to feedback, sensitive to the needs of work relationships.

Torbert's research shows that this logic is found in around 30 per cent of managers and describes the achiever leader as 'effectiveness and results oriented; the future is vivid and inspiring; feeling like an initiator rather than a pawn; tries hard to live up to his or her own standards; blind as to their own shadow; capable of choosing (but not creating) an ethical system' (Torbert and Associates, 2004: 86).

The achiever coach will arrive at supervision with more focus on goals and purpose of the coaching and the challenge of how to achieve them. They will 'start with the end in mind' and will be interested in how to enable the improved performance for both the individual client and the client's organization.

## Post-conventional action-logics

Whereas the leaders using conventional action-logics appreciate similarity and stability, those using post-conventional action-logics increasingly appreciate differences and participating in ongoing, creative transformation of the action-logics they use.

Up to this point, the leadership styles have been operating within a single frame of reference or view of the world. The post-conventional action-logics are less and less formed by implicit frames that limit one's choice, and utilize more explicit frames that highlight the multiplicity of action-logics and develop the freedom and the 'response-ability' to choose one's action-logic on different occasions.

## The individualist

> *Focused upon:* recognizing and communicating with the different action-logics, holding both present and historical contexts, awareness of conflicting emotions and dilemmas, difference and change rather than similarity and stability.

> *Characterized by:* independent, creative work; focusing upon listening and finding patterns; starts to notice own 'shadow'; being experienced as something of a maverick.

The individualist action-logic is seen in about 10 per cent of leaders. It recognizes that all the logics we use are constructed rather than God-given and true. They are partial constructions of oneself and the world. The individualist is focused on putting personalities and ways of relating into perspective and communicating effectively with those who have other action-logics.

What sets the individualist apart from the achiever is their awareness of both sides of the dilemmas facing individuals or the organization – for example between someone's principles and their actions, between the organization's values and their implementation. This awareness creates a tension, which becomes the source of future creativity and a growing desire to develop further. Individualists are also likely to ignore rules that they think are irrelevant, which can make them a source of irritation to their colleagues with conventional action-logic.

Individualist coaches will be more focused on development than immediate performance improvement and will be interested in their own action-logic and that of their clients. They will be more at home with modes 4, 5 and 6 of the Seven-eyed Model (Hawkins and Smith, 2006: 166–70) and will be interested most in growing their and their client's awareness. Their limitation can be an over-focus and reliance on insight and awareness, their own and their clients, and a less well developed ability to use the awareness and insight to create transformational change live in the room (Hawkins and Smith, 2010)

## The strategist

> *Focused upon:* the importance of principle, contract, theory and judgement (not just rules, customs and exceptions) for making and maintaining good decisions; interweaves 'short-term goal' focus with 'longer-term developmental process' focus; the awareness that perception is shaped by one's action-logic; playing a variety of roles.

> *Characterized by:* creativity in conflict resolution; witty, existential humour; using double-loop learning; testing the limits of their organization's and their leader's constraints.

Torbert and Associates (2004) describe the strategist's skill as 'self-conscious reframing of mission, strategy and timing, listening to multiple voices of stakeholders and customers'. As discussed above, this is the first level that can initiate the deeper levels of learning that are necessary to strategic success without the attempt to coerce participants into a single frame of thinking that will inevitably kill the process. The strategist is able to see all ways of perceiving the world, all frames of reference as potentially valid and is thus able to treat them with the respect necessary for deeper learning. Strategist managers will always be open to the potential of the situation, to the ways in which the different perspectives of various stakeholders can be combined. They appreciate others' frames of reference and are continually looking for one that is appropriate for the situation. They will be open to feedback from any source, whether clearly linked to their purpose or not. They will always be drawing people together to investigate difficult and challenging issues.

The ability to reframe situations and problems – see them from different angles – can make the strategist appear untrustworthy to others. If insufficiently connected to some valid purpose, the strategist can indeed become Machiavellian. Thus effective strategists will tend to have sources of support to reinforce and develop their sense of purpose. This is where supervision is crucial for the strategist coach.

Strategist coaches, in supervision, will be focused on awareness and insight, not just as an end in itself but as the foundation for considering what they need to shift in their own ways of thinking and relating, in order to shift the relationship with the client, and enable the client to shift how they are engaging with the organization or system they are leading. The strategist coach will have a transformational coaching approach that powerfully facilitates the embodied change in the here and now that is necessary to enable a change in the wider system (Hawkins and Smith, 2010). Strategist coaches can use the interplay between all seven modes of the Seven-eyed Model and are proactive supervisees and often very effective supervisors themselves.

## The alchemist

> *Focused upon:* the truth in the situation; many situations have multiple levels of activity and meaning; expressing multiple aspects of personality during the course of a day.
>
> *Characterized by:* charismatic personality; extremely aware and living by high moral standards; ability to catch the unique moments in the history of their organizations; embracing a sense of leisure and a fierce efficiency; creating symbols and metaphors that speak to people's hearts and minds; often engaged with multiple organizations and finding time for all.

The final action-logic is the alchemist; 1 per cent of the leaders Torbert studied were in this category. What seems to set them apart from strategists is their ability to renew or reinvent themselves and their organizations in historically significant ways. Leaders who operate consistently beyond the strategist stage are extremely rare – Torbert quotes Pope John XXIII and Gandhi as examples. At this level, according to Torbert, the leader begins to let go of egocentricity and surrenders the attachment to being 'right'. The alchemist leader will not so much be consciously reframing situations to achieve his or her outcomes but appears to be continually noting frames of reference arising – and then letting them go, the better to stay with the energy of the dance that emerges from the stillness of the present moment.

Nelson Mandela's behaviour at the 1995 Rugby World Cup final in Johannesburg may well have come from this level of leadership and illustrates clearly the capacity of the alchemist leader to create powerfully transformative symbols. The Springboks, the South African national rugby team, progressed to the World Cup final, which was staged at a venue that was seen as one of the bastions of white supremacy. 'Mandela attended the game. He walked onto the pitch wearing the Springbok's jersey, so hated by black South Africans, at the same time giving the clenched fist salute of the ANC, thereby appealing almost impossibly, both to black and white South Africans' (Rooke and Torbert, 2005: 72).

The rare alchemist coach possesses all the transformational effectiveness of the strategist coach, but with a greater level of humility and non-attachment. He or she will be interested in exploring coaching and supervision as modes of spiritual practice.

# Connecting action-logics to ethical dilemmas

If we return to our ethical dilemma, mentioned above where the coachee wanted the coach to help her prepare for an interview with a new organization without telling her current employer:

- Opportunists will be most concerned about holding on to their client (even in their next job) and future work from the current organization. They might be interested in planning ways to help the coachee without the organization finding out.

- Diplomats faced with this ethical dilemma will be most concerned about not offending either their individual or organizational client or their supervisor.

- Experts will focus on what is 'technically correct' and recognized as good practice by the coaching profession and will present the 'either-or dilemma' (Hawkins, 2005) of either agreeing to keep it confidential or saying that the contract does not make this possible. They may want to engage the supervisor in giving them an 'expert opinion' on how they should proceed. The expert supervisor will want to know what the contract says, and how to act correctly to the letter of the contract.
- Achievers will focus on what best serves the interests of both parties and how to create a 'win-win' arrangement.
- Individualists will be more interested in what is happening in the relationship between themselves and the coachee; how they are getting caught up in experiencing the coachee's disconnection between their individual needs and the organization's needs and how they have been left carrying the coachee's dilemma.
- Strategists will have the awareness of the individualist but will go on to focus on how to intervene to help the coachee to confront his splitting and struggle with the dilemma, in a way that the coachee shifts his own action-logic.
- The alchemist might laugh!

## Supervising coaches through transitions

As suggested above, it is possible to enable the growth of a coach's relational engagement and ethical capacity within his or her current action-logic or frame of reference, but at some point the capacity development will come up against this limiting frame, so the supervisor needs to be able to both identify this and enable the transition to a high-order frame of reference. Such transitions are most often triggered by being confronted by new challenges that cannot be met by one's current ways of engaging with the world and require transformational learning, involving the whole person.

Often in the transition process there are three recognizable stages. My approach draws on van Gennep's study of the rites of passage (1960) and Kubler-Ross's (1991) work on the transition curve.

The first stage, unlearning, involves supervisees in beginning to encounter the limits of their current way of being. They find themselves in a role or situation in which their past ways of operating no longer work so well for them. For some this is a time of frustration and loss of confidence: having been previously very successful they now start to receive negative feedback. Others can cling desperately to their old skills and habits. The task of the supervisor is to support their supervisees in letting go and to courageously face the challenges and lessons that life is currently providing them.

The second or 'liminal' stage is where supervisees have left their previous way of operating but have not yet fully entered the next stage. The supervisee will be experimenting with ways of behaving in this new manner and needs space to learn and reflect on these experiments. In this stage one can feel lost and confused and therefore need a good deal of support and reassurance that this a natural process that most people go through. There can be a tendency to want to retreat to old ways of being or rush into an assumed and false confidence, rather than stay with the uncertainty and exploration.

The final stage is incorporation. This is the stage when supervisees start to incorporate new ways of thinking, behaving and acting and make them both sustainable and their own. Recognition and appreciation of what has been established from the supervisor is often most useful at this stage.

I will now explore more specifically how this applies to supervisors enabling coaches to shift between the different action-logics.

## From expert to achiever

Expert coaches come to supervision wanting to focus on problems and to learn how to fix them. They look to the supervisor for guidance on best practice and for expanding their 'tool-bag of techniques'. Achievers, on the other hand, start 'with the end in mind' (Covey, 1989) and focus on what is necessary to best achieve the outcome. The supervisor can facilitate this developmental transition by regularly turning the coach's attention to the purpose of the coaching, the goals both for the individual client and the wider organization. Also, the supervisor can help the coach reframe problems as challenges and opportunities for new learning.

## From achiever to individualist

For supervisors to reliably support the transformation of coaches from achiever to individualist action-logic, they require an increase in their own ability to work with the unknown in an open, inquiring and experimental way. Where developing achievers focus upon results, individualists focus on a wider field of awareness that includes themselves as part of the field and embraces different worldviews. They also have to move from prescribed and rehearsed ways of communicating in order to be able to inquire about situations without knowing the answer before they start. For the transformation to be successful, the coach needs to feel able to experiment with new ideas and ways of working. The supervisor can enable this transition by encouraging more focus on the self-awareness of the coach and helping him or her to reflect on the wider coaching system and themself as part of the field (modes 3, 4 and 7 of the Seven-eyed Model; Hawkins and Smith, 2010). The supervisor can also direct attention and increase awareness of what is happening live in the supervision process using modes 5 and 6 of the Model.

## To strategist and beyond

The transformation to individualist is based upon developing a strong capacity for self-reflection and an ability to recognize the different views held by individual clients and their organizations as relative, whereas the transformation to a strategist or alchemist action-logic requires the readiness to break out of current modes of thinking altogether. To enable this transition the supervisor often has to:

- link individual and systemic change;
- use paradoxical and contradictory interventions that help coaches face their own inner contradictions;
- help them see their either-or dilemmas and find ways of transcending them; and
- encounter what they need to transform in themselves to better enable transformation in the client and their organization.

This requires the supervisor to be able to constantly reflect, flex and comment on their own process live in the supervision. To help the coach move beyond awareness and insight the supervisor can facilitate the coach experimenting live with possible ways of being, through using 'fast forward rehearsals' (Hawkins and Smith, 2010) in the supervision session.

For a supervisor to be able to facilitate such transitions, he or she needs to be able to work from a strategist's action-logic and from Laske's frame of reference, which he terms 'practical wisdom'. This does not imply the supervisor being more advanced, understanding better or knowing what is good for the coach. What is required from the supervisor is effective relational engagement, ethical maturity and the flexibility to embrace and move between different frames of reference, and the fearless compassion and moral courage to hold his or her supervisees to face up to the challenges that life and their coaching clients are so generously providing!

In Hawkins and Smith (2006) we wrote:

> The Torbert model of leadership development has a great deal to offer to mentors, executive coaches and their supervisors. It makes clear what the key elements of transition are for moving from one action-logic to the next. The model works from an assumption that we are not imprisoned in our genetic coding and habit patterns but can change the way we do things and the way we see the world, if we are prepared to put in the time and effort that is truly needed. This is where mentors, coaches and supervisors come in. They can provide the support and challenge to help make these shifts a reality.

# Conclusion

If the coaching profession is going to increase its capacity to enable the development of leaders and leadership to meet the growing demands of the 21st century, then coaches will need to be constantly expanding their own emotional, conceptual and ethical capacities and transforming their frame of reference. Supervision is the central process for enabling such development, but this requires supervisors to understand stages of adult development, recognize these in themselves, their clients and the coaches they supervise, and be skilled at facilitating the transition from one form of 'action-logic' to another. When both forming a contract for supervision and re-contracting, it is important that the supervisor and coach focus on how the supervision can best enable the development of the capacity of the coach. This should provide the framework for constantly attending to how the challenges that the coaches' practice is presenting them are pushing the bounds of the coaches' frame of reference and their action-logic, and attending to transforming the frame. I hope this chapter goes some way to supporting this process.

## *Acknowledgements*

I would like to thank my colleagues Nick Smith, Judy Ryde, Joan Wilmot and Robin Shohet for comments on this chapter, Nick Smith for generously letting me draw on our joint work on Torbert's action-logic, and Fiona Benton for her editorial work.

## References

Berglas, B (2002) The very real dangers of executive coaching, *Harvard Business Review*, June, 86–92

Broussine, M (1998) *The Society of Local Authority Chief Executives and Senior Managers (SOLACE): A scheme for continuous learning for SOLACE members*, University of the West of England, Bristol

Carroll, M (1996) *Counselling Supervision: Theory, skills and practice*, Cassells, London

Carroll, M (2009) Ethical maturity. Presentation to CSTD and Bath Consultancy Group Graduate groups Bath UK (see **www.bathconsultancygroup.com**, **www.cstd.co.uk**)

CIPD (2004) *Reorganising for Success – A survey of HR's role in change*, CIPD, London

Covey, S (1989) *The Seven Habits of Highly Effective People*, Simon & Schuster, London

Erikson, E (1968) *Identity, Youth, and Crisis*, Norton, New York

Grant, A M, Passmore, J, Cavanagh, M and Parker, H (2010) The state of play in coaching, *International Review of Industrial & Organizational Psychology*, 25, 125–68

Hawkins, P (2001) Beyond opposites. A series of talks given at the Unitarian Summer School, Great Hucklow, Derbyshire, August

Hawkins, P (2005) *The Wise Fool's Guide to Leadership*, O Books, Winchester

Hawkins, P (2006) Coaching supervision, in (ed) J Passmore, *Excellence in Coaching*, Kogan Page, London

Hawkins, P (2011) *Leadership Team Coaching*, Kogan Page, London

Hawkins, P and Schwenk, G (2006) *Coaching Supervision*, CIPD, London

Hawkins, P and Schwenk, G (2010) The interpersonal relationship in the training and supervision of coaches, in (eds) S Palmer and A McDowell, *The Coaching Relationship: Putting people first*, Routledge, London

Hawkins, P and Smith, N (2006) *Coaching, Mentoring and Organizational Consultancy: Supervision and development*, Open University Press/McGraw Hill, Maidenhead

Hawkins, P and Smith, N (2010) Transformational coaching, in (eds) E Cox, T Bachkirova and D Clutterbuck, *The Complete Handbook of Coaching*, Sage, London

Hawkins, P and Shohet, R (1989, 2006) *Supervision in the Helping Professions*, Open University Press, Milton Keynes

Kohlberg, L (1981) *Essays on Moral Development, Vol I: The philosophy of moral development*, Harper & Row, San Francisco, CA

Kubler-Ross, E (1991) *On Death and Dying*, Macmillan, London

Lachman, M E (2004), Development in midlife, *Annual Review of Psychology*, 55, 305–31

Laske, O (2003) Executive development as adult development, pp 565-584, in (eds) J Demick and C Andreoletti, *Handbook of Adult Development,* Plenum/Kluwer, New York

Laske, O (2006a) From coach training to coach education: teaching coaching within a comprehensively evidence based framework, *International Journal of Evidence Based Coaching and Mentoring,* 4 (1)

Laske, O (2006b) Why does your maturity matter? How developmental theory impacts your coaching competence, *Choice Magazine,* 4 (3) 10–13

Laske, O (2009) *Measuring Hidden Dimensions of Human Systems: Foundations of requisite organization (MHD volume 2),* IDM Press, Medford, MA

Loevinger, J (1976) *Ego Development,* Jossey-Bass, San Francisco, CA

Piaget, J (1955) *The Child's Construction of Reality,* Routledge and Kegan Paul, London

Piaget, J (1977) *The Grasp of Consciousness: Action and concept in the young child,* Routledge and Kegan Paul, London

Rooke, D and Torbert, W (2005) Seven transformations of leadership, *Harvard Business Review,* April, 67–76

Salovey, P and Mayer, J D (1990) Emotional intelligence, *Imagination, Cognition and Personality,* 9, 185–211

Stern, D N (1990) *Diary of a Baby,* Penguin, Harmondsworth

Stoltenberg, C S and Delworth, U (1987) *Supervising Counselors and Therapists: A developmental approach,* Jossey-Bass, San Francisco, CA

Torbert, W and Associates (2004) *Action Inquiry: The secret of timely and transforming leadership,* Berrett-Koehler, San Francisco, CA

van Gennep, A (1960) *The Rites of Passage,* University of Chicago Press, Chicago, IL

## 17

# Using case studies for reflective practice

**JONATHAN PASSMORE, GLADEANA MCMAHON, DIANE BRENNAN, BOB LEE, BARBARA CHRISTIAN AND MICHELLE TENZYK**

## Introduction

In this final chapter of the book we offer a case study model as a tool for learning and development. The case study approach is well recognized as a model for learning in business, where it is the dominant model for learning on many MBA programmes, as well as in education. The chapter reviews the role of case studies as a tool for continuous professional development before moving to a series of case study examples that could be used in coach training or for personal study and reflection.

## The role of case studies

Case studies or scenarios have a valuable role to play in learning as well as in continuous professional development. The benefits are five-fold for the learner – and by learner we mean all coaches. We would summarize these as:

- awareness;
- refining an ethical decision-making framework;

- case conceptualization;
- exploring values and beliefs;
- a platform for learning.

The first role is to widen the awareness of the coach. Many of us operate in different sectors and have different experiences. By sharing these experiences in a structured way they can help us recognize the depth and breadth of the work taking place within coaching and the types of issues and challenges that can occur from time to time.

The second role is the opportunity to use case studies to test out and develop more fully our own ethical decision-making frameworks, discussed in Chapter 9 in this book. Decision-making frameworks are useful in that the coach needs to move beyond a list of ethical requirements expressed in a code of practice and consider how he or she would make a decision. Case studies allow such decision frameworks to be tested and refined.

Third, case studies allow coaches to consider individual cases and learn to identify the core themes within a case, as well as to prioritize the main themes. This has links with case conceptualization, which is a common approach in therapy but has yet to be developed as a common approach in coaching.

A fourth area allows opportunities for us to consider how we interpret information. In doing so, we bring our own beliefs and values to all interventions. Case studies offer opportunities to reflect back on these interpretations and the values and beliefs that underpin them. Are such beliefs or values helpful to us? Do our beliefs make us less effective as a coach?

A final role of case studies is that they provide us with a platform to hold conversations with others. This may be in formal learning environments such as on a training course, like an MSc in Coaching, or on informal learning through peer discussions or supervision.

## The contribution of reflective practice

We have developed the case studies below mainly from our experience of coaching. In writing a case study it is only possible to reflect a slice of what has happened and what is happening within the organization and in the coaching relationship. As a result, these are simplified representations of the reality. We would encourage coaches to fill in the missing parts of a case study. This involves considering, if the missing information was X, you might decide to do A; if the missing information was Y, you would prefer to pursue course of action B. Recognizing which factors might influence a change in your behaviour and also considering why that is the case, we would consider to be part of the learning that can emerge from using case studies.

As you read the case study we would encourage you to:

- identify the issues as you see them;
- prioritize the issues and consider why one is more important than another;
- expose your interpretations of the case and consider different interpretations;
- propose responses to the situations;
- consider the consequences of your responses for the different characters involved in each case study.

## CASE STUDY 1  Jennifer

Jennifer is an assistant director of corporate services at a health trust. In her role she is responsible for human resources and some corporate functions. She is responsible for a small team of a dozen staff. Jennifer was appointed to the post six months ago and successfully completed her probation appraisal.

Her coach is Peter, a newly qualified coach who completed a short course with a local commercial training provider. Peter has worked as a manager in the retail sector for 30 years. He is in his early 50s and has a good understanding of management, having managed large teams over his career before moving into coaching. He has personal experience of the health service, but has never coached or worked in the sector. He met Jennifer at a local breakfast networking event and persuaded her of the benefits of coaching. She subsequently secured funding for six coaching sessions.

In the first coaching session Jennifer talks about the challenges of the job and the session goes well. Jennifer is interested in how she can drive performance and deal with poorly performing staff. She wants to become a better leader and work more effectively with the clinical leads. In the second meeting Jennifer is feeling more confident about the coaching process and is open. She tells Peter about the problems she is having at home with her husband and about her growing relationship with her boss. She has a performance review coming up in four months time and there is an opportunity for a performance bonus of up to 5 per cent of her salary. Jennifer wants to focus the coaching session on increasing her chances of securing the maximum bonus.

## Questions

- What are the issues in this case study for Peter and Jennifer?
- What is the most important issue and why?
- How do you make sense of what is happening
- If you were Peter what actions would you take and why?
- What might be the consequences for Jennifer?
- What might be the consequences for the director of corporate services?
- What might be the consequences for Jennifer's husband?

## Discussion

There are a number of initial issues that come to mind when reading this case study. From Jennifer's situation selecting a coach through an informal conversation may not be the best way. Making a decision at an informal networking event suggests there was little opportunity to compare what different coaches had to offer. She could have started by asking her organization rather than, having found a coach, getting the organization to agree to her coach. The process also seems as if Peter has sold himself to her, as opposed to Jennifer making the decision she needed a coach. Maybe Jennifer is unclear why she needs a coach. The organization may have preferred to offer Jennifer a coach from its pool of existing coaches or at least to have tendered the assignment to secure the best value solution. In making her selection the decision seems to be more opportunistic.

Jennifer seems to not have considered, or at least not placed any value on, the lack of sector experience Peter has to offer. Peter has a background in retail but no health sector or HR background. In her first meeting Jennifer raised issues about clinical leadership. Does Peter understand the complexities of working in the health sector and of working with clinical leads? We would take the view that coaches are at their best when they have a good understanding of the sector. If Jennifer had followed a more formal route to selecting a coach, she could have looked for someone with experience of working with or in the health service. This may prove useful if she needs help in understanding how she can enhance her relationships with clinical staff.

A further issue is the relationship with her boss. While this is not a coaching issue, as a public sector body this could be damaging to the reputation of the organization – a very different situation from working at a supermarket or mobile phone retailer. Such stories often make the local press if the characters involved are senior managers in local government or the health service. As a public sector organization, the health trust may have a policy on the matter. Jennifer's role as head of HR makes this especially sensitive. Jennifer has also mentioned a performance bonus that could be awarded to her by the person she is having the relationship with. This opens questions about the decision process and again raises potential reputational damage to the organization through media exposure of the story. Again it would be very different if the story were from a private sector company. While Jennifer may think the relationship is a secret such things are difficult to keep secret for long. If it's not already gossip among staff, it will be only a matter of time before colleagues find out. While the issue of the relationship with Jennifer's husband is outside the scope of organizational coaching, we would also recognize that this uncertainty may impact on her performance at work.

For Peter there are other issues. It sounds as if Peter may be a fairly inexperienced coach. He has sold himself to Jennifer, but is he sufficiently experienced to do a good job? How will he cope with the clinical/health aspects of the coaching assignment? Does he understanding some of the different ethical standards that might apply in the public sector when compared to his own retail background? Peter may need to think about how he can use his supervisor to help him manage these new and challenging aspects of the contract he has won.

For us the most important issue to discuss is the performance-related pay theme and how Jennifer manages this and the relationship. If Jennifer takes the maximum award and has not told the chief executive, there may be an accusation of fraud, and if Peter knows he may be implicated by this. As a supervisor I would encourage Peter to get Jennifer and her boss to tell the chief executive about the relationship and for her to ensure that a different person undertakes her performance review.

In trying to make sense of this case as a supervisor, I might be wondering why Jennifer has requested a coach. Did she want somewhere she could discuss these issues with and help her disclose them? Is she someone who is impulsive or at least willing to take large risks without considering the consequences? She appears to have made a hasty decision to appoint a coach and to enter into a relationship with her boss. In neither case did she appear to consider the consequences or alternative courses of action.

In this case the consequences can be damaging for all concerned. For Peter his inexperience of the health sector and the public sector may mean he does not spot important issues to discuss with Jennifer. Alternatively, his focus maybe different based on his retail experience and lack of understanding of the health system. Such issues can result in early termination of the contract if Jennifer feels he is not equipped to deal with the work. It could result in reputation damage or potentially (depending on what he has said) in a competence claim. I would suggest coaches should show great caution and only undertake work where they are adequately trained and competent.

For Jennifer the relationship and pay reward issue could result in her losing her job following negative coverage in the local newspaper and subsequent damage to the reputation of the health trust. Other risks are that the relationship ends badly and this makes Jennifer's ongoing relationship with her manager difficult. The director of corporate services is risking reputational damage and possible dismissal depending on his future actions over the performance reward and the organizations policy.

## CASE STUDY 2   James

James, a managing director of a large European bank, had an outstanding record in analysing business issues and delivering on agreed operational commitments. However, feedback from his manager stated that his upwards communication was too detailed and he could appear confrontational. In addition, his presentations to senior management tended to neglect the larger picture. James was perceived as being dominating and unforgiving of mistakes in relation to his direct reports. The agreed coaching objectives were to become more strategically focused, to change perceived aggression into assertiveness, to develop a more cooperative style and to manage negative feedback in a non-threatening way.

Having seen two coaches, James chose Julia to work with him. Although Julia had worked commercially, her background is that of a psychologist and therapist who had trained as a coach. She has been working as an executive coach for over 20 years. Julia is often called in to work with individuals in the area of communication, assertiveness and effective thinking skills, focusing on behavioural change. James warmed to her during the initial meeting as Julia presented a number of models that he could relate to that provided him with a structure for understanding and action. Eight 90-minute sessions were agreed and James' manager asked for a three-way feedback session to take place at the mid-point and end of the coaching programme.

During their first session Julia introduced a 'Behavioural contract' to James to capture his objectives and outcomes so that these could be added to those outlined by his manager. Julia asked James and his manager to jointly agree these so that all parties were clear about their expectations. She also positioned a 360-degree feedback exercise with James as a way of capturing how people perceived him, together with the Myers Briggs Type Inventory psychometric tool aimed at helping James gain awareness of his personality.

In addition, Julia picked up on the points that James had made at his original meeting regarding his career progression and future aspirations. The session went well and James gave Julia positive feedback about this when she sent her 'Session reflection sheet' a day later for James to complete and return.

## Questions

- When using tools such as 360-degree feedback or a psychometric test, what is important about how you position these?
- What could be the underlying factors behind the way that James behaves?
- How might Julia assist James to develop his emotional intelligence?
- How could Julia approach the issue of the three-way mid- and end-point feedback session?
- How can Julia balance the learning style of her client (eg, liking structure/models) with the more reflective aspects of coaching?
- What pitfalls could Julia run into?
- What mechanisms could Julia and James employ to measure the effectiveness of the coaching programme?

## Discussion

Julia was chosen by James because of her experience, expertise and knowledge of working with thought processes, emotional intelligence and communication styles. However, Julia has to take care to ensure that the programme remains a coaching programme and, while drawing on psychological insights, avoid falling into a more therapeutic role, which would be easy to do when you consider her background. As a coaching supervisor it is important that I understand these issues to be able to help Julia as effectively as possible.

Julia has never worked in the financial services sector and while her expertise allows her to work across sectors, it is important that she has a basic understanding of her client's role and his challenges as well understanding the corporate culture that he works in.

Although James likes models and structure, there is a danger that Julia could rely too heavily on these. She therefore has to balance the need for reflective space in the coaching relationship with her more structured approach. There is the possibility that when using such models the coaching relationship can become more of an instructional rather than coaching process. Julia also has to ensure that the tools she uses are positioned as aids to learning and that while such tools can be helpful and increase the coaching client's insight, which can helpfully speed the coaching process, they are guides rather than absolutes.

Given that agreed feedback was to take place between James, his manager and Julia at given times during the coaching programme, Julia has to ensure that her client is in agreement with what the feedback should be. Careful consideration of confidentiality and what 'agreed feedback' would look like should be part of the discussion with her client. In addition, Julia and James need to work out how they will evaluate the effectiveness of the coaching programme, for example by administering the 360-degree feedback at the end of the coaching programme or by undertaking verbal 360-degree feedback where her client would ask individuals if they would be prepared to take a call from Julia. She would then collate the themes and observations of those concerned, protecting their individual anonymity. James' manager would also provide such feedback during the agreed three-way meetings. Objective feedback is an important part of the coaching process as is the coaching client's own perceptions.

As Julia's coaching supervisor my role is to assist Julia think through the implications of her work with James. This means helping her to consider her coaching plan, use and positioning of tools, desired outcomes based on her analysis of his situation, the outcomes agreed with James and his manager and how these are being met, her relationship with James and any boundary issues that could ensue (eg therapy versus coaching). Additionally, issues of confidentiality and the impact of the work on her as an individual need to be considered.

Although Julia is an experienced coach it is still important that coaching supervision considers all of these aspects. Even when the coach has a clear idea of what he or she is doing and why, it is helpful for a third party such as a coaching supervisor to listen to what is working as well as what could be done differently and why. Such discussions continue to aid the coach to develop a sturdy 'internal coaching supervisor' model, enabling the individual to assess the effectiveness and quality of his or her work. In addition, the process allows for the coach in a confidential and safe environment to share his or her challenges. A further part of the coaching supervision is to recognize that experienced coaches may find some of the work they are engaged in as repetitive. Although coaching clients are all unique as individuals, the exercises, tools and ways of working the coach engages in may not be. It is therefore possible for experienced coaches to become bored and fall back into what they have always done. The coaching supervisor may want to discuss Julia's feelings about this aspect.

## CASE STUDY 3  Jack

This case study is about Jack, a director-level executive with a major worldwide professional services firm based in the United States. The client is two levels below the CEO. The presenting issue was that Jack's star has been falling in the organization even though his technical abilities are exceptional. He regularly alienates partners by his very directive style, which becomes dismissive and even abusive. The outcomes for a successful engagement were for Vicky, his coach, to help him use a more consultative, collaborate style, do more listening, not go to 'battle stations' on every project, and to be a lot less defensive when given feedback. Vicky has over 20 years of HR and consulting experience, and has about three years of work as an executive coach.

At their chemistry-check meeting it was quickly apparent that Vicky was being severely tested. Jack came on very strong, as if to see if Vicky would stand up to him. This created strong reactions on Vicky's part – she isn't fond of being dominated by others, yet she really wanted this high-profile assignment.

During the meeting Jack said what he hoped would happen: that at the end of three months of 'coaching' they would mutually reach the conclusion that he would need to change absolutely nothing at all about his style. He agreed with his manager that he is boisterous and abrupt but claimed it was required to get the job done – which, by the way, he always accomplishes! He also made it clear that since he did not value his partners' opinions, proceeding with a 360-degree interview questionnaire would not be useful.

At the conclusion of the exploratory meeting Jack said he would agree to try the coaching, especially since his boss pressed it on him, but he remained extremely sceptical that it would be value-added to him or the firm. He scheduled the first session with Vicky – apparently she passed the test sufficiently well to continue the relationship.

During the first coaching session Vicky brought up the topic of the prior meeting. She described how she felt as a result of Jack's style. His reaction was that his behaviour was calculated to be a test. Vicky tried to discover why he does this, and does it so strenuously. Is it to gain power or control, or to establish a climate of fear? She had no success with this direct line of inquiry. Jack's point was that this is a natural way to check out who he's dealing with. To Vicky it was insulting that Jack was so aggressively dominating, and it was frustrating that he wouldn't or couldn't talk about it.

After another session of trying to relate as a partner to Jack it was clear to Vicky that she needed another approach. Trying to connect to him on a person-to-person level just didn't seem possible at this time – if ever! Perhaps she could find a way to tie the coaching directly to business results, such as improving shareholder value, or she might lose Jack's interest entirely.

Vicky also knew she needed help from her supervisor as she was becoming increasingly uncomfortable with this client. Fantasies ran through her head, ranging from quitting the assignment to giving him a strong dose of the insulting behaviour she'd been experiencing! The account manager at her consulting firm reminded her that her role was to be the client's advocate, that this was his coaching, and she needed somehow to earn his trust. She had to find a way to invite him into the conversation. This obvious statement from the supervisor was very helpful, as she had found herself ready to do combat!

For her next meeting she decided to introduce a three-factor model that connects a shift in a client's behaviour to longer-term organizational outcomes. Jack indicated this was the best session to date. It wasn't a breakthrough, but it was progress.

As the next sessions unfolded she continued to find herself feeling – and sometimes becoming – combative with Jack. He consistently would state, 'Everyone will come around to my way.' Vicky felt she was an utter failure in this engagement, and not sure where to go. Other than allowing that the three-factor theory was potentially applicable, even though he wouldn't do the homework, Jack's only positive action was to allow Vicky to listen in on one of his leadership conference calls.

The next coaching session was dedicated to giving feedback to Jack on what Vicky heard during that call. The feedback had to do with him not letting people say much of anything because he would interrupt to make his points. Vicky asked at the beginning for him to listen to the feedback without interrupting until she was done. Jack literally looked like he was going to jump out of the window at this insolent request.

Vicky noted a number of clear behavioural incidents from the phone call, yet Jack justified and defended his role each time. Not surprisingly, Jack often wouldn't let Vicky finish her sentences, so Vicky patiently reminded him of the rules. Eventually he admitted the feedback was beginning to get him to think more before talking. Vicky was happy to hear of this step forward, and told him so. She emphasized that 'fine tuning' his performance was a valuable way to create changes.

In a final effort to gather some data to use in the coaching, Vicky requested permission to do some interviews. Jack agreed to a limited interview process, with only some of his direct reports participating. After the feedback was gathered, Vicky phoned Jack to give him the results. He was defensive and combative, and told Vicky how to do her job. Vicky reported that Jack crossed a line and became abusive in his language. She truly wanted to end the coaching engagement after this call.

Following a session with her supervisor, Vicky agreed that in the next meeting with Jack, one that would be in person rather than by phone, she would take a very solid stand. She would not give him the full feedback report, although it was rich and contained much to be learnt, until he agreed to listen and not be abusive. She would get up and leave his office after saying this unless he agreed to the terms.

When Vicky gave him this ultimatum he asked if she didn't have the report ready, which of course she did. He agreed 'to behave', so to speak. They managed to get through the feedback report in a calm manner. They were then able to formulate a development plan.

Subsequently they met with his manager to review it all, which was an extremely successful meeting. At the end of Jack's coaching he asked if Vicky would be available to coach one of his direct reports!

## Questions

- When is a client not a good client?
- How big should a goal be? What is too big?
- Is the coaching relationship a valid sample of the client's behaviour?
- What happens if the client doesn't want to be a partner?
- Coaches get emotional too – is that a problem, or is it useful data?
- How much can we expect clients to change?
- Can coaches take liberties with 'standard' procedures?

## Discussion

Coaches and other consultants often have a hard time saying 'No, thanks' to a prospective client. The underlying reason may be financial need, or bravado, or perhaps the extreme optimism we coaches enjoy feeling regarding the malleability of human behaviour. Whatever the reason, it is not uncommon for coaches to accept assignments that perhaps should have been left alone. If a good outcome occurs despite the long odds, we credit it to our skill or to luck. Perhaps this is one of those cases.

Whenever possible we look for positive signs in a new assignment – a willing and committed client, an involved boss, a compelling reason to change or grow, or at least a client with a pleasant disposition. Without enough of those signs the coach risks a lot of frustration and a black mark against his or her reputation

In this case the problem was compounded by very ambitious goals. Changing the interpersonal style of a highly successful executive is never easy, even if the client really wants to make the changes. A reluctant client with a strong record of success presents a major challenge for any coach. If the attempt is to be made it is surely best to work incrementally, step by step. Moving this client in only three months to a place where he is less defensive, a good listener, collaborative in style and not combative – that's asking the impossible. As the case unfolded Vicky discovered that small steps were important and wisely she celebrated them as they happened.

One way to try to get through to a tough case is to use 'hard' data – 360-degree feedback, performance measures and psychometric questionnaires. This case demonstrates another kind of data that can be equally or more effective: the client's actions during the coaching sessions. Jack's testy behaviour, scepticism, interruptions and overall dominating style can be observed and noted when they happen.

Using the here-and-now data is not an easy skill to acquire. It takes time and practice. It requires acknowledging that behaviour exhibited in coaching sessions is just as real as any other client behaviour. It requires a measure of confidence and courage on the coach's part. It can be powerful data, however, even if other data sources are available.

Vicky was on target in urging Jack to allow her to generate more data. She was able to listen in on the phone call, and she was able to collect some interview data. These data sources were nicely complemented by the real-time observations made by Vicky.

In her first coaching session Vicky tried to get Jack to reflect on his confrontational style, with no success. This was an admirable try on Vicky's part, but not likely to succeed. It was too early in the coaching engagement. Further, it is the unusual senior executive who is comfortable and skilled at introspection and reflection.

Jack's style had significant impact on Vicky – perhaps for reasons totally obscure to Jack and maybe not evident to Vicky herself. She reacted very strongly to his domineering ways. Fortunately she realized the extent of her feelings and sought help from her supervisor. In her supervisory conversations she came to understand that she had the backbone, the need and the permission to stand up to Jack's pushiness. She was able to change her own style without forgetting that she was there to be his advocate, but not to absorb abusive behaviour.

To her great credit Vicky did not give up on Jack or on herself. She explored every avenue to get through to him, and eventually it happened.

## CASE STUDY 4   Michael

Michael is the managing director of a physician-owned medical office practice in the United States. He decided to explore coaching three months before his 50th birthday. Michael had heard about coaching six months earlier at a national medical meeting where an inspirational speaker he enjoyed said, 'Check yourself before you wreck yourself.' The speaker talked about coaching as one way to enhance your work performance and your life.

Shortly after returning home from the meeting, Michael began his search for a coach. After interviewing three individuals he found through an internet search, he selected Jane, an individual who has a Master's degree in business, completed a coach training programme, has five years' experience as an executive coach and a professional qualification from a coaching association. She also has nearly 20 years' prior experience in the health sector.

Michael and Jane discussed coaching in-person versus coaching by telephone. They were located 3,700 kilometres apart. They agreed to telephone coaching for a six-month period. The total hours of coaching agreed to for this time-frame would be 10. The agreement also included the options to discontinue coaching prior to the 10 hours or six-month time-frame or to extend the coaching on a month-to-month basis.

Michael has a successful 20-plus years' career in the health sector. He earns a comfortable salary, and he is in a challenging job that he said he finds enjoyable. He has been with the same organization for the past 13 years. Michael mentioned he resigned from the organization 15 months ago to take a job in a research and technology organization within the health sector. After a few days in the new job he realized sales was not where he belonged. Michael called his organization and found support for his return. He was overwhelmed by the positive reception he received and re-dedicated himself to the physician organization. On the personal side, Michael is happily married and has two daughters aged six and three. He told Jane, 'Life is good, but it feels like it could be better.'

In preparation for coaching, Michael completed an initial assessment answering thought-provoking questions requiring reflection and identifying initial short- and long-term goals. Michael's short-term goals focused on improving his project management skills, increasing his visibility at work and enhancing his influence and effectiveness across the organization. Long-term he wanted to change the nature of his job, possibly moving into a larger health system and to reorganize his personal finances to ensure financial security for his family.

On their first coaching call, Michael talked about recent developments in work. Several key physicians left the organization unexpectedly and the projected revenue would not be realized, which means a financial loss for the year. Michael is accountable for the financial performance and he takes this responsibility seriously. At the same time, he has been talking to a recruiter about a potential job in another part of the country. Michael struggles with whether to pursue the new opportunity or to pass it by. He is working 12-hour days most of the week and taking work home at weekends. He does not see how he can continue in his current organization, yet he feels he will have failed if he leaves. Michael wants to focus on figuring out what to do next.

## Questions

- What issues and challenges are present for Michael as the client and for Jane as the coach?
- What is the most important issue and why?
- How would you approach the coaching with Michael and why?
- What else does Jane need to be aware of as Michael's coach?
- What might be the consequences for Michael?
- What might be the consequences for the physicians and the organization Michael works with?
- What might be the consequences for Michael's family?

## Discussion

Michael found several coaches by searching the web. He identified three that had what he saw as important in a coach. Doing a web search is not uncommon for an individual or smaller organization looking to hire a coach. Michael had clear requirements, including an advanced degree, training and a professional qualification as a coach, and a background in the health sector. Larger organizations or those with national or multinational offices often require the executive to select a coach from a pre-screened panel of professionals who meet standards such as those Michael required of his coach.

Jane's experience in the health sector is positive given Michael's selection criteria. Michael's uncertainty about his job, the problems he is experiencing with the organization's financial loss and his confusion about his career can all be areas of expertise Jane brings from her previous work in the health sector. Jane will need to be clear for herself and to ensure there is a clear understanding and agreement with Michael about the coach's role and the mutual expectations. Jane will need to keep herself in check around coaching versus consulting versus counselling. Her supervisor can serve as a support and safety net as Jane reflects on the coaching plan and her interactions and coaching with Michael.

Jane and Michael are separated by a large geographic distance. Michael chose the telephone coaching option and Jane is comfortable with this method of coaching. Have they explored all the options available to Michael? Are they both clear on the benefits and potential limitations?

Since the two will not be meeting in person, it will be important for Jane to ensure she creates a safe environment conducive to developing trust and engaging in open, honest communication with Michael in the telephone coaching. Jane and Michael will want to determine overall goals and measures of success and to assess how the coaching is working on an ongoing basis. As with any coaching, it is also important to establish agreement and identify the focus and measures of success for each session. Jane's experience with telephone coaching allows her to be open and direct with the client to get to the deeper concern. She may also use a 360-degree assessment or interview to help Michael obtain additional data as he continues in his development. Even as an experienced coach, telephone coaching may be an important area to review with her supervisor to ensure she is staying objective, away from judgement and not missing opportunities with Michael by not seeing him within his organization.

Michael presents several contradictory issues. He is happy in his work yet he is feeling like he cannot stay. He has had a successful 20-plus year career yet he is struggling with financial concerns in his current organization. He left the organization 15 months ago and he is considering leaving again. Jane will need to work with Michael to identify the real issue. He is approaching his 50th birthday and may be questioning more than work in his life. His statement to Jane about his current life infers that he is looking for more meaning. He is at a developmental stage in life where he is assessing what is important, what he has done and what he wants to do as he enters this next phase. Michael has been consumed by work at times and his expression of frustration may be his questioning the value of what he has really achieved or perhaps even his own value as a human being. Jane's work is to uncover what is really occurring with Michael. Is his uncertainty due to frustration and feeling overwhelmed, or are these due to his uncertainty? What caused him to leave the organization 15 months ago?

What is driving him now? Helping Michael reconnect with his values, practise raising his awareness, observe rather than judge, self-reflect and learn, will help him find perspective. Jane will need to reflect and learn as she continues her work with Michael as well. She is just a few years younger than Michael and she will want to make sure to stay out of his emotion or experience. Having the ability to process her experience, reflect and learn will allow Jane to strengthen herself personally and professionally.

Michael takes his responsibility for the organization's performance very seriously. He is the managing director but may take on more than is expected. He works long hours and is frustrated by the time away from family. The lines between Michael the managing director and Michael the human being are blurred. Michael may have a sense that he has to be the best in the organization, perhaps even superhuman, in his role. Jane will need to challenge Michael in his thinking so that he can separate himself from the story he created. She may need to work with him to raise his awareness of who he is being in his various roles and to rediscover who he is rather than what he does. This is another area for Jane to look at with her supervisor to stay clear on her role as a coach.

## CASE STUDY 5  Cindy

Cindy is a young professional who recently started her job as an executive assistant to a high-powered chief executive of a global not-for-profit organization. She is hoping to establish her career in this sector.

Shortly after Cindy joined she was asked to also take on the duties of personal assistant; Anne, the chief executive, plans to dismiss her current PA. The role of personal assistant is not new to Cindy, since her previous job was to be the PA for a very wealthy philanthropist.

Cindy was offered the opportunity for coaching along with a group of more senior managers in the organization. Susan, a young professional with an HR and communications background and who just completed a coaching course, is assigned to Cindy as a coach. Susan is smart, has a real passion for helping people, and is looking forward to having this coaching experience.

Cindy is very excited at being one of the people selected for coaching. She eagerly bonds with Susan in their first session, providing a lot of personal history and disclosures about the work setting. She is grateful to her former boss who used his network to place her in this job, but she's not sure how it's working out. She expresses frustration about handling both the executive assistant and personal assistant roles. She confides in Susan that she is thinking about moving to another job that will more quickly give her the professional experience she seeks. She feels she doesn't have much of a relationship with Anne, doesn't get much feedback, and feels disconnected. Cindy continuously criticizes the way Anne leads the organization, and frequently compares Anne to her former boss, who apparently trusted her in everything and involved her in all professional and personal matters.

Susan is intrigued by Cindy's story and experiences, and also is excited to be working with her. Susan feels frustrated after their first meeting because she doesn't have a clearer goal for the coaching. When she asked about having a conversation with Anne, she was told that Anne is too busy so it would be best to just get started with the coaching. Susan definitely wants to explore these issues with her own supervisor.

## Questions

- What issues do you see emerging in this coaching assignment?
- What are important relationship issues between coach and client?
- What choices and tasks does Susan have for the upcoming coaching sessions?

## Discussion

It's good that Cindy is excited about having a coach and about being part of the group of more experienced people receiving coaching. She sees it as cool and conveying certain prestige. This is perhaps adequate motivation for starting the relationship, but a caution flag needs to go up in Susan's mind. Coaching means hard work lies ahead, so Cindy's enthusiasm will need to be grounded in something more than the status of having a coach.

And that raises the question of what this coaching is about. What's the work to be done? Even before a coach meets a client and has a chance to say hello, a lot has happened in the client's organization that is not known to the coach. The decision to engage a coach can be influenced by one or more relevant factors. Sometimes the client has encountered an obstacle to higher performance that can't be addressed in the usual way, or the client has been promoted and needs to stretch into new skills. The fact that a number of people are being coached in this organization could mean that Cindy was included not because there is a specific issue to work on, but to not leave her out. Perhaps it just seemed like a good thing to do in light of her short tenure with the organization.

There is only a vague mandate for the coaching: help Cindy settle into her new job. There is no input from her boss on what Cindy should do differently to become an effective executive assistant plus personal assistant. Susan has an obligation to engage her client and the boss in determining a reasonable set of goals to be accomplished through the coaching process.

What does it mean that Anne is unavailable? Combined with Anne's very busy work life, this could indicate a hidden request that the coach take over the work of getting Cindy onboard, manage her skill development, and set realistic expectations – work that would be better done by Anne as Cindy's manager. Susan must be careful not to go beyond the boundaries of what a coach should provide. Susan's scepticism about Anne's motives needs to be resolved.

Not having previous experience with coaching, Cindy's naïve expectations may be adding to Susan's early frustrations. Cindy seems to use her coach as a girlfriend and confidante. The first session felt to Susan more like gossiping about the boss's private life and professional shortcomings than exploring what Cindy's role is and how she can establish herself as a professional. Susan should move directly to creating structure, boundaries and a goal-oriented process.

Cindy's first job out of college was with a wealthy young philanthropist. That job provided her with very exceptional experiences, benefits and lifestyle. She only has that work experience as a comparison. Now she is one of many people in the life of her boss, and she is in a larger office environment. Will she be treated in this special way again? Will she miss it? Cindy is working for the first time for a woman. Does this make a difference? Might Cindy's expectations for being 'special' be different when she has a female manager?

Susan is just a little older than Cindy and is not an experienced coach, so it is a challenge to not be drawn into the office drama. Keeping a healthy distance and perspective is important so that Susan will be able to ask useful questions and help Cindy reframe challenges.

One of Cindy's challenges is the shift in her role. Cindy was hired to be an executive assistant and now is taking on an additional personal assistant role. How will she handle this in terms of priorities and in terms of her self-image? What will she do with the resentment that isn't being expressed to Anne?

Cindy hasn't managed so far to establish a relationship with Anne that would make her feel connected and comfortable. Cindy has a very critical view of Anne personally and as the leader of the organization. Cindy is still questioning her career decision and contemplates moving to another job. These and other factors suggest possible confusion as to what kind of coaching is appropriate here: onboarding, role clarification, relationship management with a boss, career planning, etc. This confusion contributes to Susan's unease and should be motivating her to design a fairly structured second session with her client.

The coaching case looks like a good developmental opportunity for Susan as well as for Cindy. It doesn't present itself as a problematic case; on the other hand it is not trivial and bears a certain amount of complexity that can accelerate her learning as a coach. Susan does the right thing in involving a professional supervisor and making sure not only that the coaching is on track but that she continues to develop her skills.

Susan knows she has a very accommodating style and therefore tends to focus too much on the client's comfort. This sometimes prevents her from constructively challenging the client. For Susan, pushing back on issues feels like jeopardizing their relationship. Susan established a good relationship with her client and they are off to a productive start; now she needs to develop a business-like coaching relationship with Cindy.

The next step for Susan is to contract with Cindy about coaching goals and boundaries. What can be included in coaching and what are they leaving out? What do Susan and Cindy feel is realistic to achieve in the three months they plan to work together? There are many possible goals they could focus on, including Cindy's professional growth, setting boundaries on the personal assistant role, dealing with Cindy's negative perspectives and what causes them, and designing a realistic development plan. Regardless of the coaching goals, Susan needs to discuss with Cindy how to involve Anne in this effort and how to build a better relationship with her.

# INDEX